GREAT BRITISH ECCENTRICS

S. D. TUCKER

AMBERLEY

First published 2015

Amberley Publishing
The Hill, Stroud
Gloucestershire, GL5 4EP

www.amberley-books.com

British Library Cataloguing in Publication Data.
A catalogue record for this book is available from the British Library.

ISBN 978 1 4456 4770 8 (hardback)
ISBN 978 1 4456 4771 5 (ebook)

Map design by Thomas Bohm, User design.
Typesetting and Origination by Amberley Publishing.
Printed in the UK.

Contents

Introduction:
In an Orbit of Their Own

'I'm not mad; I've just read different books.' Ken Campbell[1]

At the beginning of the year 1724, a forty-eight-year-old man named John Tallis (1676–1755), from the small village of Burcot in Worcestershire, decided that he had had enough of the outside world, and determined to retreat away from it forever. It is the kind of impulse that I am sure we have all had at some point or another during our lives – the difference is that John Tallis really meant it.

This was not the kind of momentary fit of depression or mental unease that could be dismissed by the simple prescription for its sufferer to go on a refreshing holiday and take in some fresh air, however – indeed, it was fresh air itself that was Tallis' whole problem. For some inexplicable reason which he never saw fit to reveal, Tallis had arrived at the erroneous conclusion that the cause of all ill health and death in humans was nothing less than the very air that we are all compelled to breathe in through our lungs each and every day. As such, he ordered his bedroom to be modified so as to be as airtight as was practicably possible, having all but one of his windows bricked up, and the glass in this solitary portal onto the world outside constructed to a special design in which the panes were at least three times as thick as was the normal practice.

Still, however, this was not enough for John Tallis. Seeing as he was still able to breathe in the room, clearly it cannot have been entirely airtight; so, in 1725, this strange man decided to take his plan a step further. He retreated permanently into his bed, tucking himself in tightly under its covers so that his head was the only exposed part of his body. Then, he had his entire head wrapped up with various coverings, caps and bandages made up of around

100 yards of flannel, like some kind of living Egyptian mummy, and fitted stoppers into both of his nostrils to stop any air getting into him that way. A piece of ivory placed within his mouth also acted to lessen the inflow of deadly air to his lungs, Tallis thought, and, just to complete the picture, he often had a piece of woollen cloth laid over his bandaged face, just in case. He stayed in his bed for nearly thirty years, during which time his sheets were never once changed, a new bed being brought into Tallis' room once per year instead, whereupon his servants had to roll him into it, his leg muscles eventually having atrophied from lack of use during his long lie-in.[2]

Eventually, of course, in the year 1755, Tallis did in fact breathe his last – much against his own will, admittedly – but his legend has lived on, in a way in which it would surely not have done had he simply led an ordinary lung-powered and oxygen-fuelled existence like the rest of us. Known to history as 'The Burcot Eccentric', Tallis' life has been held up over the past 300 or so years not, as you may initially expect, as an object of pity, disgust or incomprehension, but as a source largely of wonder and amusement. He first came to public attention in an issue of *The Gentleman's Magazine* for March 1753, where news of him was billed in a headline as 'Mr Tallis' Extraordinary Method of Life', the *Magazine*'s fascinated correspondent in Burcot ultimately concluding that Tallis should be left alone to rest in his bed on the reasonable grounds that 'though he is not useful, he is at least harmless'. After all, there was no need, wrote the publication's man on the spot, to start sermonising to 'caution mankind against his peculiar extravagances', on account of the obvious fact that nobody else in the country would want to follow his bizarre example in any case![3]

Such a laissez-faire and almost even admiring attitude is often held up as being characteristically English in its nature. While, from today's perspective, we can see that the man must have had some pretty severe mental problems, Tallis ultimately became known specifically by that typically English word, 'eccentric', not as a 'madman' or a 'disturbed' person, as he might have done had he had the misfortune to be born elsewhere than in these isles. If Tallis had been born in America or Australia, for instance, he might have been termed a 'crank' or a 'kook', a 'freak' or a 'nutter', a 'misfit' or a 'crackpot'. The difference in terminology is very telling. All nations have their strange people, but it seems to be only the British – and the English especially – who have made something of a cult out of them. It is not that Britain has eccentric people living here that makes us unusual as such – it is our *attitude* towards them that is, in itself, the eccentric thing about our land.

These islands have long been a stronghold of peculiar behaviour among their people. From William Lauder Lindsay, the Scottish psychiatrist who acclaimed lobsters as capable of love and damned crabs as having hearts of stone, to Joe Meek, the paranoid music-producer who turned down the Beatles in favour of a talking cat, to Sir George Sitwell, the peculiar aristocrat who invented a tiny gun for shooting wasps and attempted to write a complete scholarly history of the fork, all have been more than tolerated here, and this book will tell the story of some of the very strangest. For whatever reason, eccentricity has traditionally been enthusiastically embraced as being one of the British people's defining characteristics, one of the many things that add up to make us what we are – a fact that has been being exploited by those in the publishing industry for over 200 years now. According to one recent study, for instance, it has been estimated that, between the years 1790 and 1901 alone, over sixty works dealing with the lives of eccentrics were published in England, with titles like Henry Wilson's 1821 *Wonderful Characters* and William Russell's 1868 *Eccentric Personages* fighting for shelf space with books adopting a more specific approach to the subject, like Cyrus Reddings' 1863 *Memoirs of Remarkable Misers*.[4] Such titles, as this present book proves, continue to appear, year after year, and show no discernible sign of stopping. Perhaps they never will stop – the lives of our fellow countrymen provide writers like me with such a rich seam of bizarre and unbelievable biographies to be written and recycled that it is hard to believe the mine will ever be exhausted.

But why is this? Is it our status as an island people, set apart from the rest of the world, that has made so many of our countrymen turn in on themselves and go a little strange? Has our long libertarian tradition of the idea of the freedom of the individual to live his own life as he pleases, just so long as he does no harm to anybody else, allowed weirdness to flourish within our land? Or is there just something dodgy in the water? Surprisingly, some of our nation's greatest minds have seen fit to try and consider the question, which is a testament to the centrality of the whole notion of eccentricity to our native culture.

For John Stuart Mill, for instance, the great nineteenth-century liberal philosopher, MP and champion of personal and political liberty, the degree to which a person had the right to be eccentric in their way of life was a visible sign of the health and vigour of democracy itself, and a central pillar of the strength of the British state. As he wrote in his 1859 masterpiece *On Liberty*, eccentricity and genius themselves tended to walk together hand in hand, due to the 'originality in thought and action' that people in possession of such qualities tended to display. However, as he then admitted,

> Originality is the one thing which unoriginal minds cannot feel the use of. They cannot see what it is to do for them: how should they? If they could see what it would do for them, it would not be originality.[5]

The great danger facing British society during his day, Mill thought, was what he saw as an increasing trend towards social conformity among the masses, with their derided 'unoriginal minds'. After all, he argued, 'Nothing was ever yet done which someone was not the first to do,' and, while many independent thinkers might well be leading themselves down blind alleys, how could anyone ever be able to tell a hopeless crank apart from the next Isaac Newton with any real degree of certainty? Because of such reasoning, Mill thought that the great British tradition of tolerating eccentricity was one which was worth defending.

> In this age, the mere example of nonconformity, the mere refusal to bend the knee to custom, is itself a service. Precisely because the tyranny of opinion is such as to make eccentricity a reproach, it is desirable, in order to break through that tyranny, that people should be eccentric. Eccentricity has always abounded when and where strength of character has abounded; and the amount of eccentricity in a society has generally been proportional to the amount of genius, mental vigour and moral courage that it contained.[6]

Indeed, for Mill, so central was the idea of tolerating eccentrics to our national character that a lack of visible eccentricity in our land could actually be seen as being a kind of 'canary in the mine' – or 'the chief danger of the time', as he put it – and a warning that something was in the process of going badly wrong in the British body politic. To Mill, the right of an Englishman to quietly go a bit loopy without being unduly bothered by his peers was virtually an extra, hidden clause of Magna Carta itself; the right to be eccentric was not only a kind of guarantor of individual liberty, but also of national greatness. This is because, paradoxically, while by definition the typical eccentric tends to operate upon the margins of society, when on the odd occasion his ideas do actually manage to come off successfully, in a truly healthy civilisation he will end up in some sense being embraced back into that society's centre somehow, and not simply be rejected or have his ideas suppressed. The number of borderline madmen who stand among the pantheon of a nation's true greats, Mill implies, can thus effectively be seen as being a fairly accurate (if somewhat surprising) indication of that same nation itself's own claim to greatness.

Ancient Greece was full of slightly odd yet simultaneously brilliant eccentrics like Archimides and Pythagoras, for instance – and just look at the immortal legacy that that particular great civilisation left to the world. It is telling that even the ancient Greeks' non-eccentric geniuses, like the philosopher Empedocles, and the mathematician and astronomer Thales, had silly little stories invented about them which can be read as having been intended to illustrate that their intellect and their supposed lunacy went hand in hand. Empedocles, for instance, was meant to have thrown himself into the volcano of Mount Etna, in order to demonstrate to his followers that he was immortal (it turned out that he wasn't), and Thales ultimately became better-known for a fable told about him supposedly falling down a well while gazing up in absorbed contemplation of the stars above his head instead of looking where he was going properly.[7] According to no less an authority than Bertrand Russell, 'philosophy begins with Thales'[8] – and yet the people who came after him still felt the need to paint him as nothing more than an absentminded odd bod who went around falling into holes like some early Hellenic version of Mr Bean.

Was Thales being mocked or celebrated in this fabricated tale, then? It is hard to say; perhaps it is both at once. There is certainly an uneasy tension present in the British people's customary love of eccentrics, in which most people who read or hear about them seem torn between a certain admiration for such people's determination to plough their own furrow in spite of everything and simply laughing at them as bizarre but amiable nutcases. Whatever the case may be, though, never (except perhaps in the present day, as we shall see at the end of this book) could the British people be accused of ever simply ignoring their eccentrics or, worse, of actively persecuting them. Instead, as a rule, they seem to have been actively cherished, or at least tolerated, so long as they don't do anybody else any obvious harm. So evident has this aspect of our national character been that foreign visitors, too, have frequently seen cause to comment upon it. In 1787, for instance, the Prussian military officer and political historian Johann Wilhelm von Archenholz saw fit to publish an entire chapter called 'The Peculiarities of the British' in his book *England*, where his own particular celebration of English eccentricities sounded almost as if it could have come from the pen of John Stuart Mill himself. This is what Archenholz wrote:

> In England peculiar behaviour of all kinds is so frequent that people have a name for it. Such a thing is called a 'whim', and the person who frequently practices it 'a whimsical man'. In other countries such people are taken for crazy, but because here freedom is abetted by every possible means if it causes no damage, people aren't very surprised about such things: a bizarre story makes just another something about which people laugh or shrug their shoulders ... It would be possible to fill entire volumes with the peculiar behaviour of the British, which are daily occurrences in England and are a peculiarity of only these islanders because they, of all large and small peoples and tribes on earth, live most after their own fancies and can act on them because in their country they feel people to be individuals.[9]

To von Archenholz, given the land of his birth, such facts must have seemed particularly startling; the stereotypically regimented social structure in which the average Prussian military-man had to live was perhaps the direct spiritual opposite to Britain's long-held toleration for a man's own personal foibles. The contrast between the traditional British tolerance of eclecticism and the more regimented ways of certain societies abroad has perhaps never been so loudly and persistently pointed out, however, as during times of war and national crisis. For the writer and polemicist George Orwell, for example, in his 1941 essay *England, Your England*, one of the defining qualities of our national character was what he termed 'the addiction to hobbies and spare-time occupations, the *privateness* of English life'.

Celebrating the English as 'a nation of flower-lovers, but also a nation of stamp-collectors, pigeon-fanciers, amateur carpenters, coupon-snippers, darts-players [and] crossword-puzzle fans', Orwell contrasted the natural right of the free-born Englishman to live his own life the way he himself pleased, and to hold whatever opinions he chose to see fit, with the lack of personal liberty seemingly afforded among the ranks of our then war-time enemies in Nazi Germany, the twentieth-century heirs to the old Prussian military conventions of the likes of von Archenholz. As he put it, the in-born inclination of the British citizen to chart his own course in life, against any and all official attempts to make him conform to 'official' attitudes, meant that in Britain there could be 'no party rallies, no Youth Movements, no coloured shirts ... No Gestapo either, in all probability'.[10]

This seems comforting news, but Orwell, in a curious echo of John Stuart Mill writing almost a century earlier, then warns us that this peculiarly British way of life is coming more and more under threat in the modern world – and not only from the attentions of potential militaristic foreign invaders. There is, it would seem, a prospective enemy within. Later on in the same essay, Orwell decries how, 'in a narrowing world, more and more governed from Whitehall', there may in the future be rather less space for the true British eccentric or individualist to operate in the mainstream of national life. He explains this theory with reference to the then still-extensive British Empire, which he saw as having undergone a process of 'stagnation' since the 1920s. While certainly no fan of Imperialism, to say the least, Orwell still sought to contrast the lively, independent-minded and frequently heroic (some of them arguably to the point of insanity) giants of the earlier years of the Empire, men such as Admiral Nelson, General Gordon, Lawrence of Arabia and Clive of India, with the modern, centralised mode of government in which 'well-meaning, over-civilised men in dark suits and black felt hats, with neatly rolled umbrellas crooked over the left forearm, were imposing their constipated view of life on Malaya and Nigeria, Mombasa and Mandalay', thus reducing the modern equivalents of such folk heroes as Nelson and Gordon down to 'the status of clerks, buried deeper and deeper under mounds of paper and red tape'.[11]

This was worrying news indeed for a society that had, to a very great degree, been governed by a kind of benign 'cult of the amateur'. It has often been said that Britain gained her Empire by mistake, and it has to be admitted that a disproportionate number of our nation's greatest successes in conquest, commerce, science and other such important fields have been made by persons operating from well outside of the mainstream, and at the behest of no pre-defined 'great plan' imposed upon them from the centre by government or other traditional strongholds of administrative power. Soviet-style 'five-year plans' or Chairman Mao-esque 'Great

Leaps Forward' are fundamentally alien to a society many of whose
most important developments seem to happen as much by accident
as anything else, and whose economy is governed more by the
so-called 'invisible hand' of the great eighteenth-century Scottish
economic theorist Adam Smith than by the sadly increasingly
visible 'dead hand' of the state.

Many of our greatest minds and most celebrated figures – from
Isaac Newton to Winston Churchill, from Dr Johnson to Lord
Byron – have, at least for part of their lives, ploughed a lone
furrow, pursuing their own unusual ideas privately to a point
most people would have found to be profoundly odd, all the while
engaged in various personal foibles, from compulsively seeking
hidden messages from God in the Bible (Newton), to rolling down
hills for fun and collecting old orange-peels for no apparent reason
(Johnson), to keeping a tame bear in his university-rooms as a
pet (Byron), to obsessively building brick-walls for recreational
purposes (Churchill), which definitely qualify them as having been
highly eccentric by anyone's standards.

But the monomanias of such people ended up having truly
remarkable results, from the discovery and formulation of the laws
of gravity, to the defeat of Hitler, to the creation of some of our
tongue's finest poetry, to the compilation of the English language's
first true dictionary; incredible achievements, which would clearly
have been beyond the ability of most ordinary people such as
John Stuart Mill's bland, amoeba-like masses with their uniformly
'unoriginal minds', or George Orwell's constipated, felt hat-wearing,
umbrella-wielding Whitehall mandarins, to even conceive of, let
alone see come to fruition. The idea of there being a fine line between
madness and genius is not entirely without reason when it comes to
such people, clearly; and perhaps it is because of this fact that we
should examine the origins of the word 'eccentric' more closely, for
its curious history is more complex than it may initially seem ...

The word 'eccentric' was originally an astronomical term,
deriving ultimately from the Greek word *ekkentros*, meaning 'out
of the centre', and was used from 1551 onwards to describe the way
in which a planet or other heavenly body's path often deviates from
a perfect circle around the body which it is orbiting. By 1685, we
can find examples of it being used to describe unusual behaviour,
and it finally became a noun, describing an actual eccentric
person, in 1832.[12] We can see how the term came eventually to be
applied to people and their behaviour, not just the movement of
astronomical bodies, by examining Dr Johnson's definition of the

word 'ECCENTRICK', from his celebrated *Dictionary* of 1755. Rather than simply printing a picture of himself rolling down a hill beneath the word and saying 'That's one!', Johnson was at pains to give as accurate a definition of the concept as was possible, giving four possible senses in which it could be used. Firstly, he provides the explanation 'Deviating from the centre', then 'Not having the same centre with another circle', thirdly, 'Not terminating in the same point; not directed by the same principle' and finally 'Irregular, anomalous; deviating from stated and constant methods'.[13] This would seem to describe the path traced out by many eccentrics' own thought patterns perfectly, making it easy to see how the word could eventually come to be used in its present sense. But are such thought patterns necessarily a bad thing?

John Stuart Mill would not have said so. Eccentrics' habits of seeing things from a different point of view, and approaching problems from new and previously unconsidered angles, of existing in a different kind of orbit from the vast mass of humanity, were, for Mill, precisely what allowed them to achieve such extraordinary things. Take away Dr Johnson's hill-rolling and orange peel-collecting, and you might well end up taking away his magnificent *Dictionary*, too; you could easily argue that the notion of spending nine solid years of your life trying to collect and define an example of every word in the English language and then publishing 42,773 of them in a giant book of some 2,300-plus pages was every bit as much of a lunatic exploit as some of his other, less celebrated, personal activities were. This, after all, was a man who occasionally spent his spare time investigating ghosts, who once physically assaulted his employer by battering him to the floor with a large book, and who made the practice of deliberately insulting other people's feelings almost into an art form. The average person, perhaps, might not think that any of those particular undertakings were a particularly good idea; but then the average person does not create the very concept of the modern dictionary. The general orbit of their mind occupies altogether too ordinary and rational a path for them ever to be able to even think about doing such a thing.

But is this all just a kind of slightly patronising attempt to romanticise certain aspects of mental illness? Occasionally, some people's fondness for eccentricity could be viewed in such a negative light, and there is no doubt that, like the Surrealists occasionally did over in France, a kind of 'cult of madness' can sometimes be built up, in which people's eccentricities become so celebrated that, eventually, they end up taking things too far and make the fatal step over that hazy borderline which undoubtedly exists between mere oddness and outright insanity. The French poet André Breton, for instance, the founder of the Surrealist movement, actively sought out the company of unusual persons, especially those of an artistic and literary bent, finding their company to be both stimulating and amusing to him. Here, for instance, is his admiring description of one of the most marked public eccentricities of the celebrated English painter Leonora Carrington (1917–2011), a sometime fellow-traveller of Breton's own movement:

> Who today could answer that description [of a bewitching young eccentric] better than Leonora Carrington? The respectable persons who invited her to dine in an elegant restaurant a dozen or so years ago have still not forgotten their embarrassment at noticing that, all the while taking part in the conversation, she had removed her shoes and was patiently slathering her feet in mustard.[14]

Most amusing, of course – and yet Leonora Carrington ended up spending time in a mental institution. So did several other of Breton's fellow Surrealists. So did one of Breton's own lovers. And yet, after admiring some of Carrington's later canvases, painted after her release from the madhouse, this is what the much-vaunted 'Pope of Surrealism' had to say about them:

> Leonora Carrington has retained a nostalgia for the shores [of insanity] that she once approached and that she has not despaired of reaching anew, this time without brooking any resistance, as if granted a permit to travel in either direction at will.[15]

If Breton himself, for all his own undoubted genius, had ever stepped over onto those same shores of insanity, then perhaps he would have discovered for himself that gaining a permit for travel back from them to the land of the sane was not always quite so easy as he might have imagined.

The so-called 'anti-psychiatry movement' which began to spring up across Europe and America during the 1960s and 70s could also be viewed in light of such romantic wishful thinking. When the French historian and philosopher Michel Foucault published his classic study *Madness and Civilisation: A History of Insanity in the Age of Reason* in 1961, for instance, it seemed initially to be a largely admirable and commendably compassionate plea for wider society to reconsider the welfare of some of its more unfortunate outcasts, who had been locked away in mental institutions for years on end and then simply forgotten about. Foucault argued that, way back during the Renaissance, so long as they were not actively dangerous, mad people and extreme eccentrics were once given some kind of credit by many people as having access to a sort of 'different truth' from the rest of us. 'Melancholics', for instance – what we might now call 'depressives' – were often associated with sudden flashes of inspiration and genius that the sane were ordinarily denied access to. Instead of automatically being locked up or drugged, such people were often engaged with by others, to the benefit of all. During the Enlightenment, however, said Foucault, such ideas began to be denied and suppressed, with the mad being 'quarantined' away from society in asylums, even when their behaviour was essentially benign and they were of no danger to themselves or others, leading to what he called the 'dialogue' between the sane and the insane being brought to an abrupt end.

While in an abstract sense Foucault's ideas were seemingly humane enough, however, some people who have since been influenced by them – whether directly or indirectly – have undoubtedly gone too far in their attempts to put them into action. Some people, after all, are placed inside institutions for very good reasons indeed! Perhaps chief among these offenders against common sense was the famous Scottish psychiatrist R. D. Laing (1927–1989). Laing was not only a psychiatrist – and an incurable eccentric himself, in many ways – but also an extreme left-wing thinker, who, like many a wannabe-revolutionary, thought that in various ways Western capitalist society itself was insane, and that as such the madness of the insane individual was, paradoxically, by far the sanest response a person could have to the cruel world they were forced to live in by 'The System'. As such, Laing didn't think that madness was something to be 'cured', so much as 'worked through'. In a recent interview with the intrepid investigative journalist Jon Ronson, Laing's son Adrian explained his parent's thinking thus:

> My father believed that if you allowed madness to take its natural course without intervention – without lobotomies and drugs and straight-jackets and all the awful things they were doing at the time in mental hospitals – it would burn itself out, like an LSD trip through the system.[16]

The reference to mind-altering substances here is perhaps telling. It seems that Laing grew to have a rather over-exaggerated respect for insanity, sometimes feeling the same awe about those who suffered from it as Renaissance medical men could do for the melancholics they were called on to treat. As such, the treatment regime at London's Kingsley Hall, the infamous 'therapeutic community' Laing helped set up for mental patients in 1965, was rather an unorthodox one. Patients were encouraged to be creative, to sing and dance in rooms hung with soft and colourful Indian silks, while celebrities of the day like Sean Connery, attracted by Laing's fashionable theories, wandered about the place observing matters and attending specially arranged poetry evenings put on for their benefit. This all sounds very pleasant and enlightened – but, as Laing's son Adrian later told Ronson, there was really rather an 'unhealthy' level of respect for madness about the place.

Exhibit A was a rather smelly place in the basement known as 'Mary Barnes' Shit-Room'. Here, in a bizarre new experiment, Laing had attempted to get a schizophrenic patient named Mary Barnes (1923–2001) to regress down to the mental level of a new-born baby, so that she could then be encouraged to grow back up sane again. The plan didn't really seem to work that well, however. Inhabiting her new-found infantile state, Mary had begun sleeping in a wooden chest for a crib, crawling around the place naked, abandoned all human language in favour of a system of baby-like squeals, and was refusing to eat unless fed direct from a bottle. Worse, she had begun defecating all over the place, smearing her brown stuff across the walls and her own body like an uncontrolled toddler. Rather than simply stepping in and putting a stop to all this, however, Laing instead engaged in an earnest discussion with his colleagues about Mary's 'right' to protest against the madness of the world by rolling around in her own filth like this, and debated how this could be made to fit in with his other patients' equally valid right not to have to live in a part of the building that was increasingly beginning to smell like a public toilet.

Clearly, this was idolisation of madness and eccentricity taken to its wholly illogical extreme. However, while Laing never did manage to coherently explain just how it was he expected to cure a schizophrenic by having her strip naked and then soil herself in front of James Bond, the story does, somewhat surprisingly, have a happy ending to it. Noticing that Mary had begun painting pictures on the wall with her poo, one of Laing's colleagues suggested that they give her some crayons and a painting-set to see if this might calm her down a bit. Amazingly, it did – and Mary Barnes later went on to be an acclaimed artist, whose paintings were praised, exhibited, and sold for large amounts of money, with a celebratory play being put on about her journey out of insanity and into genius at London's Royal Court theatre in 1979.[17] Maybe Laing did have a certain point about great things sometimes lurking away inside some mental patients after all ...

Or, then again, maybe not. Most mental patients who go around perpetrating dirty-protests do not later go on to be acclaimed artists – and nor, indeed, do most acclaimed artists later go on to perpetrate any dirty protests. However, artists and creative-types like writers and musicians are, as a whole, often viewed by the average person as being highly eccentric in their nature nonetheless, as we shall eventually see in the chapter in this book which is devoted to some of their most noted British examples. On account of their remarkable creative exploits, society seems happy to give such persons a little leeway to go around acting in a way which, if they were simply ordinary people with nine-to-five jobs, might bring them to the inescapable attention of psychiatrists.

An undeniable difficulty, though, then clearly begins to arise – namely, where should we draw the dividing-line between mere eccentricity and outright madness? Is such a thing even possible? How could such a thing be done? These are difficult questions indeed, and perhaps this is the reason why surprisingly few doctors and psychiatrists have ever made a concerted attempt to answer them. One man who finally did take these perplexing and burdensome problems upon himself, however, was Dr David Weeks, the author (with Jamie James) of the influential 1995 book *Eccentrics: A Study of Sanity and Strangeness*, and a prominent neuropsychiatrist at the Royal Edinburgh Hospital.

Weeks came to fame in 1984, when he started leaving cards in everyday locations across the Scottish capital, places like pubs, supermarkets, laundrettes and libraries. These cards read simply 'ECCENTRIC? If you feel that you might be, contact Dr David Weeks at the Royal Edinburgh Hospital.' One person who picked up Dr Weeks' card, though, was not a local eccentric at all, but a journalist. A story about Dr Weeks and his quest soon appeared in a regional newspaper, was picked up on by *The Scotsman*, and thence was regurgitated again and again by media organisations around the whole world. Tabloids, magazines and news programmes which carried the story quickly spread the word much farther than Edinburgh, and between the years 1984–87, Dr Weeks estimated that around 30 million people in the UK alone were made aware of his plea.

But what, precisely, was Dr Weeks trying to do? An original native of New Jersey, Weeks had long had a fascination with eccentrics, something that may well have been sparked by tales of his own slightly odd sci-fi-nut grandfather supposedly driving his car off a pier in 1938 in an attempt to escape from a Martian invasion of America, which he had managed to convince himself was then in the process of taking place. Dr Weeks realised that here was a potentially interesting field of study, especially once he discovered that he would essentially have it all to himself, given that no previous formal clinical research into the topic of eccentrics had ever been made.

Ultimately, around 800 volunteers were recruited for study by Dr Weeks, some of whom were very strange indeed. For instance, there was the person who kept a collection of coffins in his house and invited guests to try them out for size in order to help prepare themselves for their own inevitable deaths, the cave-dwelling ex-Royal Marine who liked hiking around the Scottish coastline in his bare feet and clad only in his pyjamas, the man whose only interest in life was the history of potatoes, and who had managed to secure his dream employment as a potato inspector so as to be able to spend his every waking hour in the root vegetables' company, the man who camped out inside dumpsters, wandering the streets with a mattress until he could find one that looked comfortable enough to make a bed for the night in, and the woman who gained an inexplicable sense of joy from going around town and wallpapering public toilets in her spare time.

Dr Weeks certainly managed to unearth some fascinating case-studies, but of course his real aim with the study was not simply to provide the general public with some amusing anecdotes about weird people, but to draw as many interesting and useful conclusions from his subjects as he could. He was able to estimate that, for instance, there were probably around 6,000 eccentrics living in the UK in 1984 (that is, about one in 10,000 people), that most eccentrics were highly intelligent, his subjects having an average IQ of 115–120, as compared to a UK-wide average of 104, and that male eccentrics outnumbered their female counterparts by a ratio of two to one.[18] Weeks' greatest desire, however, was to find out what exactly it was that made an eccentric *into* an eccentric, as opposed to a full-on psychotic. His basic answer, given in a 1986 interview to an American tabloid magazine, makes perfect sense.

Eccentrics are the most diverse people in the world, and among the hardest to define. In general they are loners and nonconformists who are curious, creative [and] obsessive. They don't give a hoot about what other people think about them. They see the rest of the world as rather mundane and out of step with them … [However] eccentrics have not lost touch with reality. They have insight into their behaviour and usually don't show any of the positive symptoms of [mental] illness, such as delusions and hallucinations.[19]

These facts probably account for the otherwise bemusing truth that nobody had ever performed a full-scale clinical study into the issue of eccentricity before. If eccentrics were neither delusional nor psychotic, and of no meaningful danger to themselves or others, then this meant that the very word 'eccentricity' merely denoted a certain slightly unusual personality type, and not a specific mental disorder or diagnosis as such. For instance, we all know people who are optimists, and people who are pessimists; but they would never be diagnosed as such by a psychiatrist and given medical treatment, as these are not states of mental illness. Nobody has ever been locked away in a mental asylum just for being a bit too gloomy or a tad too chirpy first thing in the morning, after all. Eccentricity, Dr Weeks stated, is therefore better thought of simply as being a way to describe a man or woman's personal character than of describing a form of mental disorder. Eccentrics, it seems, were not mad after all – just a bit 'different' from the norm. You might as well call an exceptionally attractive person a freak, as an eccentric person insane.

In order to help us better measure and define the so-called 'eccentric personality', Dr Weeks eventually came up with a flexible basic check-list of things a typical eccentric (if there is such a thing) may reasonably be expected to do, have or be, namely:

Be a nonconformist or loner, with little interest in mainstream society or popular culture.

Be creative, whether artistically, mechanically or in other ways.

Be idealistic, wishing to make the world a better place.

Be excessively but happily obsessed with around one to six hobbies or subjects.

Be aware from childhood that he or she is different from most other people.

Be more intelligent than the average person.

Be opinionated, often convinced that they are right and everyone else wrong.

Be non-competitive with others in a material sense, unconcerned with money/possessions.
Be unusual in their living and/or eating arrangements.
Be in possession of an extreme or unusual sense of humour.
Be single, and/or have no children.
Be an eldest or only child.
Be a bad speller.[20]

Surprisingly, this final apparently trivial characteristic is in some ways actually the most telling one – it seems that many ostensibly dyslexic eccentrics are perfectly capable of spelling words properly if they want to, it's just that they think their own self-invented way is better than the dictionary's! Maybe that's the real reason why Dr Johnson felt the need to write his own ...

The main difference between the madman and the eccentric, though, may well be that the eccentric almost always *knows* he is eccentric, being too intelligent and self-aware to think otherwise, and is perfectly content about the fact. As Dr Weeks once put it, 'Without exception, eccentrics are happy in their eccentricity.'[21] While I'm not entirely sure that this is *always* true (some of the eccentrics we shall meet in this book have ended up committing suicide, for example), it does seem to *generally* be so. As Dr Weeks has wisely suggested, people with a mental illness *suffer* from their condition, whereas eccentrics seem usually to actively *enjoy* their lot in life. Thus, even in spite of her heartening later artistic success, Mary Barnes was clearly quite severely mentally ill while still under the care of R. D. Laing in the 1960s, as she reportedly 'hated being mad', finding this state to be 'agony', and 'desperately wishing to be normal',[22] whereas, say, Dr Johnson was quite happy to have a few unusual ways, was able generally to lead a full and useful life, and so could be classified as having been merely eccentric, rather than disturbed.

This does seem a sensible way to look at matters, as we can see that even some of the most extreme eccentrics appear to derive far more pleasure from their weirdness than sorrow. You may, for instance, imagine John Tallis, the fresh-air-phobic eighteenth-century bed-dweller of Burcot, to have been a miserable and choleric old soul – but not a bit of it, apparently. According to Johann Wilhelm von Archenholz, who mentioned Tallis in his book *England* as an illustration of a typical English eccentric,

He was an intelligent man and, even more remarkably, a vivacious one. He ate and drank with good appetite [presumably

after having removed the ivory stopper from his mouth first ...]
and remained continually healthy [apart from his withered legs!]
to a great age.[23]

The earlier-cited correspondent of *The Gentleman's Magazine*,
who visited Tallis in 1753 and gained a sight of the noted sleeper
at first-hand, was likewise impressed with his talkativeness and
gregarious nature, once his host had managed to wake himself up
fully from his habitual slumbers. According to the correspondent:

> When I beheld him, he opened his eyes and stretched himself like
> a bat that is just awaking from a sleep of six or seven months; but,
> as he awaked thirsty and disordered, he reached his cup, which
> was constantly placed near him with some cooling liquor, and
> having drank, he exhibited his right hand decorated with many
> rings, which he surveyed with great appearance of satisfaction
> and complacency, and entered into a description of [The Tower
> of] Babel, the Nile and crocodiles.[24]

There can be few people who, when faced with a stranger
standing around in their bedroom, would feel happy not to miss
a beat but simply to start showing off their jewellery and opening
up a completely random-sounding conversation about Egyptian
crocodiles with their visitor, but clearly Mr Tallis was one of them.
Obviously, the Burcot Eccentric was perfectly happy in his own
skin, even if most of the rest of us would not be. This brings us
to another aspect of Dr Weeks' discoveries, one which was given
much publicity at the time and which still pops up in the popular
press occasionally today – namely that, on apparent account of
their greater levels of happiness with their lives than the general
population, the typical eccentric enjoys better health and a longer
life-span than the usual non-eccentric in the street does, seeing
a doctor on average only once every eight-and-a-half years, an
amazing twenty times less often than most people do. Significantly,
quite apart from having fewer physiological problems, eccentrics
are also far less prone to suffering from genuine mental illnesses
and conditions like depression than the general population.[25]

But why is this? Dr Weeks' answer was simple. Locked up in
their sheds beavering away on their unworkable perpetual-motion
machines like benign cousins of Professor Frankenstein, or engaged
in endless labours on their unpublishable 10,000-page books about
the history of the potato like misguided versions of Dr Johnson,

eccentrics, being quite happy floating around in their own little bubbles away from the myriad pressures and strains of the everyday world in which most citizens are forced to live, simply suffer from far less stress than the average person does. Rather than ending up as a nervous wreck like Reggie Perrin through trying to conform all day at the office and then again at home in curtain-twitching suburbia of an evening, they are able to unwind by devoting time to their own chosen hobby horses at home, relieving stressful feelings from their persons in a way which proves to be highly effective. Less stress means a better immune system, said Dr Weeks – and hence, fewer visits for eccentrics to the doctor, the psychiatrist and the hospital, and a probable delayed appointment with the local undertaker, too. Being an eccentric is good for you, it would seem!

One other curious aspect of eccentricity worth noting here to finish with, though, is eccentrics' frequent fascination with other figures of their kind – it is the case, for instance, that one of the most unusual persons chosen for greater discussion in this book, the poet Dame Edith Sitwell, published a notable book about the lives of her fellow eccentrics, as we shall soon see. Another source upon which I have drawn while writing this text, meanwhile, is the 1984 book *Eccentric Lives and Peculiar Notions* by a man named John Michell (1933–2009), a fascinating and admirable character who, during a long and varied career, edited a magazine about crop-circles, helped put Glastonbury on the New Age map, and wrote best-selling books with titles like *The Flying Saucer Vision* and *The View Over Atlantis*, in which he laid out the theory that UFOs and other such alleged paranormal phenomena were, in his own words, 'portents of a radical change in human consciousness coinciding with the Dawn of the Aquarian Age.'[26] Odd people like to know information about other odd people, it would appear. Perhaps they find some comfort in knowing that, in some sense, they are not alone. But, if this pattern of finding enjoyment in hearing about the lives of eccentrics is a personality trait which, in itself, is slightly eccentric in its nature, then stop and think about this fact for a moment; for what does it say about *you* for having chosen to obtain and read this present book in the first place – or, indeed, about me for having chosen to write it?

Ah well, look on the bright side. At least you probably won't be taking a trip to the doctor or the funeral parlour any time soon.

Aberrant Aristocrats:
Upper-Class Eccentrics

The chief inmates of the stately homes of England who really were an entire breed apart.

If there's one thing that having blue blood running through your veins gives you, then it's a sense of supreme and easy confidence; take, for example, the life of Sir Claude Champion de Crespigny (1847–1935), a sportsman, soldier and adventurer of the very first order, and one who could only ever have been born an Englishman. The author of the 1910 memoir *Forty Years of a Sportsman's Life*, Sir Claude's definition of what constituted 'sportsmanship' was rather far removed from the idea which may be held by pampered millionaire Premier League footballers or F1 racing drivers today. His abiding maxim in life was that 'wherever there is a daring deed to be done in any part of the world, an Englishman should leap to the front to accomplish it', advice he himself followed at every available opportunity.

His first career was that of a warrior; he started early, entering the Royal Navy aged only thirteen, and transferring to the King's Royal Rifle Corp in 1866, but it seems that a life of regimented order was not for him. Typically, Sir Claude wanted more action than even the armed forces could provide, and in 1870 he resigned his commission to devote himself to far less relaxing exploits than mere warfare. A keen huntsman, known as the 'Mad Rider' due to his wild style in the saddle, Sir Claude had already tried his hand at steeplechasing, winning his first race in 1867 and continuing to compete successfully until as late as 1914, when he was an amazing sixty-seven years old. Apparently, he had chosen steeplechasing as his preferred discipline because flat racing simply wasn't dangerous enough. One time, after falling from his horse and being rendered unconscious by a heavy hoof-kick to the head, de Crespigny was so delighted by the experience that he was back on horseback within a mere four days – having previously attempted to recuperate from his injury by rolling his cricket ground flat single-handed. Other sports he tried included swimming, big-game hunting, diving and canoeing, becoming, in 1889, the first European to swim the rapids of the Nile.

This still wasn't enough to quench his adventure-lust, though; in 1869, despite having no relevant experience whatsoever, he generously offered his services to Henry Morton Stanley on his expedition into darkest Africa in search of the missing Dr Livingstone, but was promptly turned down. He was likewise disappointed when turned away from Niagara Falls one day after asking to be allowed to try and walk across it via tightrope, and was most annoyed, after securing a position as war correspondent for *The Sporting Times*, to be turned back from a combat zone in Egypt by military officials who were sceptical that this publication would employ someone to write about anything other than horse racing. Bored beyond endurance, in 1882 de Crespigny felt compelled to take up hot air ballooning, winning the Balloon Society's gold medal for being the first man to cross the North Sea in such a vehicle in July 1883. Another way Sir Claude discovered of staving off ennui, meanwhile, was to volunteer as a hangman. In 1886, having been advised that he might be asked to serve as the High Sheriff of Essex, he considered it his duty to see what it took to hang a man, travelling up to Carlisle to assist during the execution of a trio of convicted murderers.

Fighting, however, was his real passion, whether with fists, swords, knives or pistols, and he continued to engage in regular bouts of violent fisticuffs right into his seventies, considering such pursuits to be a good test of character. After inheriting his baronetcy in 1868, de Crespigny decided to implement a programme of unconventional job interviews for anyone applying to be taken on as a male servant at his ancestral home at Heybridge in Essex; he began punching them in the face to see if they fought back. Regardless of whether or not they lost the fight, if Sir Claude considered them to have put up a good enough show, he took them onto his staff – pacifists need not apply. Even passing tramps were not safe from the Baronet's flailing fists; he used to offer them a hot dinner if they agreed to spar with him. Sir Claude usually won – except on one occasion, when some of his friends paid a professional boxer to disguise himself as a vagrant and administer a sound thrashing. Defeated, de Crespigny was as good as his word, and gave the 'tramp' his meal, finding his injuries to be highly amusing.

Naturally, Sir Claude was eager for his children to follow in his footsteps and prove themselves real men – even though four of them were in fact females. Proud of his swimming skills, he decided to throw them all in at the deep end – literally. Sir Claude's chosen method of teaching his offspring to swim consisted of taking them out in a boat and then unceremoniously pushing them over the side, leaving them to work out how to make it back to dry land themselves. None of them actually drowned, though, so the technique must have worked! Certainly, Sir Claude's sons grew up to be brave; one, Norman, was killed during the First World War while attempting to capture some German artillery armed with only a revolver, and another son, also called Claude, was twice recommended to receive the Victoria Cross during the Second Boer War. Sadly, in May 1910 Claude Jr committed suicide aged thirty-seven, the coroner concluding that perhaps he had been damaged in the head through falling off his horse too often while playing polo. Maybe something similar had happened to his father, too, that day he got his skull kicked in by a racehorse.[1]

Of course, such supreme self-confidence could easily tip over into outright arrogance among certain members of the British aristocracy. Consider, for instance, the case of Percy Sholto Douglas, 10th Marquess of Queensberry (1868–1920), who so disliked the new-fangled motorcars that were springing up towards the end of his life that he attempted to get a court permit allowing him to shoot their drivers dead on sight.[2] In 1995, meanwhile, one Lord Erskine of Rerrick (1926–1995) was so outraged that RBS, with whom he banked, had dared to cross him that he threatened to leave it his testicles in his will, seeing as in his view the institution 'had no balls'.[3] Another supremely arrogant aristocrat was Charles Seymour, 6th Duke of Somerset (1662–1748), dubbed 'The Proud Duke' on account of his hatred of the lower orders. Seymour considered his servants so inferior that he refused ever to speak to them, communicating his wishes via written notes or rudimentary sign language, and was so disturbed by the idea of encountering a commoner on his way down to London to see King George I that he used to send outriders on ahead to clear the road of riff-raff. He also had a series of houses built at intervals along his route so he could sleep overnight in them instead of having to lodge at any

inns with the great unwashed. He wasn't much more generous to
his own kith and kin either, once partially disinheriting a daughter
after she had committed the heinous crime of sitting down on a
chair without his permission.[4]

Maybe it was suffering such unfeeling abuse at the hands of
their parents which has made so many of our aristocrats go a bit
loopy. Certainly, this seems to have been partly the case with Sir
Tatton Sykes (1826–1913), whose father (another Sir Tatton) was
so keen on thrashing his son and heir that he was once seen running
through the Yorkshire village of Sledmere after him, barefoot and
screaming, brandishing a whip. Once this old tyrant had died,
the younger Sir Tatton wasted no time in gaining his revenge by
systematically uprooting every single flower from the grounds of
Sledmere House, whose gardens had been his father's pride and
joy. Throughout the rest of his life, Sir Tatton retained such a
pathological hatred of flowers that, if he ever saw one while out
for a walk, he would immediately flog it to death with his walking
stick. Tenants on his lands, meanwhile, were expressly forbidden
from growing any such 'nasty, untidy things' in the gardens of their
cottages. 'If you want to grow flowers, grow cauliflowers!' was his
habitual mantra.

Another of Sir Tatton's pet hates was women. Such was his
apparent dislike of seeing females stood around on the doorstep
gossiping to one another that every cottage on his lands was fitted
with a false front door, his tenants' wives having to use the back or
side entrances as settings for their idle chitchat. It was somewhat
surprising then, that in 1874, at the age of forty-eight, he took an
eighteen-year-old bride, Jessie Cavendish-Bentinck. Predictably,
the marriage was not a happy one. Jessie was a pretty and spirited
girl and her husband a miserable old recluse and hypochondriac
who obsessively followed various bizarre health fads of his own
invention. He lived off an exclusive diet of cold rice pudding and
meat juice (chewing up pieces of meat, then sucking out the blood
and sap before spitting out the actual flesh) and, so the story
goes, in 1911 refused to leave Sledmere House during a blazing
fire until he had finished his rice pudding, the consumption of
which he is alleged to have felt was the key to immortality. 'I must
eat my pudding!' he is said to have told his servants while the
flames consumed his property, 'I must eat my pudding!' Worse,
feeling that it was imperative to always maintain a constant body
temperature, he used to order his coats in sets of six to eight, all of
slightly different sizes, and then wear them on top of one another

in layers, like some living Russian doll. Then, when he began to get too warm, he would simply remove one coat at a time and discard it on the ground, relying upon local boys to pick them up and bring them back to Sledmere for a small reward. Apparently, he had a similar arrangement with his trousers.

It was no wonder that Jessie fled to London, where she maintained an apartment, entertained various lovers and ran up huge debts in her husband's name, soon earning the nickname 'Lady Satin-Tights' for her extravagance. When creditors came knocking, asking Sir Tatton to pay off his wife's arrears, he refused, taking advantage of a legal loophole by placing a public advert in *The Times* to the effect that his wife was a ne'er-do-well and that he could accept no responsibility for any money she owed. A scandalous court case – in which all of Sir Tatton's eccentricities were publicly revealed – backed him up in the matter. Jessie claimed that her husband's 'health fads' of rice pudding and multiple coats were merely an excuse for not having to buy proper food or pay for the house to be heated, but in fact the real miser in the family was from Jessie's own bloodline, namely Venetia Cavendish-Bentinck (1855–1948), a woman who, despite marrying a millionaire, recycled milk from the cat's bowl for her guests, bought bacon on a use-or-return basis, and attempted to get vets to examine her household staff when they were ill, seeing as their fees were lower. Given such a disastrous family background, it is unsurprising that Sir Tatton's son Mark had a miserable childhood too, the undoubted nadir coming when he came across the corpses of his adored pet terriers dangling down from a tree in the garden one day, his dad having elected to hang them from its branches through pure spite. The Sykes, incidentally, are distantly related to our present Royal Family – which explains a lot, no doubt.[5]

Perhaps being a miser was better than being a spendthrift, though; at least, taking into account the strange case of Henry Lee Warner (1722–1804), who was so generous with his money that he openly allowed the tenants on his Norfolk estate to steal from him, being too timid to object. If someone wanted firewood, they cut down one of his trees; if anyone wanted a horse, they walked right into his stables and took it, returning it when they pleased, if at all. He kept pigs and poultry, but refused to kill them, letting them wander free and feeding them breakfast before he even thought about having his own. When one of his tenant farmers, a drunkard, tried to relinquish his tenancy even though he had it rent-free, Warner paid men to work his land for him to get him to stay, the farmer then wasting all the profits in the local inn. Even insects were the recipients of Warner's insane and self-ruinous charity; when he found a housefly caught up in a spider-web one day, he abandoned his guests, carefully unwound the creature, then laid it out on his handkerchief and provided it with love and encouragement until it recovered. Eventually, Warner took to sleeping during the day and only walking about by night, under cover of darkness; perhaps he just wanted to avoid all the people who had been taking advantage of him? Even Lord Longford might have considered Mr Warner to be a little too forgiving.[6]

Not all eccentric aristocrats have been quite so self-destructive or malign, though. For instance, Sir Thomas Parkyns (1663–1741), the owner of Bunny Hall near Nottingham, was perfectly harmless, both to others and himself. It wasn't his fault that he was so obsessed with wrestling that he employed two full-time fighters at his mansion to take on all-comers, grappled with his own servants, and held an annual Wrestle-Mania in what is now the garden of a local pub. Adopting the wrestling name of 'Luctator' ('The Struggler'), in 1713 Sir Thomas penned an instructional pamphlet on his favourite sport, entitled *Inn Play: Or, Cornish Hugg-Wrestler*, and dedicated it to King George I. Fixated with his own mortality, Parkyns' other main hobby was collecting large numbers of stone coffins, and he arranged for a bizarre monument to himself to be erected in the chancel of his local church, where he appears in a wrestling stance which makes him appear slightly constipated, while an accompanying Latin verse details how, in death, Sir Thomas has been 'thrown' by the strongest tag-team opponents of all: Death and Time. 'Luctator' warns them, however, that, come the Resurrection, he will be itching for a rematch.[7]

Another benign noble whose high birth made him feel supremely comfortable in his own skin was 'Amphibious' Lord Rokeby (1713–1800), or Matthew Robinson, to give him his full name, who seemed relatively normal during his youth, studying Law at Cambridge and serving as the MP for Canterbury from 1747. Dismayed by the corruption of the Commons, however, in 1761 he retired to his family estate in Kent and returned to nature. Rokeby surprised his estate managers by telling them to remove all fences from his lands to allow the cattle and sheep to roam wild, and surprised his cooks even more by deciding to live off only local produce, burning peas and pouring hot water over them to create his own brand of 'coffee', for instance. Believing that God was found in nature, not the pulpit, he let his private chapel go to ruin, and spent hours instead pacing through a favourite grove, meditating. One day, though, disaster loomed; his relative, the Archbishop of Armagh, was visiting, and Rokeby suddenly realised that, the next day being Sunday, the Bishop would want to attend Mass. Immediately, he summoned every carpenter, painter and labourer he could get his hands on, and ordered them to work flat-out on repairing the chapel. Once the service ended, the church was left to return to rack and ruin – it must have been the most expensive religious ceremony ever held.

Following a spa holiday abroad, Rokeby later gained a new obsession – fresh water, which he believed was the key to life itself. He took to drinking virtually nothing else, and had a series of stone water fountains erected across the landscape; he always carried a supply of half-crowns upon his person to reward anyone he saw drinking from them, a habit easily abused. Meanwhile, the majority of his spare time was soon spent floating in water, either in the sea at nearby Hythe, where he would swim about all day until he actually fainted and had to be dragged to safety by servants, or in a specially constructed immersion bath he had constructed in a greenhouse-like structure near his mansion. Here, he would spend hours immersed up to his neck allowing his waist-length forked white beard to spread out across the water, where joints of veal also bobbed about in case Rokeby got hungry, obsessing about his pet idea that the Bank of England was on the verge of collapse, and writing inflammatory pamphlets about the Prime Minister, presumably on waterproof paper. Due to his bizarre lifestyle and weird appearance (he had a crooked back and two separate moustaches, which were so long he pinned them back over his shoulders) rumours that he was secretly a cannibal began to spread, and he was once besieged by curious citizens who thought he was a wild Turk, but Rokeby survived these outrages and died peacefully in his bed – and not his bath, surprisingly – in November 1800.[8]

John 'Mad Jack' Mytton (1796–1834) was even more his own man. The Squire of Halston Hall in Shropshire, Mytton used the £10,000 annual income from his lands (over £700,000 today) to lead a life of what he considered leisure, although few others might agree. A boisterous child, Jack was expelled from Westminster School for fighting one of his teachers, and saw off many of his subsequent home-tutors by playing bizarre practical jokes on them, such as placing live horses inside their bedrooms. Pressurised by relations, Mytton eventually agreed to go up to Cambridge, carting with him an astonishing 2,000 bottles of port to get him through the boring lectures. In 1819 he secured immediate election to Parliament as the Tory candidate for Shrewsbury by wandering around town offering voters ten-pound notes – a ploy which cost him the modern-day equivalent of £750,000. However, attending the Commons for the first time, the half-deaf Mytton spent only half an hour there, decided the speeches were too boring and inaudible to be bothered with, packed his bags and went home, never to return.

Back at Halston, 'Mad Jack' began truly to earn his nickname, devoting his life to hunting and field sports, amassing 2,000 dogs, some of which he fed on steak and champagne, and allowing his favourite horse, Baronet, to live inside the house with him. Another horse, however, he accidentally killed by getting it drunk on port. Such was his devotion to sportsmanship that he amassed a hunting-wardrobe of 700 pairs of boots, 1,000 hats and 3,000 shirts – a pointless extravagance seeing as, during an especially exciting fox-chase, he would often strip off and ride around fully nude or in his underwear, even during snow and wintry weather. One time he was observed running across a frozen pond naked, in hot pursuit of a duck. Such was his enthusiasm for sports involving animals that he felt moved to invent a few of his own, such as punching bulldogs, biting mastiffs and attempting to lift them into the air with his bare teeth, wrestling with bears, and equipping his stable boys with ice skates and leading them off on wild, slippery rat hunts. One time, sick of merely jumping over hedges on horseback, he attempted to see if one of his steeds could leap over a toll gate while pulling him in his carriage behind it – with predictable results. The constantly inebriated Mytton actively enjoyed being involved in painful accidents, especially when they broke his ribs; once, appalled by a passenger's admission that he had never been involved in a road crash, Mytton deliberately drove his carriage up a steep bank at top speed and tipped it over, to show the timid little fool what he was missing out on.

Squire Mytton's most notorious two exploits also involved acts of insane, self-induced peril. Firstly, there was the time he dressed up in full hunting gear, jumped onto the back of his pet brown bear Nell and rode it into his dining-room to surprise some guests. They certainly were surprised – particularly when Nell threw her master off, bit into his leg and began to eat it. Secondly, there was the infamous occasion when, bothered by hiccups one evening while in Calais, Mytton decided to 'scare' them away by deliberately setting fire to himself. After two witnesses to this act of utter lunacy had helped beat out the resultant inferno and put Mytton into bed, his body covered in horrible burns, Mad Jack expressed deep satisfaction at the success of his plan. 'The hiccup is gone, by God!' he said, and went straight off to sleep.

Mytton was only in Calais at the time in an attempt to escape from his angry creditors, of whom there were many. So careless was he of money that visitors would frequently find banknotes lying around his grounds in random places, having been dropped by Mytton and just left there. Being a generous man, he didn't seem to care who picked up his money. Even his methods of finding a mate were expensive. Following his second wife, Caroline Gifford, upping sticks and fleeing Halston Hall in 1830, Mytton appears to have become lonely. Walking across London's Westminster Bridge one day, however, he perceived a solution to this problem; noticing an attractive young woman whom he had never met before, he simply walked up to her and, out of nowhere, offered her the sum of £500 per annum if she would be his lover. She agreed, and Mytton and his concubine stayed together until the Squire's ultimate death in 1834, following a stretch in Debtor's Prison. Mytton was only thirty-eight, but seeing as he had taken to drinking eight pints of port and brandy a day and living off a diet almost exclusively of filbert nuts, perhaps it was not that surprising that 'Mango, King of the Pickles', as his neighbours bizarrely dubbed him, was not long for this world.[9]

Nearly as untamed as Mytton, meanwhile, was Henry de la Poer Beresford, 3rd Marquess of Waterford (1811–1859), a notorious Anglo-Irish drunkard and scrapper who enjoyed beating up night watchmen and playing sick jokes on people, such as the time he wrote off to the London and Greenwich Railway Company offering them the then huge sum of £10,000 if they would arrange a deliberate train crash for him to observe so he could laugh at the victims. Known as 'The Mad Marquess', he was known to do anything for a bet, and was suspected by some at the time of being Spring-Heeled Jack, a notorious half-real, half-folkloric Victorian bogeyman figure who had perpetrated a series of bizarre assaults on women during the late 1830s. Whether or not Beresford really was Jack, one of his exploits was so extreme that it has since entered the language, in the popular phrase 'painting the town red'.

While the derivation is disputed, this idiom is popularly said to have its origins in the illegal late-night activities of Beresford and some of his friends in the Leicestershire town of Melton Mowbray during the early morning hours of 6 April 1837. A keen horseman (in 1840, he rode his own horse in the Grand National, finishing last), Beresford was on his way back from the Croxton Park Races, where he had spent his time drinking with pals, when his way into town was barred by a toll gate keeper, who demanded he pay the standard fee. Sadly for the tollkeeper, his gate and sentry-post were in the process of being repaired, and some brushes and tins of red paint lay nearby, which the Marquess, refusing to pay, seized hold of, before proceeding to daub the tollkeeper a fetching shade of deepest scarlet. Barricading the tollkeeper inside his hut with nails and planks of wood, the Marquess and his friends then rampaged through the centre of Melton Mowbray, painting doors, ripping down signs, attempting to tip over an occupied caravan, and beating up policemen before painting them all red too. When one of Beresford's companions, Edward Raynard, was eventually arrested, the Marquess and his other drinking partners stormed the lock-up, broke down the doors and released him.

Just as extreme, meanwhile, was the time the noble nutter took several large casks of gin and stood in London's Haymarket handing out mugs of the stuff to random passers-by for free to see what would happen. Eventually, everyone got so drunk that a riot broke out and Beresford had to be arrested by the police for his own safety. Even more outrageous was his conduct after being summoned before a magistrate after riding his horse at high speed through a crowded street, heedless of any injuries he might cause. The story goes that he turned up at court on horseback and demanded that his steed be let in to serve as his star defence-witness. Denying his crime, the Marquess demanded that the animal be questioned in the dock – after all, he explained, 'only he knows how fast he was going.' The case seems to have been rapidly dismissed. Somewhat surprisingly, in 1842 Henry Beresford was eventually tamed and reformed by a happy marriage; but he still kept up his horseriding, dying in Ireland after a bad fall in 1859 which broke his neck.[10]

Some eccentric aristocrats' whimsies are more concrete, meanwhile – namely, in the form of those pointless and whimsical building works termed 'follies' which litter the country-estates of Britain like visible reminders of the fact that their creators once had far more money than they knew what to do with. The best explanation of the purpose (or lack of) of such buildings was aptly summed up by one Lord Berners, whom we shall meet properly in a future chapter, who spoke of a folly he had constructed in the grounds of his own Oxfordshire estate thus: 'The great point of the tower is that it will be entirely useless.'[11] You just can't argue with logic like that.

Undoubtedly the most acute case of compulsive aristocratic folly-building was that exhibited by William John Cavendish-Scott-Bentinck, 5th Duke of Portland (1800–1879), a recluse who spent what would now be tens of millions having various underground tunnels built around his Nottinghamshire estate of Welbeck Abbey. The tales told about the Duke's apparently pathological shyness are actually quite contradictory in nature. On the one hand, we are told he delivered strict instructions to the reputed 1,500 workmen he employed on his land that they were under no circumstances to speak to or even acknowledge him; instead they should simply pass him by 'as they would a tree'. This may not always have been possible, however, as the Duke provided a rather more notable sight than a mere oak or elm, often dressing weirdly in any combination of the following items: wig, two foot tall hat, old-fashioned frock coat, two or three Russian Doll-style overcoats like Sir Tatton Sykes, white tie with high collar, and checked trousers which were held up a few inches above the ankle with knotted string. He also carried along an umbrella, which he used to open and hide behind if anyone dared to take a peek at him. Going out after darkness, however, the Duke is said to have employed a maidservant to walk forty feet ahead of him bearing a lantern and warning people away. When a passing workman doffed his cap to him one day, he is supposed to have sacked the disobedient fellow on the spot.

Most of his dealings with others were conducted via post; even his own servants received their orders through written notes. After writing one, the Duke would ring a bell, place the note into a letter box marked 'outgoing mail', and wait to have his words read and obeyed in silence. Even his doctor wasn't allowed into his room to see him – and even if he had been, the Duke would have remained hidden from view inside a bizarre, custom-made square bed surrounded by doors and screens which made it impossible to know whether it was occupied or not. His carriage, too, was constructed so that it was impossible to peer into; although it did have hidden spy-holes through which he could look out. Whenever he visited his property in London, Harcourt House, meanwhile, the domestics were ordered to hide while he rushed through the hallway and into his private apartments so he wouldn't be seen. Other peculiarities of the Duke included the fact that he would not handle coins until they had been washed, that he insisted upon a whole chicken being continually roasted somewhere in his kitchens twenty-four hours a day, and his obsessive collecting of newspapers and journals, both national and provincial, which he ordered four copies at a time so he could keep a set in each of his properties, and upon which he spent £1,300 per year – hundreds of thousands in today's money. The reasons for the Duke's reclusive oddness were the subject of intense speculation at the time; some said he had leprosy, and couldn't bear to be seen, others that he had conceived a great hatred for all humanity following a failed proposal of marriage to an opera singer during his youth.

However, you do have to wonder if some of these tales of Cavendish's undoubted shyness were not a mite exaggerated; after all, as a young man the Duke had been in the army, and served as an MP from 1824 to 1826, during which time he did actually attend the Commons Chamber rather than simply hiding outside in the toilets. He even arranged roller skating sessions for his workmen in a specially-constructed rink, and coached them in rowing on his lake. Indeed, he was highly popular among his employees, famously providing them with a donkey and an umbrella each to aid their journey to work every morning. Furthermore, he was a keen horse-lover, with a huge stable complex and riding school which he inspected often, and he did have some friends among the local aristocracy. Moreover, while at times he would hide from his workmen, at other times he would deliberately jump out on them; he had a trap door in his room leading to his underground tunnels, through which he would roam in secret, before surprising his men with his presence. At other times, far from fleeing strangers, he would start shouting at them, telling them to get off his land. Presumably, then, the Duke's reclusiveness would come and go, or only began partway through his life. Perhaps the most plausible reason why he paid to have his tunnel network constructed was annoyance that the authorities had not allowed him to close the public right of way which existed through part of his estate. To get around this nuisance, he decided to become a kind of mole-man instead, creating subterranean dens into which the public dared not enter.

Whatever the reason for the Duke's architectural follies, they were certainly remarkable. He is said to have spent £100,000 a year on creating them, for perhaps twenty or so years, the tunnels reputedly running for some fifteen miles below ground in total, some of which were large enough for a horse and cart to be driven through and all of which were lit by gas jets. Even stranger were the subterranean rooms he had constructed, which included an underground observatory (a contradiction in terms, you might have thought), a billiards room, library and giant picture gallery-cum-ballroom in which he never held a dance, filling it up instead with canvases by genuine Old Masters and priceless historical curiosities, all displayed for his eyes only. All but four of the rooms of his actual above-ground home of Welbeck Abbey, meanwhile, he had entirely stripped of furniture, painted pink and abandoned to ruin – although, before leaving them, he did take the inexplicable step of having a toilet fitted in the corner of each one. Such was the Duke's famed weirdness that, following his death in 1879, another odd bod, a widow by the name of Anna Maria Druce, hatched the plan of claiming that the Duke had secretly been her father-in-law, a deceased London upholsterer named Thomas Charles Druce, and that her son was thus the rightful heir to the family fortune. Ms Druce claimed that the Duke had been impersonating Thomas in order to live a care-free life away from the pressures of his estate, but had faked Thomas' death in 1864 in order to retreat away underground. In 1907, following legal action on behalf of one of Ms Druce's relatives, Thomas' coffin was finally exhumed – and found to contain Thomas after all. As for the 5th Duke of Portland himself, meanwhile, he now resides six feet under in a plot in North London's Kensal Green Cemetery, perhaps the only man in history to dwell in death somewhat nearer the Earth's surface than he did during life.[12]

The Duke of Portland's reclusive ways rather pale, however, in comparison to those of Henry Cavendish (1731–1810), a perfect illustration of that now all-but-extinct species of humanity, the 'gentleman scientist'. Long before the days of massive multi-national chemical companies or giant, publicly funded physics laboratories, the pursuit of scientific knowledge was often a much more private affair, left to those who had the time and the money to do so – many of whom, quite naturally, were wealthy and leisured aristocrats. This was certainly the case with Henry Cavendish, who came into a massive fortune when, aged forty, his uncle the 3rd Duke of Devonshire died, transforming him overnight into one of the richest men in England. Prior to that point he had been kept in relatively straitened circumstances by his own father, Lord Charles Cavendish, who may have been stingy with his son's allowance, but proved rather more generous in introducing him to the world of science. Lord Charles was himself an eminent meteorologist and mathematician, awarded a Gold Medal by the Royal Society for inventing a new type of thermometer, and he used to allow his infant son to assist him in performing experiments. Following Lord Charles' death, Henry came into even more money, becoming the single largest owner of bank stock in all of England.

Like many newly rich persons, Henry Cavendish used his new-found wealth to purchase property, buying two London town houses. What Cavendish did with these houses, though, was much more unusual. One of them he turned into a massive library full of scientific books and journals, which grew so extensive that he ended up hiring a German scholar to run it for him full time, devising an elaborate series of receipts and chits that he took to filling in himself whenever he wished to take a book out. His other property, meanwhile, the one in which he actually lived, became effectively a kind of personal laboratory, with its own private observatory, forge and weather observation station, and filled up with hundreds of scientific instruments, many of which had been made specifically for Henry by his own salaried instrument-maker. However, having been kept so short by his father up until the age of forty, being obliged to live in a set of converted stables and manage on a comparative pittance, Cavendish could never quite fully adapt to being rich. He maintained various habits of frugality, never paying more than five shillings for a meal, this being the sum of dinner money Lord Charles had given to him every day, and only ever eating cheap mutton at home. Meanwhile, he wore the same clothes (a three-cornered hat and faded velvet purple frock coat) day-in, day-out, items so old they could easily have served as props for a costume-drama.

Clearly, Henry Cavendish cared for little but science, eschewing any kind of social life to devote himself to various researches, in 1766 discovering the gas hydrogen (which he called 'inflammable air'), and in 1781 being the first to demonstrate that water was composed of two parts hydrogen to one part oxygen. More bizarrely, he tried to devise a scale for measuring electric currents by giving himself shocks and then attempting to estimate the magnitude of pain caused by each effort. However, Henry was less than eager to receive credit for everything he found out, not bothering to tell anybody about some of his discoveries at all. It was not until decades after his death, when his papers were being sorted through by the Scottish physicist James Clerk-Maxwell, that it was realised that many recent discoveries attributed to various other scientists had actually been anticipated by Cavendish nearly a century beforehand.

As this suggests, the noble scientist was not overly keen to court attention; notoriously shy and retiring, attempts have been made in recent years to diagnose him posthumously as having had some form of autism. So shy of his servants, particularly the female ones, that he preferred to communicate with them by letter, developing a complicated series of double doors and internal mailboxes so he wouldn't have to set eyes on them, Cavendish is even alleged to have had a separate staircase installed so that he wouldn't accidentally encounter his housekeeper. Henry's only friends appear to have been his fellow scientists, his only topic of conversation science itself. As a young man, his father had dragged Henry along to dinners at the Royal Society, London's premier scientific association, and, never one to break a routine, he continued to attend such occasions throughout his entire life, though he was hardly the model of sociability. If someone said something to him which he found uninteresting, he simply refused to reply and sat there in stony silence, or else emitted a weird squeak and then ran away into a corner, talking to himself about more appealing matters instead. Whenever he did speak, it was in a bizarre, high-pitched tone like he had swallowed helium, and it took him some time to pluck up the courage to enter the dining room each time in any case, loitering around outside nervously with a strange gait prior to the meal, steeling himself to face his fellow men. In particular, he feared strangers. When, one day, an Austrian visitor approached Cavendish, praised him as a genius and informed him that he had travelled all the way from his homeland to meet him, Henry panicked and ran straight from the building without a word, speeding away to safety and solitude. Another time, when a bank employee called at his house unexpectedly, wanting to know what Henry wanted him to do with some £80,000 of interest he had accumulated, Cavendish was so alarmed that he threatened to close all his accounts down on the spot if the man didn't leave his presence immediately.[13]

Another gentleman scientist, but one who preferred to apply his genius practically rather than theoretically, was Colonel Thomas Thorneycroft (1822–1903), whose family were late entrants to Britain's landed classes, their fortune coming from industry. Indeed, the Thorneycrofts were not really nobles at all, but the family's immense wealth allowed Thomas to purchase his stately Wolverhampton home of Tettenhall Towers in 1853 and begin playing at being the local Squire. Thomas' father George had been something of an engineering genius, inventing a new and improved method of smelting iron which had helped make his fortune, and Thomas seemed set to follow in the family footsteps. While living at Tettenhall, he was responsible for many unusual schemes, some of which were sensible, and others of which were not. Among this latter category was a proposed steam gun which Thorneycroft thought should be fitted to Royal Navy vessels to fire jets of scalding-hot gas and water vapour at opponents, a scheme for pumping in fresh air to London from the coast to willing subscribers, and a kind of fan which could be fitted to hot air balloons in order to blow them away from danger should they pass too close by to factory chimneys and start to be sucked in. Most famously, he created a pair of mechanical wings to enable a man to fly – a device which he is said to have tested out by fitting them to his butler and then pushing him off Tettenhall's roof to see what would happen. I'm sure you can guess what did.[14]

By far the most eccentric gentleman scientist in this country's history, though, was undoubtedly Sir Francis Galton (1822–1911), a controversial figure nowadays due to his status as the father of eugenics, a branch of science which has had rather a bad name since a certain Mr A. Hitler woefully abused its teachings during the 1930s and 40s. A half-cousin of Charles Darwin, Galton was one of the greatest men of his age, whose achievements ranged from creating the world's first-ever printed weather map to pioneering the use of fingerprinting, while other interests included statistics, anthropology, currency reform, the best way of flashing signals to Martians, inherited lunacy among cats, the fluctuating weight of British noblemen, and even psychical research.

A staunch atheist, Galton conducted a statistical study into whether or not prayers had any beneficial effect, concluding that they didn't on the twin grounds that priests had shorter average lifespans than either doctors or lawyers and that ships carrying missionaries were just as likely to sink as any others. However, recognising that prayer still had psychological value, Galton continued to make use of the practice himself, making a private plea to a God he didn't believe in that every paper he wrote would prove successful. The God to whom Galton prayed wasn't necessarily always the usual Christian one, however; as an experiment, he decided to see if it was possible to recreate the religious feelings African tribesmen felt for their wooden idols by attempting to convince himself that a puppet of Mr Punch was in fact a deity. By sheer force of will, Galton eventually managed to convince himself that Mr Punch did indeed possess divine powers, feeling it impossible to look upon his hook-nosed and red-cheeked face without feeling a mixture of awe and reverence in the presence of his new, wife-beating puppet-God.

Every bit as bizarre as Galton's experiments were some of his many weird and wonderful inventions, which ranged from a steam-powered flying-machine he designed when only thirteen, to a modified hour glass to be used as a speedometer on bicycles, to a so-called 'Gumption-Reviver', which dropped water onto his head to maintain his alertness during periods of study. By placing pressure gauges under the legs of chairs at dinner-parties, meanwhile, he aimed to record empirically how much his guests fancied each other, his theory being that, the more each male leaned towards each female at the table, and vice versa, the more suitable marriage-partners they were. Best of all, though, was a special hat Galton invented in order to prevent the wearer's brain overheating during periods of strenuous thought. Claiming to have once 'sprained' his own brain while studying mathematics at Cambridge, Galton was determined that his head should never again become too warm through over-use, leading to the embarrassing sight of him potentially falling down to the floor in front of guests and having a fit. To this end, he devised a special 'ventilating hat', whose top featured a valve which opened and closed whenever a rubber bulb dangling down from its brim was squeezed, thus preventing disaster. The fact that this aim could have been achieved rather more easily by simply not wearing a hat indoors seems never to have occurred to Sir Francis.

Undoubtedly an original thinker, to Galton every problem had its solution, and mere embarrassment at its nature should never be allowed to get in the way of its inherent logic. To keep your clothes dry during a rainstorm, for instance, Galton recommended you remove and then sit on them, providing shelter; if your shoes were too hard, meanwhile, he advised you crack eggs into them for lubrication; if you needed to vomit, then why not simply swallow a handful of gunpowder?

Most alarming of all was Galton's mania for classifying and then ranking people in order of what he saw as being their level of moral, intellectual or physical worth. For instance, by studying large numbers of court reports and examining whether or not witnesses had lied in the dock, he was able to 'prove' statistically that British citizens were the most honest people of all, while Greeks were the biggest liars. Classifying criminals was another enthusiasm of Galton's, with the great man pioneering a technique called 'composite photography' to try and identify a specific criminal 'type' so that a likely thief or murderer could be spotted instantly just by looking at him. The idea was to take photographs of dozens of muggers, say, and then lay them all over the top of one another, one by one, on the same plate until some kind of 'average' image of such a miscreant emerged in the final photo, via a process of superimposition. Galton thought this would work well with lunatics, too, visiting an asylum and getting all the patients to line up in a row and await their turn in front of the camera. Sadly, one of the madmen, who thought he was a member of the Royal Family, was annoyed at not being placed first in the queue as royal protocol demanded, and bit the photographer's posterior in protest.

This wasn't the only time Galton's practical studies went wrong, either; while travelling in Africa he attempted to gain statistical evidence of the native women's average shape by sizing up their bums and breasts with a tape measure, something which proved open to obvious misinterpretation. Eventually, he took to estimating the women's chests and posteriors from a distance, using just his naked eye and a ship's sextant. Apparently, he was greatly impressed by the large size of both! Just as dubious a field of study was his attempt to create what he called a 'Beauty Map of Great Britain', the research for which consisted of Galton travelling to various cities up and down the land, walking through the streets and staring at women, in order to determine whether or not he would like to have sex with them. Hidden inside one of Galton's pockets was a piece of paper divided into three sections, marked 'Beautiful', 'Average' or 'Ugly', which would receive a pinprick from Galton in the appropriate column, delivered through a special thimble-mounted pin he wore, once he had eyed up each female he encountered for levels of pulchritude. Through such dedicated and selfless research, Galton claimed to have proved objectively that London had the greatest proportion of pretty girls, while Aberdeen was home to the most hideous slab-faced harridans in the entire kingdom.

Of course, Galton's idea of what precisely a pretty girl looked like was somewhat subjective, and this was the whole problem with his most famous creation, the science (or pseudoscience, perhaps) of eugenics. Impressed by his half-cousin Darwin's theory of natural selection, Galton hit upon the idea of applying such reasoning to human beings as well as the plant and animal kingdoms. Knowing how racehorse breeders purposely bred their swiftest and healthiest animals together in order to produce even faster and more healthy steeds, Galton saw no reason why such methods could not be applied to people as well, in order to speed up the process of evolution artificially and create a race of genetic supermen. He envisaged establishing a 'Register of Superior Families' whose members would be paired off to mate with one another, while the inferior criminal classes, the insane, the disabled and the feckless poor would be sterilised or otherwise discouraged from polluting the nation's gene-pool any further.

In a limited sense, Galton's reasoning was sound – if you want a tall child, then two tall parents, whose parents and grandparents were also tall, will make that outcome more likely (though not certain). The problem was how to decide what characteristics it was desirable to have in a genetic super-child of the future; the fact that, at one point, Galton took to using his special pocket-thimble to measure the incidence of blue eyes and blonde hair in passers-by is a good indication of how such reasoning can all go horribly wrong. A novel of Galton's, written in the last year of his life and named *Kantsaywhere*, in which the chosen master race live happy, productive lives, while the genetic under-class are forced into exile or labour camps, was to prove both horribly prophetic of life in 1930s Germany, and utterly unpublishable for the next hundred years – when Galton's niece read it after his death, she decided that its content (particularly the embarrassing eugenic sex scenes) was simply too disturbing for public consumption and consigned parts of it to the fireplace. Perhaps this was for the best. Quite apart from everything else, in any world in which babies are born effectively to design, there would almost certainly be little room given over to encouraging any more eccentric persons to be born; those who did not fit the pre-agreed template would quickly find themselves being simply discarded. The greatest irony of all about Galton's ideas, then, is that if they really had been put into practice, then someone like himself – or many of the other aberrant aristocrats examined in this chapter – would never have been allowed to be born ever again![15]

The Strangest Family in England: The Sitwells

The bizarre brood who wrote poems, hunted ghosts and tried to paint cows to fit in with the crockery.

Nobody writing a modern book about eccentricity can avoid putting pen to paper in the shadow of Dame Edith Sitwell (1887–1964). Not only was she the author of perhaps the most celebrated book upon the topic of all, 1933's *The English Eccentrics* – a tome so well-regarded it was later turned into a comic opera[1] – she was also a member of what is arguably the strangest family ever to have lived. The exploits of the three Sitwell siblings, Edith and her younger brothers Sir Osbert Sitwell (1892–1969) and Sir Sacheverell Sitwell (1897–1988) were legendary, so much so that tales of their incredible eccentricities have often overshadowed recognition of their very real achievements in the fields of literature, music and the arts. Not that the Sitwells seemed to mind; according to their friend Evelyn Waugh, the trio revelled in the publicity they attracted so much that each kept a bowl filled with press-cuttings of their adventures on their dressing tables for visitors to examine, where most others might have nuts or sweets for callers to nibble.[2]

Sitwell's book itself contains one of the most popular quotes upon our topic, namely the opinion that eccentricity is endemic in our land largely on account of 'that peculiar and satisfactory knowledge of infallibility that is the hallmark and birthright of the British nation.'[3] Many contemporary reviewers agreed, E. M. Forster in *The Spectator*, for instance, writing that 'the lesson to be drawn' from the book was that 'eccentricity ranks as a national asset, and ... so long as it is respected there is some hope that our country might not go mad as a whole.'[4] Maybe so. In an extended metaphor, Sitwell talks of a great heap of cinders that had once covered several acres following 1666's Great Fire of London, through which the eager locals had combed, seeking buried treasures. Even the blackest of dust can sometimes contain hidden nuggets of gold within it, she implies – and it is the same with life. As a cure for the boredom and melancholy which modern existence so often induces, she suggests that the 'dust heap' of mainstream history can be rooted through by people like her, the literary equivalents of the old cinder-scavengers, looking for amusing anecdotes about neglected eccentrics from whose examination 'dusty laughter may arise'.[5]

Laughter is the best medicine, as they say, and undoubtedly Sitwell presents her eccentrics as worthy of being laughed at – but laughed at in a peculiar, indulgent way. She clearly admires these people, saluting their 'rigidity' and stubborn refusal to conform.[6] Nonetheless, mock such people Edith sometimes did. After achieving fame, she and Osbert composed a questionnaire to send out to any correspondents whose fan mail seemed weird enough for their authors to be considered potential loons. As well as asking for deliberately nonsensical information like the 'Age, sex and weight of your wife' and demanding they provide passport photos signed by clergymen, the siblings also made several personal queries relating to the mental health of the letter-writers' families. 'Has any relative of yours ever been confined in a mental home?' was one such question; 'If not, why not?' was another. Sadly, Edith's secretary seems to have discreetly neglected to actually post these forms out – a real shame, as you feel certain her employer would have thoroughly enjoyed leafing through any replies.[7]

After all, during their extreme infancy during the 1890s, the three Sitwell siblings had temporarily occupied an old stone structure named Belvoir House in Scarborough, whose nursery backed onto an alley which was something of a meeting spot for the town's most mentally disturbed tramps. Looking out of the nursery-window, the toddlers would thrill to the exploits of such vagrants as the 'Cat-Man', who would wander around meowing to himself, an unnamed organ grinder with his monkey, and various other human flotsam and jetsam. Far from being intimidated by their antics, the Sitwells enjoyed them – so much so that, in later life, Osbert would implausibly but rather proudly claim that his first words were 'Rag and bones! Rag and bones!'[8]

Given this taste for the agreeably grotesque, it is perhaps no surprise that Edith Sitwell chose to write a book about eccentrics, even if ultimately she did so largely to earn cash to help support a cancer-stricken friend of hers, Helen Rootham (1875–1938), rather than for its own sake.[9] Rootham herself, though, was a striking example of the kind of unusual acquaintance the Sitwells liked to cultivate. Coming from a difficult background – an insane sister of hers occasionally tried to murder people – Helen first became known to Edith after being appointed her governess in 1903. A talented musician, as well as a translator of French poets like Rimbaud, Rootham became an important influence upon the young Edith, and it has been suggested that, without her governess' artistic ways, Sitwell would never have become the famous poet she did as an adult.[10]

Another influence that may have rubbed off on Edith, though, was Helen's undoubted eccentricity. As well as translating Rimbaud, Rootham had tried to help introduce the nineteenth-century Russian mystic Vladimir Solovyov to the English-speaking world; an inspiration for both Tolstoy and Dostoyevsky, Solovyov had argued for a synthesis of Christianity with Buddhism, the Jewish Kabbala and the teachings of Plato, and claimed to have had mystical encounters with a being named 'Sophia', the very personification of Divine Wisdom itself.[11] Rootham had a weakness for this kind of thing, being drawn to arcane quasi-Spiritualist movements like Theosophy and its offshoots, engaging in barefooted 'nature-dances', and becoming convinced that she was the reincarnation of an esteemed medieval Yugoslavian princess named Yelena. At one point, Helen became abnormally obsessed with a dream of hers in which a giant leaf had emerged from the body of what she rather vaguely termed 'a Being', going around and asking everyone she met if they knew what it meant – many said they did, but, being English, were much too polite to add out loud that 'it means you're mental'.[12]

Marching to Her Own Drum

The weirdest incident involving Rootham and the Sitwells occurred in 1915, however, when the governess took it upon herself to expel a demon – or 'elemental', as she had it – from the family home of Renishaw Hall in Derbyshire. Built in 1625 and occupied by successive generations of the Sitwell family ever since, the Hall certainly had plenty of time to acquire some ghosts to haunt its lonelier corridors and stairwells, but the one which Rootham claimed to have expelled was particularly horrible in its nature. Edith claimed to have met it herself, as a child; lame-sounding footsteps were heard by her dragging their way across empty rooms, and on one occasion, in the company of a cousin, Edith saw a door handle repeatedly turning around by itself before the door then burst open, revealing ... nothing, other than the melancholy sound of the invisible spook, limping away into the distance.

Clearly this was a poltergeist infestation, and on a visit back to Renishaw during the First World War, Rootham took it upon herself to play ghost-buster, wandering around the place with Edith and Osbert, saying prayers for the dead. Suddenly, standing at the bottom of a staircase, Rootham announced 'It is coming!' – and, lo and behold, the sound of the halting footsteps began once more. Overcome by a sense of evil, Helen retreated down some further stairs to join Edith and Osbert, the latter of whom pronounced that 'It is coming for *us*.' Seemingly, it was; a sound like whispering waves filled the trio's heads, and a shapeless black mist appeared, floating down the steps and interfering with their brains in a strange, trance-inducing fashion. Perhaps scared off by all the praying, the ghost then veered off at the last moment and passed through a doorway. Rootham later swore blind that the elemental had visited her again in bed that night, where she engaged in a 'battle' with it, of which precise details have sadly never been revealed.[13]

Osbert wrote a poem about this uncanny event, *Night*, and Edith herself was also inspired to versify by poltergeist phenomena, her poem *The Drum* being based upon one of the most celebrated of all English hauntings, that of the so-called 'Demon Drummer of Tedworth'. The poem's lines reveal that she was intimately familiar with this case; references to 'mocking money' turning black in people's pockets and 'scratching under the children's bed' are taken directly from contemporary accounts of the haunting, which occurred in Wiltshire during 1661–63.[14] The poem presents an interesting representation of Sitwell's own peculiar poetic craft; in much of her poetry, Sitwell was concerned above all with the sound the lines made when read aloud, as seen in her most famous piece, 1940's *Still Falls the Rain*, in which a peculiar rhythm is built up whereby the sequence of words is supposed to imitate the steady beats of rainfall, falling Nazi bombs, a person's pulse and the hammering of nails into Christ's body on the Cross, creating a dizzying conflation (and mystical redemption) of all human suffering from the Crucifixion to the Blitz.[15] The rhythm of *The Drum*, however, is even stranger – for it is surely the only poem in the English language to take its tempo direct from the noises allegedly made by a real-life ghost.

Edith had discovered the story of the Tedworth Drummer in a 1682 edition of Joseph Glanvill's well-known tract *Saducismus Triumphatus*, a book of witchcraft tales which provided the first comprehensive account of the haunting. The story, which has a real fairytale air to it, begins with a Wiltshire magistrate named John Mompesson confiscating the drum of a local beggar named William Drury, and banishing him from the area. Robbed of his livelihood, Drury is then supposed to have cursed the official, leading to his home being plagued by poltergeist phenomena, including the loud rapping and knocking noises characteristic of such spooks. Seeing as these raps and knocks seemed to play distinct tunes from thin air, they were interpreted by contemporary observers as being drumbeats caused by the supernatural agency of William Drury in revenge for his instrument being confiscated.[16] Sitwell's poem was supposed directly to imitate the sound of this unearthly tattoo – and lines like 'Dust doth clack/Clatter and quack/To a shadow black' do indeed sound like the regular beatings of an invisible drum if you read them correctly.

The Drum was prominently appended to the front of a book published by Sacheverell Sitwell in 1940, called simply *Poltergeists* – together with another short poem which, trying to go one better than his sister, he claimed had actually been 'written by a poltergeist.' In fact, this was a joke; the poem was simply a traditional human-penned rhyme which Sacheverell had copied out of J. O. Orchard-Halliwell's 1849 book *Nursery Rhymes and Nursery Tales of England*, where it had been placed into the mouth of a spook-like 'goblin', but the deceit is typical of the pinch of humour with which the Sitwell siblings approached these (and most other) matters.[17] This humorous attitude does not, though, mean that the Sitwells did not believe in ghosts – because they undoubtedly did. However, it was Sacheverell's book which marked him out as the family's true expert on such matters. Sacheverell made a point of gathering information about local hauntings, such as one at a place called Toadpool Farm, only around a mile or so from Renishaw. Sacheverell saw this place as being 'enchanted ground', surrounded by mushroom rings, and interpreted its name as meaning 'suicide pond', 'Tod' being the old Anglo-Saxon term for 'death'. Here, said Sacheverell, inexplicable Tedworth-style rappings had been heard by successive tenants, and even more inexplicable showers of stones seen to fall down onto the roof or rattle against the windows. Stranger yet, when the stables were opened of a morning, the horses inside were sometimes found to have been ready-saddled by hands unseen – or so the story went.[18]

Family Skeletons

In truth, though, if Sacheverell really wanted to find some ghosts, then he need not have left Renishaw Hall, where it sometimes seemed there were more dead occupants than living ones. The voice of his great-great-grandfather Sitwell Sitwell – so odd they named him twice – for instance, could apparently still be heard echoing around the place on occasion, calling out for his wife Alice.[19] Particularly bizarre was an episode contributed to the 1936 publication *Lord Halifax's Ghost-Book*, a compendium of the uncanny experiences of England's aristocracy, by the father of Edith et al., Sir George Reresby Sitwell (1860–1943).

Sir George was one of the oddest men of all time, as we shall soon see, but when it came to ghosts, he was utterly orthodox in his opinions; he didn't believe in them one little bit. He accepted that people *saw* ghosts, certainly, but thought they were hallucinations – or 'reverse impressions of something seen in the past, and now projected from an overtired and excited brain', as he had it.[20] Nonetheless, he still sent off to Lord Halifax the tale of how his wife Lady Ida Sitwell (1869–1937) had seen a ghost one day in September 1909. Talking to a friend, she happened to glance out into a passageway, where she saw some unknown grey-haired lady dressed in a white cap, moving in a 'very slow, furtive, gliding motion' with outstretched arms and clasped hands, who had disappeared into nothing by the time Lady Ida got outside to ask who she was.

Stranger yet, though, were certain events of 1885, when Sir George had held a party at Renishaw to celebrate his twenty-fifth birthday, with one of the invited revellers complaining that her sleep had been disturbed by the sensation of being given three cold, wet kisses in her borrowed bed. Sir George found these claims amusing, but another acquaintance, a Mr Turnbull, told him not to be so dismissive; while visiting Renishaw some years previously, Turnbull said, one of his own wife's friends had reported being awoken by exactly the same phenomenon. Sir George remained sceptical, but still felt bound to report to Lord Halifax a strange coda to the story. Sometime later, when a staircase was being enlarged, the floorboards of the haunted guest bedroom were ripped up and an old, empty coffin discovered, dating from the seventeenth or eighteenth century. It was fastened to the floor joists with iron clamps and had no cover, this function being fulfilled by the floorboards directly above so that, whenever you walked across the room, you were essentially treading on a giant coffin lid. A legend later sprang up that the casket had once contained the bones of a tragic 'Boy In Pink' who had drowned in a pond at Renishaw back in 1724, thus accounting for the coldness of the ghost's kisses – an eerie echo of Sacheverell's theories about the spirit at nearby Toadpool Farm.[21]

While these stories may have had a great effect upon his children – Edith used the image of the cold kiss in several of her poems, for instance – Sir George simply saw them as silly 'women's matters', caused by the supposed inferiority of the female nervous system. 'Ghosts are sometimes met with, but they are not ghosts,' he said.[22] When it came to his own wife's nervous system, Sir George may have had a point – an unstable alcoholic with a taste for self-dramatisation, Lady Ida was given to explaining away any sleepless nights by reference to Renishaw's ghosts being noisy, kept an expensively acquired hangman's noose on display at the top of her bed for luck, and squandered a fortune of her husband's money upon a pet pig she was convinced was psychic.[23]

Perhaps Sir George's cynicism stemmed from a youthful experience while up at Oxford. Attending a séance put on by the British National Association of Spiritualists on 9 January 1880, George had witnessed a notoriously dubious twenty-four-year-old medium named Florence Cook walk behind a curtain only to re-emerge moments later disguised as a dead twelve-year-old girl called Marie. On a previous visit to the séance room, however, George had noticed something suspicious about Marie – beneath her white shroud-like robes, the dead child was sporting a corset. Pondering this fact later, George had concluded that ghosts were unlikely to require any underwear and that, even if they did need to purchase fresh knickers in case of ectoplasmic accidents, there was no reason for a twelve-year-old spook to wear such an adult undergarment. This time, however, Sitwell had come prepared. When 'Marie' emerged from behind the curtain, George jumped up and grabbed her, establishing that, beneath her shroud, the 'little girl' was indeed wearing only her undies, thus no doubt allowing him to observe that she was unusually well-developed for a girl of such alleged tender years. Tearing down the curtain between two worlds, Sitwell was unsurprised to find Florence Cook's discarded clothing scattered all over the floor behind it. The séance then broke up in shouting and abuse, but Sir George later appeared in the pages of *The Times* and *The Telegraph*, where he was praised for having exposed a fraud.[24]

A Class Apart

As we progress through this book, it will become apparent that a surprisingly large number of our eccentrics have maintained an interest in paranormal phenomena – no doubt it is something to do with the typical eccentric's desire to arrive at their own conclusions about the way the world works, rather than just taking the 'official' line society tries to peddle us for granted. Such an idea is also reflected in another of Dame Edith's opinions about eccentricity, taken from her posthumously-published 1965 autobiography, *Taken Care Of*:

> Eccentricity is not, as dull people would have us believe, a form of madness. It is often a kind of innocent pride, and the man of genius and the aristocrat are frequently regarded as eccentrics because the genius and the aristocrat are entirely unafraid of and uninfluenced by the opinions and vagaries of the crowd.[25]

This is, surely, highly perceptive. The seventeenth-century jurist Sir Edward Coke's famous assertion that 'an Englishman's home is his castle' has held true historically best of all for the titled classes, some of whose homes literally *were* castles, and behind whose walls, once upon a time, they could more or less do whatever they wanted to do with their time and their money, no matter how eccentric the project – as we have already seen. Nonetheless, to many modern palates, Sitwell's equation of aristocracy with genius might smack unpleasantly of snobbery; ours is, supposedly, a democratic age, and such things are not meant to be said. Certainly, if any small-minded peddlers of the modern mantra of 'equality' wanted to, it would be very easy to portray Sitwell as being a stuck-up snoot; in June 1928, for instance, after a letter had been printed in the *Daily Mail* complaining about the 'acid' tone of some of her recent articles there, Sitwell penned an even more caustic reply in which she thanked the complainant for having 'taught me the value of birth-control for the masses'. Perhaps, a critic could say, it surprised Dame Edith that such people were able to pick up pens at all, let alone use them to write with.[26] Her oft-repeated claim to be 'an electric eel in a pool of catfish', meanwhile,[27] could also be slandered as showing that she thought of herself as being inherently better than other people. The fuller context surrounding this well-known quote makes her sound even worse:

> The reason I am thought eccentric is I will not be taught my job by a lot of pipsqueaks. I will not allow people to bore me. Nobody has ever been more alive than I![28]

A closer look at Sitwell's opinions about the matter of peculiarity among the nobility may give us a different viewpoint, however. As she wrote in her 1933 book about the topic, perhaps the human quality of eccentricity itself was simply 'the ordinary carried to a high degree of pictorial perfection.'[29] Maybe so. We must ask ourselves what it is that, historically, has enabled the gentility to indulge their most eccentric whims; surely it is the fact that, due to a simple accident of birth, they have found themselves in a position to do so. Prior to Lloyd George's 'People's Budget' of 1909/10, which introduced Land Taxes on the wealthy to help fund the fledgling welfare state, it was often enough for a land-owning aristocrat simply to exist for the money to come rolling in to them through rents, year after year, without them necessarily having to lift a finger. Born into poverty, however, those same landed gentry would have had to go and work for a pittance in a cotton mill or on a farm for all the hours God sent like everybody else did – hence, an alternative life normally lived, and not eccentrically, even for the likes of Sir Tatton Sykes and the Marquess of Waterford.

When the situation is reversed, however, and a working-class lad or lass unexpectedly makes it big, then they essentially come to occupy the traditional position (and, often, the former stately homes) of the old aristocracy. Footballers, pop singers, film and TV stars – all are famous nowadays for frequently spending their unimaginable fortunes on bizarre things. The comedian Vic Reeves (b.1959), for example, who started out as a humble mechanical engineering apprentice, has used the cash from his subsequent TV career to do things like buy an antique Austin A40 Somerset car and embed it standing up vertically in the middle of his back garden for no apparent reason, and devotes some of his no doubt extensive leisure-time to the self-invented hobby of going around and photographing big piles of dog dirt in the street.[30] Had Reeves been working for the minimum wage on the factory floor, then he would not have been able to do any of this. Wealth and leisure, however, free such people from the usual constraints that would otherwise have hemmed in their natural impulses – with the end result that they end up going around acting like the very maddest lords and ladies of our nation's past. Sitwell's idea of 'the ordinary, carried to a high degree of pictorial perfection' seems almost to be embodied in people like Reeves, and naturally raises a surprising question: given the means and the opportunity, are we *all* natural aristocratic-style eccentrics? It could well be so.

Born to be Wild

Edith Sitwell, though, was living and writing in a post-Lloyd George world, and so had to dedicate at least some of her time to earning a living – for much of her adult life, she was actually quite poor. In *The English Eccentrics*, Dame Edith gave over much of her space to detailing the lives of the high-born mad – people we have already met, like 'Amphibious' Lord Rokeby and the bear-riding 'Mad Jack' Mytton – and there seems almost a tinge of envy in her words when she writes about them. No doubt Rokeby and Mytton's amazing exploits represented perfectly the kind of profligate, leisured and wildly eccentric aristocratic lifestyles that Edith, Osbert and Sacheverell would have liked to have led if they could, but modern financial and social circumstances, regrettably, meant that they could not – or, at least, not individually. While most of the Sitwells were more than a bit abnormal on their own, it was on a collective basis that the family's true eccentric strength lay, and where they may well in fact have been invincible. Where to begin when describing the almost impossible heights of combined looniness to which that ancient line once climbed? Edith and her brothers had been introduced to the traditional Sitwell ways from a young age, being taken to Christmas family gatherings at which the adults had gone around concealing live lobsters inside people's beds, and racing around the rooms killing rats for a bit of festive fun, but that was not the half of it.[31]

Profound oddity descended down through both sides of the family-tree. Edith's maternal grandmother Lady Londesborough (1838–1915), for example, required her children to wear gloves at all times, even indoors, as it was her dream for them to grow up with lovely smooth hands, and was of such unusual appearance, wearing bizarre tall white wigs and old-fashioned clothes, that in old age she was reputedly once mistaken for a bonfire-night guy while being wheeled through the street in a bath chair, a passing clergyman tossing coins into her lap in innocent misunderstanding.[32] Likewise, Lady Londesborough's mother, the Dowager Duchess of Beaufort (1800–1889), was so gaga that she demanded her coachman take her and her beloved pet parrot on a different scenic drive each day as entertainment, never once noticing that the coachman always took the same route, and that her parrot had in fact been dead for several years and now sat stuffed and entirely immobile in the carriage alongside her.[33]

On the paternal side of the family, meanwhile, was Edith's other grandmother, Lady Louisa Sitwell (1827–1911), an excessively religious woman whose favourite pastime was driving through the streets of Scarborough in her coach together with a suffragan bishop, kidnapping prostitutes (or, more accurately, women she thought *resembled* prostitutes) and carting them off to a home for 'fallen women' she funded. Here, the whores were stripped naked, forcibly bathed by a burly matron to wash away their sins, and then dressed up in navy-blue uniforms like policemen, before being put to work as laundresses behind closed doors.[34] Cousins and second cousins provided further weird delights, most notably one Reginald Farrer (1880–1920), a Yorkshireman with a cleft palate who turned both vegetarian and Buddhist after accidentally eating his pet cat while visiting Japan, and became the world's leading authority on oriental rock gardens, adopting the bizarre alpine-planting method of filling his shotgun up with rare Himalayan seeds and then firing them into cliffs in order to lend an element of chance to his horticultural compositions. In 1913, Farrer stood for Parliament, but lost after blowing his entire campaign budget on flower bulbs.[35]

As a family, then, the Sitwells could take on the entire world in the ever-popular sport of competitive nuttiness – but their only real hope of a solo world champion lay with the father of Edith and her brothers, Sir George Reresby Sitwell, the 4th Baronet of his line. Sir George was a fan of gardening, too, just like Reginald Farrer had been, devoting much of his time – and his fortune – to planning alterations to his estate, constructing numerous tall wooden pillars upon which he would sit perched with an umbrella for hours on end, surveying his lands through a telescope, fantasising about adding lakes and statues, and bulldozing away annoying hills which interfered with his line of sight.[36] Today, visitors to Renishaw Hall's beautiful formal gardens may well be pleased that Sir George took such troubles over his hobby; but most people will no doubt be rather more pleased that his son Osbert took equal pains over the careful presentation of his father's life story in his five-volume 1945–50 autobiography *Left Hand, Right Hand!*.

Daddy Queerest

Osbert's book is very funny, being a treasure-trove of mad anecdotes about his parent. Eager to present his father as having been crazy from birth, Osbert told of how, after inheriting his title as a toddler following the early death of his father in 1862, the young Sir George immediately began to feel a sense of superiority and entitlement. There was the time, for instance, when travelling on a train with his nurse, that an avuncular old man sat opposite asked him 'And who are you, young fellow?' The enquiry was to elicit an alarmingly precocious response. 'I am Sir George Sitwell, Baronet,' the tiny tot answered. 'I am four years old and the youngest Baronet in England.'

Sir George's unusual ways continued while away at Eton between 1873 and 1878, where he is alleged to have devised and built two amazing inventions; a musical toothbrush that played as you scrubbed your teeth, and a tiny revolver for firing miniature projectiles at wasps – devices which are still being searched for by his descendants. As an adult, Sir George's unsuccessful marriage to the alcoholic Lady Ida, whose spending, solipsism and general stupidity rather cancelled out her extreme beauty, sent him retreating further and further inside himself. He would sometimes walk straight past his own children in the street without noticing, such was his level of self-absorption, and he once advised Osbert that it was 'such a mistake to have friends', as they only ended up costing one money. Convinced he was always right about everything, ever, Sir George once published a pamphlet pointing out to Einstein where he was going wrong, and deliberately tried to alienate any visitors to Renishaw by having a notice made, reading, 'I must ask anyone entering the house never to contradict me or differ from me in any way, as it interferes with the functioning of the gastric juices and prevents my sleeping at night.'

Appalled by modernity, he became an expert on the Middle Ages, a period he thought better than his own day in every respect, and tried to convince everybody else that life should be lived on a medieval model, too. He banned electricity from his presence until the 1940s, rationing visitors to two candles apiece during their stays, and calculating Osbert's allowance upon the basis of the amount one of his ancestors had given to his own son during the years of the Black Death. He even affected not to understand how telephones functioned – when somebody promised to 'give you a ring on Thursday', he is supposed to have been annoyed at not having later received a gift of jewellery. Appropriately enough,

Sir George began devoting much of his time to highly specialist historical research, writing a series of utterly unpublishable books whose titles ranged from the wilfully obscure – *The History of the Fork*, *The Use of the Bed*, *Leper's Squints* – to the absurdly specific – *Domestic Manners in Sheffield in the Year 1250*, *The Origins of the Word 'Gentleman'*, *Acorns as an Article of Medieval Diet*. So desperate was he to see his name in print that Sir George ended up purchasing the publishers behind *The Scarborough Post*, and forcing them to put out a book in 1889 with the stupidly long sixty-three-word title *The Barons of Pulford in the Eleventh and Twelfth Centuries and Their Descendants, the Reresbys of Thrybegh and Ashover, the Ormesbys of South Ormesby, and the Pulfords of Pulford Castle, Being an Historical Account of the Lost Baronies of Pulford and Dodleston in Cheshire, of Seven Knights' Fees in Lincolnshire Attached to Them, and of Many Manors, Townships and Families in Both Counties.*

A weird mixture of miser and spendthrift, Sir George was perfectly happy to buy a medieval Italian castle upon pure whim, but once attempted to persuade Eton to accept Osbert's school-fees in the form of potatoes. Frequently, he would question trivial household expenses, buying his children utilitarian presents like bars of soap at Christmas, and yet when it came to his own interests of landscape gardening and antiquities, money was no object. Even the cows that wandered through the fields of Renishaw were not safe from Sir George's aesthetic attentions; he seriously conceived the idea of paint-stencilling their hides with blue and white willow patterns to match his tasteful Chinese crockery.

Despite his passion for the past, Sir George still continued trying to invent new things. Some of these innovations were actually quite sensible, such as a self-assembling mosquito net weighted down with lead – but his insistence upon using it himself at home in malaria-free Derbyshire was not. He even tried his hand as a gourmand. During a visit to Selfridge's in London, he demanded to see Mr Selfridge himself, in order to offer him a new concoction he called 'The Sitwell Egg'. This spherical abomination consisted of a 'yolk' of smoked-meat, a 'white' of compressed rice, and a 'shell' of artificial lime. The synthetic shell was supposed to ensure that the contents would never go off, making it an ideal snack for explorers; even in the icy tundra, all a man had to do was boil it up, wait for the shell to disintegrate, and fresh nutrition would be his! Unsurprisingly, Gordon Selfridge refused this kind offer. In 1925, Sir George left England for good to live in his castle near Florence, writing a wholly unnecessary explanatory note to the Chancellor of the Exchequer and the Archbishop of Canterbury, telling them he had left Britain because the taxes were so high. He died in Switzerland in 1942, though for him, in many respects, it may as well have been 1342.[37]

Jeeves and Bluster

So eager was Osbert to portray his father as the modern-day Don Quixote that he even gave him his own Sancho Panza figure, Sir George's faithful long-term butler, Henry Moat (1871–1940). Moat may have described his master as 'the strangest old bugger you ever met',[38] but he was a little odd himself, too. Described by Edith as resembling a benevolent purple hippopotamus, the burly Moat was forever having bust ups with Sir George and walking out on him before returning to patch it up again, like an old gay couple. Brought up in a large family along with eighteen brothers, one sister and a tame seal, Moat's chief role was to try and curb Sir George's madder schemes as tactfully as was possible. There was the time, for instance, that Sir George called Moat into his presence and informed him excitedly of his new idea that, from now on, all knife handles 'should always be made from condensed milk'. Taking his time to ponder this bizarre suggestion, Moat eventually came up with the following droll response: 'Yes, Sir George ... but what if the cat gets at them?'[39] When Lady Ida died and was buried in 1937, meanwhile, Moat attempted to console the household thus: 'Well at least now Sir George will know where Her Ladyship spends her afternoons.'[40]

Another of Moat's roles was to accompany Sir George on his frequent foreign travels and keep a sharp eye on his medicines. This was particularly important because Sir George, wary of sinister foreigners trying to steal his tonics, had deliberately mislabelled their contents so as to potentially cause any thieves a severe medical mishap.[41] When Moat finally died in 1940, some forty-three years after first entering the Sitwells' service, Sacheverell, typically, thought he heard his ghost banging about in the pantry at Renishaw. When she heard, Edith fondly imagined that Moat was returning back home to check up on the poor neglected children whom he had tried his best to protect from their parents' harsh inadequacies during their earliest and most tender years.[42]

These are marvellous stories. The only question is – how accurate are they? Osbert Sitwell did not like his father, for a variety of reasons. Perhaps he had bad memories of receiving bars of soap from him for Christmas – but, worse, he resented the way Sir George tried to make him live a niggardly lifestyle while wasting money on his own mad schemes with abandon, and was also probably jealous of his intellect. Osbert may have tried to make his father seem mad, but he was undoubtedly also abnormally intelligent, like so many great eccentrics. For instance, he was an extremely shrewd investor on the Stock Exchange, and made easily as much money this way as he wasted on gardens and castles. What must be remembered with the paternal portrait painted in *Left Hand, Right Hand!* is that it is extremely partial. Nothing in it is untrue, as such, but Sir George's numerous episodes of weirdness were stitched together by his unfaithful son in such a way as to obscure the general day-to-day pattern of his life. While he was undoubtedly very strange, for most of the time Sir George acted in a reasonably rational manner, and no doubt whole months could sometimes pass without him acting like he belonged in a straitjacket. He was, for example, a perfectly well-respected Conservative MP, sitting for five years in the Commons. I looked up the contributions he made there – there aren't many – hoping they would be filled with insane ramblings, but they were not. Even Sacheverell complained his father was not quite as advertised, once admitting that:

> He wasn't nearly as comic a figure as [Osbert] made him appear. He was a much nicer person. I think he was much nicer than Osbert.[43]

By the time Sacheverell spoke out, though, the damage was already done, and 'Ginger', as his children sometimes called him (out of earshot) had become a bit of a legend. He appears repeatedly in disguised form in contemporary novels written by well-connected literary types such as Aldous Huxley and Wyndham Lewis and, worse, people's previous entirely normal encounters with Sir George soon began to be reinterpreted in light of Osbert's cartoon caricature. Osbert's friend Evelyn Waugh, for instance, contributed a wildly exaggerated description of a single meeting he had once enjoyed with Sir George as an appendix to the fourth volume of *Left Hand, Right Hand!*. Here, Waugh alleged that the great man's red Van Dyke beard had some kind of mysterious capacity to make his face shape-shift so as to closely resemble various literary characters from King Lear to Robinson Crusoe as he spoke, which obviously wasn't true at all.[44]

In some ways, of course, this is all most unfair – and yet, at the same time, Osbert's skewed version of Sir George Reresby Sitwell is undeniably a great literary creation. Had he not exaggerated his father's genuine foibles in such a way, then it is unlikely he would be remembered at all today, after all. This slightly disingenuous method of biography has some real parallels with the process described by Edith Sitwell at the start of her own *English Eccentrics* book; namely, the sifting through of piles of quotidian rubbish in search of small morsels of valuable treasure. That is, essentially, the method of all eccentric biography, including this present one; a presentation of unusual lives with all the dull bits taken out in order to leave us with a slightly inaccurate, yet hardly untrue, heightened picture of the person thus treated. You can make more-or-less anyone look like a fruitcake via such a method, I would suggest – as can be ably demonstrated by applying the process to the life of Edith Sitwell herself.

An Absurd Façade

One of Sir George's many unpublished master works was called *The Errors of Modern Parents* – a subject upon which he really was qualified to write, particularly in relation to Edith's childhood. Sir George was not deliberately vindictive towards his daughter, but many of his kindnesses seemed to her very much like cruelties. For example, genuinely concerned about her well-being, Sir George allowed himself to be convinced by misguided doctors that the eleven-year-old Edith was in danger of growing up with both a crooked spine and a severely misshapen nose, thus condemning her to spend years locked up within a kind of artificial bodily prison. Specially made iron-lined boots and a weighty metal and leather corset restricted Edith's movements during the day, while at night her legs were sealed up within a locked cage which rendered it impossible for Edith to leave her bed – even, as she complained, if there should be a fire. She was also made to wear a nose-truss, with two steel prongs constantly locked into place against either side of her nose, forcing it to grow straight. So odd did this apparatus look that, callously, her hated mother used to encourage her friends to visit Edith during her home-schooling lessons, in order to peer at the infant freak show.[45]

With a childhood this gothic, no wonder Edith grew up to be somewhat unusual. The very word 'gothic', for example, is surely the best way to describe the manner of dress she adopted during adulthood; long flowing velvet dresses, fingers filled with rings, and strange, medieval-style headwear and golden turbans were far indeed from the usual fashions of the day. With her tall, thin frame, elegant, elongated fingers, highly unusual nose (in spite of the childhood truss) and even more unusual clothing and jewellery, Edith certainly made a striking figure, but to many she was simply a strikingly ridiculous one. In reality, she took much of this strange personal style from that of her flamboyant maternal grandmother Lady Londesborough, but, ever the self-dramatist, later claimed to have actually modelled her appearance on that of Queen Elizabeth I, about whom she wrote two best-selling books. So strongly did she begin to identify with the Virgin Queen that Sitwell, finding they shared a birthday, hired a professional astrologer to cast their charts for comparison. According to Sitwell, the astrologer tentatively concluded his client may well have been the reincarnation of Good Queen Bess, an idea she found pleasing.[46]

As all this suggests, Edith Sitwell felt a very real need to engage in acts of self-reinvention, perhaps in an attempt to escape from the miseries of her childhood. Deciding upon life as a poet, she started to view herself as different from most other people, more 'sensitive'. She believed, for instance, that she and her brothers were slightly psychic, having access to what she called 'a leakage in time', which facilitated prophetic dreams, and claimed that, when asked as a toddler what she would be when grown, had answered, 'A genius!' – a prediction which, it was implied, had since come true.[47] Determined to embark upon the life literary, as a young woman Edith began performing acts of faintly embarrassing poetic pilgrimage, travelling to Algernon Swinburne's grave on the Isle of Wight and pouring libations of milk over it as an offering to his soul, for instance, or leaving red roses on the doorstep of W. B. Yeats then running away before he could catch her.[48]

I suppose you could easily argue that this whole weird public persona was merely a façade behind which the real Edith hid – certainly, that was the opinion of her London char lady, who once told her that a public performance of her poems she was busily preparing at the time was merely 'a carry on' and 'just one big façade'.[49] Far from being offended by this comment, Edith was delighted by it, and took the word *Façade* as the title of her show. First performed in public at London's Aeolian Hall on 12 June 1923, *Façade* went down as being the most notorious of all the Sitwells' escapades. Exemplifying Edith's belief that the best poetry was really a kind of music, *Façade* represented a collaboration between herself and the composer William Walton, in which a number of Edith's poems were read out by her in a fashion intended to be complementary to Walton's accompanying musical score. Sadly, however, this act of artistic innovation was not appreciated by many among the audience on the opening night for a number of reasons.

Most bemusing, at least for those not familiar with the Modernist movement then sweeping through the arts, was the extremely bizarre way in which the poems – in themselves fairly obscure in content – were actually read out. A curtain was hung across the stage, concealing Edith from view, and decorated with three arches. In the central arch was painted a formalised female face mask, with a hole cut in the middle for a mouth. Behind this stood Edith, her real mouth filling this hole so it looked as if the curtain had come to life. Sadly, however, the curtain tended to muffle Edith's speech, so she was provided with a Sengerphone – a type of early megaphone made from compressed grass – which stuck out from the mask, making the whole performance look even more absurd. The majority of the crowd did not like it, and greeted the end of the show with boos and hisses. Fearing violence, Edith hid behind the curtain until they had dispersed; reportedly, a 'sex maniac' had attended with the sole aim of molesting Edith on-stage, and an angry old woman brandishing an umbrella was ready to give her a damn good thrashing once the pervert had had his wicked way. The newspapers didn't like it either, 'Drivel That They Paid to Hear' being one typical assessment.[50]

Coward's Way Out

As the contemporary reaction to *Façade* shows, it was extremely easy to mock the Sitwells, and disparaging assessments of their contribution to the arts, such as the Cambridge Don F. R. Leavis' famous 1932 observation that 'the Sitwells belong to the history of publicity rather than poetry'[51] were not uncommon. Partly, this was their own fault. In *Who's Who*, for instance, under the heading 'Career', Osbert once provided the following rather immodest summary of his life:

> For the past thirty years has conducted, in conjunction with his brother and sister, a series of skirmishes and hand-to-hand battles against the Philistine. Though outnumbered, has occasionally succeeded in denting the line, though not without damage to himself.[52]

While obviously intended as a joke, you can see how some people could have taken such statements the wrong way. By far their worst guying, however, was perpetrated by the impish playwright Noël Coward in his 1923 stage-revue *London Calling!*. The rough equivalent of a modern TV sketch-show, *London Calling!* featured one particular skit involving a trio of deeply pretentious poetic siblings called the Swiss Family Whittlebot. Coward had been present at the Aeolian Hall performance of *Façade* and, thinking it silly show-off rubbish, had very ostentatiously walked out, making his disapproval clear for all to see. His transformation of the Sitwells into the Whittlebots was his revenge for being bored.[53]

Looking at Coward's sketch today, it is still funny. Edith herself is transformed into the monstrous Hernia Whittlebot, while her brothers become Gob and Sago. Coward's stage directions make it clear that the trio's appearance is wilfully absurd; Hernia is 'effectively and charmingly dressed' in dyed sacking, with 'a little clump of bacchanalian fruit' hanging below each ear, while Gob and Sago come bearing a series of wholly invented musical instruments – of which, rather ominously, it is said they 'have many' – described as being 'rather queer in shape'. Then, Hernia begins spouting forth various pretentious and nonsensical statements – 'Life is essentially a curve, and Art is an oblong within that curve', 'I wrote most of the first part [of this poem] in a Lighthouse' – before reciting some of her awful verse. Throughout, the Whittlebots demonstrate precisely zero understanding of the contempt the public hold them in, Hernia misinterpreting the fact that people frequently jeer at the siblings and hurl vegetables at them in the street to be merely 'all colour and humour' on behalf of the working classes.[54]

This would have been humiliating enough, but soon the Whittlebots escaped their stage-origins and became popular comic characters, Coward referring to them constantly in his radio broadcasts and getting their names inserted into gossip columns, as if they were real people. He even had a collection of Hernia's fake verses printed at his own expense, in which he strongly implied that she – and by implication Edith – was a raving lesbian.[55] Edith and Coward remained enemies until as late as 1962, when they finally made up; although, in private, her former tormentor still maintained that fully 'three-quarters' of her poems were simply meaningless 'gibberish'.[56]

Coward's ultimate (partial) repentance has since been mirrored by the wider literary world, with the Sitwells nowadays being regarded a little more respectfully than was once the case. Nonetheless, it remains an inescapable fact that the family are still much more celebrated for their bizarre lifestyle and humorous escapades than they are for their artistic achievements. But is it really such a terrible fate to be remembered as being slightly mad by the multitude? Not necessarily. The last word, as ever, must go to the formidable Dame Edith, who assessed her family's reputation for insanity and weirdness thus, in a 1923 lecture given at the London School of Economics:

> Let us speak of our madness. We are always being called mad. If we are mad ... at least we are mad in company with most of our great predecessors and all the most intelligent foreigners. Beethoven, Schuman and Wagner, Shelley, Blake, Keats, Coleridge, Wordsworth, were all mad in turn. We shall be proud to join them in the Asylum to which they are now consigned.[57]

So, surely, would anybody else remotely sane.

House of Uncommons: Political Eccentrics

The clowns on the Left and jokers on the Right whose antics were anything but 'politics as usual'.

To have the self-belief to put yourself up for election to public office must require many qualities which tend to be shared by eccentrics; idealism, unshakable self-confidence, a sense that you are always right, and an unwillingness to back down in your beliefs in the face of public opposition, indifference or even outright mockery. Maybe this is why so many our politicians down the years have been so incredibly strange.

Admittedly, Britain, like all stable western democracies, does have a certain tradition of grey, boring behaviour among its elected representatives, though. One of our nation's finest statesmen, for instance, Lord Salisbury (1830–1903), three times PM during Victoria's reign, was so bored by proceedings in the House of Commons that he audibly yawned in the middle of his own Maiden Speech, and kept a penknife hidden in his pocket to jab into his leg whenever he felt in danger of dozing off during meetings. Lord Salisbury himself was not a figure to induce somnolence in others, however; he could frequently be seen riding a tricycle through St James' Park wearing a top hat, and, while possessing a sharp mind for policy, could be notoriously absent-minded about other matters, once having to ask a colleague who the strange young man who kept on smiling at him during some official ceremony was. 'It's your son,' came the bemused reply.[1]

Quite how Salisbury could forget this particular son, Lord Hugh Cecil (1869–1956), is perplexing; he was a man of very odd convictions. Disturbed by the idea that Sussex was infested with poisonous snakes, he claimed to only ever sit out in the garden in a very high chair while talking loudly – 'reciting poetry, perhaps' – to scare such serpents away, advising his constituents to follow his example or risk certain death. Lord Cecil was a tireless campaigner upon the issues that really mattered, taking up the ever-popular cause of banning air-raid shelters during the Second World War, once writing a letter to *The Times*, asking, 'Would it matter a jot if a theatre full of people were bombed?' and having a fanatical belief that beards were immoral. When he found his cousin had grown one, he immediately confronted him about the matter, only to be told that 'Our Lord wore a beard.' 'Our Lord wasn't a *gentleman*!' replied Lord Cecil, shocked.[2]

Also not a gentleman, despite his name, was Screaming Lord Sutch (1940–1999), the founder and leader of the Monster Raving Loony Party. No actual member of the nobility, David Edward Sutch started out as a novelty pop-singer who dressed up as Jack the Ripper, set his hair on fire and performed various horror-themed stage shows involving coffins and skulls, which we shall examine in a future chapter. Sutch's first taste of the political limelight came in 1963 when he stood for election on behalf of the National Teenage Party, founding his more famous Monster Raving Loonies in 1983. Seemingly inspired by a 1970 *Monty Python* sketch entitled 'Election Night Special', in which a strangely dressed man named Tarquin Fin-tim-lin-bin-whin-bim-lim-bus-stop-F'tang-F'tang-Olé-Biscuitbarrel stood as candidate for the Silly Party, Sutch's Loonies fulfilled an essentially satirical role in the political landscape, espousing deliberately bizarre policies such as banning January and February to make winter shorter, reducing class sizes by making pupils sit closer together, and marking all vegetables with the phrase 'for oral use only'. Most notably, his observation that there was only *one* Monopolies Commission, and that this in itself technically constituted an illegal monopoly, did actually make a sort of twisted sense.

Attitudes towards Sutch and his followers varied, with some finding their big joke amusing, and others thinking them merely tedious, attention-seeking show-offs – most notably Margaret Thatcher, against whom Sutch stood in the Finchley constituency in 1983, following her around holding a giant tin opener as part of his campaign to 'open up the Iron Lady'. The famously humourless Thatcher gained revenge on Sutch in 1985 when the electoral deposit fee was raised from £150 to £500 in an attempt to put more Loonies off from standing, but the ploy did not work and, astonishingly, some of Sutch's silly proposals have since found their way onto the statute-books; the notion of having 'passports for pets', for instance, was originally his idea. The Loony slogan 'Vote for insanity – you know it makes sense!' evidently did make sense for a lot of voters, with Sutch standing for office nearly forty times, gaining around 15,000 votes in total, forfeiting over £10,000 in lost deposits and spending a further £85,000 on campaign-expenses. Clearly, Sutch was abnormally committed to his role of electoral jester, and fully admitted he loved the glare of publicity it provided. So keen was Sutch for attention that, when his partner found him hanged dead in 1999, she thought it was just yet another jape and took a celebratory photograph of the scene, not realising that Sutch, depressed after the death of his mother, really had taken his own life.[3]

Another eccentric British political organisation was the Natural Law Party, whose leader Dr Geoffrey Clements spent the early 1990s trying to persuade the electorate to vote for his laudable but unlikely manifesto promise of 'Bringing the individual and the country into tune with Natural Law so that unfavourable planetary influences are neutralised.' But what was this 'Natural Law' of which Dr Clements spoke? Named after a term describing a mystical Hindu principle supposedly underlying all Creation, the NLP was the brainchild of one Maharishi Mahesh Yogi, an Indian holy-man who had mixed with the Beatles and spent decades promoting the practice of Transcendental Meditation (TM) around the world. Essentially, adherents of this technique spend their time meditating and trying to bring body and mind into harmony with the universe. Practised en masse, however, the Maharishi and his man in the UK, Dr Clements, claimed that TM could have some kind of paranormal effect upon reality as a whole, leading to the NLP's main policy programme of training advanced TM masters to sit around meditating for hours, beaming out positive thoughts to bring an end to war, crime and violence.

Founded in the UK in March 1992, just in time to contest the General Election in April, the NLP gained initial publicity by persuading ex-Beatle George Harrison to perform a fund-raising concert, and reportedly spent nearly £1 million putting up 310 candidates – all of whom lost their deposits. Perhaps if George Harrison, Paul McCartney and Ringo Starr had agreed to stand for the NLP in Liverpool, as the Mahirishi had requested, they would have fared a little better, but the remaining Beatles refused. This was a shame, as Merseyside seemed the centre of NLP activity in

Britain, with Dr Clements himself standing for election in nearby Southport, and an 'Ideal Village' for TM-adherents being created in Skelmersdale in 1988. Skelmersdale was also the location of a curious experiment held between 1988 and 1991, when 100 advanced TM-masters engaged in regular sessions of meditation and so-called 'yogic flying' in an attempt to reduce Merseyside's crime rate (which did actually fall some 16 per cent by the end of the trial). Clements' plan was to spread the word about TM and yogic flying until eventually so many people were at it that our missile defence systems could be replaced with a kind of psychic force-field, or 'integrated national consciousness', which would render Britain invincible.

Sadly, the NLP's own publicity soon proved its downfall. Given a TV spot for a Party Political Broadcast in 1994, Dr Clements foolishly used it to show footage of TM-masters engaging in bouts of yogic flying, which is supposed to be an advanced meditational technique enabling practitioners briefly to levitate. In practice, however, this 'levitation' came across on film simply as a group of men jumping across crash-mats with their legs crossed, a highly amusing sight which led to widespread public ridicule. Following a poor return of 0.1 per cent of the total vote during the 1997 General Election, Dr Clements officially deregistered the NLP with the Electoral Commission in 2003. He need not have bothered; in 2005, the Mahirishi himself, outraged by Britain's participation in the Iraq War, condemned the UK as 'the destroyer of the world' and a 'scorpion', forbidding his followers to teach TM here from that point on. He had previously ordered his yogic fliers to beam out thoughts to the British electorate telling them to overthrow the Labour Government, but when war-mongering Tony Blair was re-elected as prime minister in May 2005, that was the final straw.[4]

The compromises necessary to succeed in ordinary party politics just don't suit some would-be statesmen, meanwhile, who have had ideas so unusual they felt no option but to stand for office as Independents. In the General Election of May 2015, for instance, voters in the Brighton Pavilion ward had the option of voting for a self-described 'high-class courtesan' named Charlotte Rose, who campaigned upon a platform of getting prostitutes to take sex education classes in schools, seeing as they were the real experts on the matter, not teachers, while constituents in nearby Hove could vote for one Matt Taylor, whose personal political crusade centred around ridding his borough's public spaces of street drinkers and heroin addicts – specifically, his own sister and nieces. In his election literature, Mr Taylor also claimed to be 'the only politician in 1,500 years to conjure up the spirit of King Arthur II in a British General Election', which is in fact inaccurate, seeing as in 2010 a man claiming to *be* King Arthur stood for election in Salisbury, gaining some 257 votes – more than enough potential knights to fill a Round Table.[5]

Another Independent with an unusual line in campaign literature was Mark Ellis (1942–2014), a retired customs officer who twice ran for office in Sevenoaks on an anti-EU platform which made UKIP's thinking look positively cosmopolitan. Mr Ellis was a well-known Sevenoaks figure on account of his hobby of pushing a shopping trolley through the streets and filling it up with rubbish 'in order to help society accumulate wealth', and because he once appeared in the local newspaper boasting that he shared his home with a stray duck. Ellis hated the EU for a variety of reasons, including its alleged desire to remove the words 'Kent' and 'England' from maps, its love of low-energy lightbulbs, and, worst of all, its 'needless spoiling of the fireworks trade'. Mr Ellis was clearly a man of conservative opinions, seeing as his other complaints about modern life included the RAF no longer using 1950s Vulcans or Dakotas in its air-fleet, and the fact that Rhodesia was now called Zimbabwe. However, the Conservative Party, he said, were no longer really the Conservative Party – instead they were the CON-servative Party perpetrating a giant CON-spiracy against England, the biggest CON-trick of all time. Sadly, Ellis' 'evidence' for his assertions that the Tories and Brussels were engaged in a secret plot to destroy Britain's firework-industry were drawn largely from something called *The Protocols of the Elders of Zion*, a notoriously racist (and notoriously fake) document claiming that Jews run the world, which rather undermined his credibility somewhat. [6]

Britain's most notable current Independent candidate, though, is undoubtedly Barry Kirk, a former computer-worker from the Welsh town of Port Talbot who is now better known as Captain Beany (b.1954), having officially changed his name by deed poll in 1991. The leader (and sole member) of the New Millennium Bean Party, Captain Beany claims to be an orange alien from the Planet Beanus, and to this end wanders through the streets of his Aberavon constituency with dyed orange skin, wearing a cape, visor and orange superhero costume featuring gold-coloured boots and what seem to be externally-worn underpants, seeking people's votes come election time. In case he gets attacked by extraterrestrial invaders on the campaign trail, Beany carries a

'Laser Bean Gun' on a kind of utility belt, and has taken out an insurance-policy against being abducted by aliens. While Beany's manifesto appears to consist largely of terrible bean-related puns, the first time he stood for office in 1990 he beat the local Lib Dem candidate by nine votes! Captain Beany appears to be genuinely obsessed by beans. He has performed several bean-related stunts for charity, raising large sums, runs the world's only 'Baked Bean Museum of Excellence' from his council flat, and has appeared on the front-page of a tabloid under the headline 'BAKED BEAN FREAK'S BUM EXPLODES!' (even though it didn't). On his official website, Beany describes himself thus: 'He hails from another warped time and dimension and he has 'beaned' down to spread much 'hap-BEAN-ness' for all 'human beans' on Planet Earth!!' How on earth did Mr Kirk's life come to this?

By his own admission, Barry Kirk has always been a joker, 'acting the gong', as he puts it, since childhood. He is the kind of man who, upon meeting a male stripper on a night out, decided to outdo him by shedding his own clothes, and who once repeatedly exposed himself to local women in a so-called 'flashathon', with only a box of strategically placed 'Flash' cleaning-fluid to hide his rude bits (all in the aid of charity, I hasten to add). According to interviews, his obsession with baked beans began one day in 1986 when he was sorting through his record collection and came across an album by the Who, the cover of which featured lead-singer Roger Daltrey sitting in a bath of baked beans. Deciding to copy the feat for charity, Beany wangled 360 free tins of beans from a local supermarket and informed the press. Trying to set a world record, Beany remained in his bean-bath for days on end, getting so little sleep that he actually began 'hallucinating baked beans'. However, the media lapped his feat up, he raised £1,500, and decided he was onto something. After officially changing his name to Captain Beany, Kirk found it hard to get work, for obvious reasons, so decided to become Beany full time. In April 2009, Beany's odd career culminated in him being awarded the title 'Eccentric of the Year', an accolade it seems difficult to argue with.[7]

This is an award which, had it existed during his own lifetime, would surely also have been won by Britain's finest ever Independent candidate, Lieutenant-Commander Bill Boaks (1904–1986), a comically obsessive road-safety campaigner. After thirty years in the Royal Navy, Boaks emerged into civilian life in 1945 in need of a new foe to fight, and found it in the rise of the motorcar. Boaks didn't object to all motor vehicles per se, but to the sheer volume of traffic which was starting to spring up, and to the increasingly careless behaviour he saw on Britain's roads. In particular, he had it in for Violet Attlee, the wife of Britain's first post-war PM, Clement Attlee, a notoriously bad driver who kept on crashing her vehicle while chauffeuring her husband on the campaign-trail. It was for this reason that Boaks decided to stand against Attlee in his own constituency of Walthamstow West in the General Election of 1951, in order to highlight the issue. Sadly, Boaks filled in the forms incorrectly and ended up standing for the seat of Walthamstow *East* instead.

Bill Boaks didn't let this mishap get the better of him, though, and he was soon out canvassing upon behalf of his ADMIRAL ('Association of Democratic Monarchists Representing All Ladies') Party, of which he was the only member, riding his campaign-vehicle up and down the streets. This vehicle was most curious; it was basically an armoured bicycle upon which Boaks had mounted a giant cardboard box emblazoned with various anti-car slogans, inside which he sat, sheltered from the elements. As his mishap with the registration forms implied, Boaks was not the most literate of men, and his block-capital slogans wishing harm upon various dangerous drivers he had read about in the newspapers left something to be desired in terms of their grammar: 'BILL BOAKS SAYS: CAN ? BATTERSEA CAR KILLER DAVID V. BLOOR BE BLINDED!' being one such example. Other illiterate slogans included 'GOOD MILES RIDE SAFELY! SHOULD MAKE YOU PONDER', 'BILL BOAKS AIR ROAD PUBLIC SAFETY WHITE RESIDENT PRIME MINISTER M.P. CANDIDIATE SEEKS YOUR CLAPHAM VOTE' and the frankly baffling 'PARENTS WATCH UNDER TAKER OVERTAKERS COLDLY ANGRY POLICE CAN ASK WHY! GIVEN INDICES'. Unsurprisingly, Boaks received only 174 votes in Walthamstow East, out of some 40,001 cast, but this only further convinced Bill he was in the right. In his view, 'It's the ones who *don't* vote [whose votes] you really want, because they're the ones who *think*.' Therefore, the fewer votes Boaks gained, the greater his victory had been – sort of.

Keeping this unique conclusion in mind, Boaks was soon back in the public eye, demanding that all goods be delivered by freight train, not van or lorry, and that all roads become giant zebra crossings so that pedestrians had permanent right of way. His aim with this latter plan was to cause such traffic chaos that citizens spontaneously gave up their cars and began travelling by bus or helicopter instead, landing pads for which he insisted be installed in all major city centres. To achieve publicity for these proposals, Boaks took to holding up traffic by repeatedly walking up and down zebra crossings wheeling a pram filled with bricks, or sitting in the middle of the A40 in a deckchair reading *The Daily Telegraph*. At other times, he would commandeer roundabouts and harangue passing motorists until moved on by the police, or roller-skate along roads wearing a bowler hat and clutching an umbrella and briefcase. Most impressively, he once stopped his van on a zebra crossing in front of Wembley Stadium and refused to start it up again until all 100,000 England fans had crossed the road safely on their way into the arena. He also attempted a series of private prosecutions against people he thought had been driving dangerously, including the Home Secretary and the Duke of Edinburgh. In trying to bring this latter case, which revolved around Prince Philip accidentally pranging another vehicle, Boaks tried to summons the Queen to court for 'aiding and abetting' Philip by being his passenger. 'I don't care whether the driver was a Duke or a bloody dustman!' he said, when asked whether he really thought this was a sensible course to pursue.

Boaks' few non-traffic-related policies were somewhat old-school, centring as they did around combating the twin evils of Communism and homosexuality in the Civil Service, and he eventually changed his Party's name to PSDMWR, or 'Public Safety Democratic Monarchist White Resident', seeing this as a good description of its right-wing leader. Boaks ran in around forty elections of various sorts from 1951 to 1982, receiving a then-record low of only five votes at the Glasgow Hill-Head by-election in 1982, rather desperately telling the media afterwards, 'Had I been elected, I would have become the next Prime Minister.' It was time to quit, but his work had not been in vain; Boaks had been one of the main inspirations for Screaming Lord Sutch, and in 1983 he was down to be the official Monster Raving Loony candidate in Streatham, though this never came to pass. Inevitably, when Boaks died in 1986, it was because of injuries he had sustained in a traffic-accident – two years earlier he had fallen off a bus and banged his head, which later led to complications. Perhaps he should have travelled by car after all?[8]

Local councillors, too, can have their foibles, as regular readers of *Private Eye* magazine's 'Rotten Boroughs' section will know. That particular column, however, tends to deal with issues surrounding corruption, incompetence and nepotism – none of which Britain's strangest local official, Simon Parkes, could ever be accused of.

Indeed, Mr Parkes, who was elected as a Labour councillor on Whitby Town Council in February 2012, appears to be a model of propriety. By all accounts, he has been a hard-working and competent public servant, with a respected and useful day job as a driving instructor, and a past existence as a lecturer at London's Natural History Museum. It is just that, away from the council offices, Parkes claims to be in regular contact with alien beings. Indeed, rather more sensationally, he claims *himself* to be a part-alien being, whose mother is a nine-foot-tall green reptile from outer space.

Mr Parkes first became aware of this fact, he said, aged around six months, when a giant lizard appeared standing over his cot wearing a purple cloak. Far from being scared, baby Simon was reassured when the creature beamed a psychic message into his brain, telling him that she was his real and 'more important' mother, not the inferior human female who was currently filling that role. His next encounter with aliens came aged three when his human mother left him alone at home suffering from chickenpox one day, at which point an eight-foot-tall extraterrestrial doctor appeared on the scene, dressed as a waiter, and helped the child out, accompanied by several armed 'human enforcement officers' who stepped out of Simon's wardrobe to monitor events. Aged eleven, Parkes was finally taken onboard a flying saucer and told the horrible truth about mankind – his mum's race had interfered with humanity's genes some time ago, to deliberately 'dumb down' our species somehow. It is unclear quite why the reptiles did this, exactly, but at least they had the good grace to apologise to Simon for this crime; they did so 'several times', apparently, and in 1971 he signed some kind of 'Soul-Agreement' with them, whose terms seem a little unclear.

Parkes is a most remarkable man, claiming to encounter strange entities on a regular basis, seeing so-called 'shadow-beings' wandering the streets of Whitby in disguise. To most ordinary humans, with their dumbed-down, non-reptilian genes, they may appear to be simply ordinary cats, owls, clowns and policemen, but Councillor Parkes knows better. Other claims reportedly made by Parkes include that he himself has fathered a half-alien love child called Zarka, that he lost his virginity to a hologram at the age of five, and that having regular sex with an alien he calls 'Cat Woman' four times a year on an Earth-orbiting spaceship has caused tension in his marriage. His most recent appearance in the headlines at time of writing came in March 2015, when Parkes gave a speech claiming that Russian President Vladimir Putin's military aggression in the Ukraine was being performed at the behest of a race of ETs called 'The Nordics', who were supplying Putin with advanced technology and encouraging him to annoy America. Mr Parkes advised his audience not to worry about this development, however, as 'it's not really a big deal, this sort of thing happens all the time'.

Seemingly, Whitby's voters did *not* much worry about this kind of thing. According to Parkes, interviewed in 2012, his alien-related beliefs rarely came up as a topic of pressing interest on the doorstep, his opinions being merely 'a personal matter' which 'doesn't affect my work'. As he said, 'I'm more interested in fixing someone's leaking roof or potholes' than discussing the lizard-people, although he did admit that 'I get more sense out of aliens than out of [the] Town Hall.' I hesitate to say it, but maybe the attitude of Whitby's electorate was a sensible one. Just so long as Councillor Parkes made sure the bins were emptied on time, then his extraordinary private beliefs were, strictly speaking, irrelevant – which makes it all the sadder that, in April 2015, he finally felt compelled to step down from his role, citing pressures of workload.[9]

Perhaps the pressures of work had also been getting to a Liberal Democrat councillor for Winchester named Adrian Hicks, who in 2004 was walking down his constituency's high-street when he claims to have seen that most unexpected of sights, an alien wearing a tutu. This entity, said Hicks, was waddling by his local branch of The Works discount bookshop like a happy penguin. 'She had very large, prominent eyes, and was twirling her hands in a circular motion. She seemed friendly, and totally at ease,' said Mr Hicks. Apparently, the extraterrestrial tutu-wearer was 'very interested in the clock over Lloyds Bank' and presented such a strange appearance that Hicks considered approaching her and saying, 'Excuse me, you're not from around here, are you?' but then thought better of it. Most of us, thinking we had seen an alien ballet dancer wobbling down the street like Pingu, might have kept quiet about the fact, but not Councillor Hicks – following his election to office in 2007, he approached his local paper, asking other witnesses to come forward and confirm what he had seen. I may be wrong, but as I far as I am aware, nobody ever did.[10] And they say that politicians today lack courage in their own convictions.

One Lord A-Looning: John Conrad Russell, 4th Earl Russell (1921–1987)

The loony Lord with a manifesto for madness, who thought humans were no better than toads.

In 1999, an act of great political vandalism was perpetrated against the age-old and age-tested constitution of this, our United Kingdom; Tony Blair's appalling House of Lords Act was signed into law on 11 November of that year, bringing to an end the centuries-old 'hereditary principle', which had allowed the eldest sons of several hundred of the nation's oldest and grandest families to take a seat in the Chamber of the House automatically, as soon as they had inherited their title.[1] This wholly regrettable measure was said to have been introduced in the name of such alleged qualities as 'democracy', 'equality' and 'fairness', which sounds admirable enough at first – but was it really?

Just stop and think about what exactly the hereditary principle meant for one moment; that there was once a legislative Chamber in this land whose members were beholden to nobody but Fate for their positions, and who thus had no necessity to slavishly toe any Party line. Being therefore able to make their own minds up about things without jeopardising their careers, they often fulfilled the immensely useful function of holding the Government of the day, whatever its stripes, to outside account. Independent-minded, independent men, who thought what they wanted and spoke as they thought – what sane person *wouldn't* want such a thing in their country? Especially seeing as, due to the fact that all hereditary Peers were essentially chosen through a process of random genetic chance, rather than active, rational selection, a fair number of them down the years have been, quite simply, monumental nutcases.

Take, for instance, Lord Michael Onslow (1938–2011), the 7th Earl of his line and, regrettably, the final Lord Onslow to take his place in the House. Disliking Mr Blair's innovations, he openly described himself as 'a pustule on the rump of the body-politic' and saw his role during his final years to act as a walking advertisement for the benefits of inherited peerages. Far from being insane himself, Lord Onslow was an articulate critic of New Labour's reforms, pointing out that, just because his family had been given their initial peerage two centuries ago by William Pitt, and some modern Members of the Lords had been given their own more recently by people like Neil Kinnock and Blair himself, it didn't make such people's appointments any more democratic, nor his own presence in the House any less valuable. Indeed, given that Lord Onslow had once ridden a horse down the A3 in pursuit of an escaped bull, kept a carved antique Roman testicle beneath his wife's pillow, gave speeches which were actually amusing and memorable (sample quote: 'One hundred years ago the Church was in favour of fox-hunting and against buggery; now it is in favour of buggery and against fox-hunting') and had once lost a pet monkey while journeying on the Tube, I think his presence in the Chamber was very valuable indeed. The pink bow tie-wearing, thrash-metal and acid-jazz-loving Peer fully admitted that his position in politics was utterly 'illogical', but so are a great many of the things our *elected* politicians do during their time in office, too ...[2]

Interplanetary Parliament

Mostly, such eccentric Lords kept their foibles separate from their role in the House – but this impulse was not universal, as we can see from the Westminster activities of one Lord Clancarty, better known to his friends on the occult fringe as Brinsley le Poer Trench (1911–1995), the former editor of the world's leading UFO-publication, *Flying Saucer Review*. Prior to inheriting his earldom in 1976, Clancarty had been busily writing a series of books with titles like *The Sky People*, laying out his unusual view that aliens had been visiting Earth for millions of years, that they had created the human race itself around 30,000 years ago, and that these same space-beings had secret bases hidden away inside our surprisingly hollow planet, which they accessed via two giant holes concealed at the North and South Poles. Worse, some of these aliens were unfriendly, he said, and occasionally surfaced to kidnap humans, taking them down below and programming them to be their slaves, in preparation for some future invasion-attempt. In 1964, he helped found a body called Contact International, linking up ufologists from all across the globe. Originally called the International Sky Scouts in order to appeal to the world's saucer-hungry children, this name soon had to be dropped after the real Boy Scouts threatened Clancarty with legal action!

Clancarty was particularly popular in Japan, and in 1966 was invited there by a saucer cult named The Cosmic Brotherhood Association to take part in a weird quasi-religious ceremony on top of a so-called 'Sun-Pyramid', where his Japanese hosts thought an alien astronaut had descended down to Earth thousands of years ago to teach people how to grow vegetables. Clancarty was particularly interested in the issue of UFO propulsion-systems, a problem he devoted much time and effort to; in 1983, he said that a high-up from the Japanese car giant Honda had paid him a visit in London, asking to be let in on his secret knowledge, something to which he readily agreed. So, if Honda ever do manage to create an affordable family-saloon spaceship, you know who to thank.[3]

As soon as Clancarty succeeded his half-brother as earl in 1976, he started using his new powers to call for the British Government to release all the information he thought they were concealing about ETs. This made the MoD nervous; an official named Patrick Stevens admitted that Clancarty was an acknowledged expert on UFOs, but that the MoD themselves did not have one, 'for much the same reasons as we have no experts on levitation or black magic.' Eventually, Clancarty managed to force UFOs onto the official agenda, the Lords holding a three-hour session beginning at 7.00 p.m. on Wednesday 17 January 1979, right in the middle of Britain's 'Winter of Discontent'. Predictably, the Debate drew more onlookers than was usual, including several prominent ufologists, all hoping to hear something weird; they were not disappointed. While Clancarty himself took the opportunity to warn the House that the number of UFO landings was increasing all across the globe and really ought to be looked into, several other Peers recalled their own (largely dubious) UFO sightings, while Lord Davies of Leek took the opportunity to ask the House if any of them believed in angels. Lord Kimberley, Liberal spokesman on aerospace, claimed to know of a dastardly conspiracy in which the US and Soviets had secretly agreed to exchange data on saucer-sightings but conceal it from other nations, including Britain. The Bishop of Norwich, meanwhile, stood up and wondered aloud about God's plans for the possible salvation of alien races, finally concluding, according to one observer, that 'redemption through Christ obtains throughout the galaxies'.[4]

There is no way that Clancarty would ever have been elected to office on a platform of trying to force the Government to reveal the 'truth' about UFOs lying in wait inside our hollow planet; and yet, thanks to the caprices of the old hereditary principle, he got his chance to entertain us by challenging them about it anyway. Blair and his cronies have robbed us all of this kind of thing forever. Personally, I think that modern politics is much the poorer for it.

Eminent Victorians

The maddest lord of all, however, was surely John Conrad Russell, the 4th Earl Russell, who was a truly excellent illustration of how the chance whims of genetics can throw up people with issues in even the most previously celebrated of families. Russell's father was one of the most famous men of his age, the mathematician, peace campaigner and philosopher Bertrand Russell, and his great-grandfather, Lord John Russell, had once led the country, being one of the most significant Prime Ministers of Queen Victoria's long and happy reign; under his premiership, various important measures, such as the 1832 Reform Act, had been passed, giving him an exalted reputation as one of the great proponents of liberalism. Indeed, so great was this reputation that one of the Russell family's many influential acquaintances was none other than our old libertarian friend John Stuart Mill, who acted as Bertrand's godfather. This was not the kind of glorious lineage you would have suspected might end up culminating in such a bizarre person as Earl Russell – or was it?

In fact, there was a certain amount of insanity, as well as brilliance, running through the Russell family. Bertrand Russell's most un-Wodehousian Aunt Agatha was mentally unstable, for instance, and his Uncle William had been incarcerated in an asylum after murdering a tramp. Bertrand himself endured a deeply unhappy youth, and began to fear that he might go mad too; feeling fundamentally isolated from others, he started to think he was a ghost, and had repeated nightmares about being trapped behind a pane of glass, cut off forever from his fellow men. Despondent, he began to consider suicide, these impulses fading away only when he discovered mathematics – for most people, it is the other way around. Perhaps the young Bertrand's feelings of loneliness were not too surprising, though; both his parents had died while he was still a toddler, and he had been packed off to live with his dour religious grandmother Lady Russell at her Richmond mansion, Pembroke Lodge. When Lady Russell observed her grandson's depression, her response was less than comforting; she curtly told the boy that, when he grew up, he had better not have any children himself, as they would 'probably be deranged'. Prior to Bertrand's first marriage, to the American feminist Alys Pearsall Smith in 1894, Lady Russell's opinion was backed up by the family doctor. At Lady Russell's behest, this hired quack told Russell that his children would undoubtedly 'be born lunatics' and that the union should be cancelled immediately on the nonsensical grounds that using condoms on their wedding night would turn him and Alys epileptic.[5]

While the happy couple thankfully failed to suffer any sudden fits during their honeymoon, however, Bertrand and Alys' marriage was nonetheless still a failure, collapsing without any children having been born after all, insane or otherwise. In 1921, the philosopher married for a second time, to another feminist, Dora Black. On 16 November 1921, their first child, John Conrad Russell, the future Earl, was born, followed by a little girl, Katharine Jane, in December 1923.[6] Katharine grew up normally, but for John Conrad this was very much not the case. John's middle name was taken from the surname of the great Polish-born writer Joseph Conrad, with whom his father had been friendly. Like Bertrand, the novelist feared insanity and had a horrible fear that Western civilisation itself was a mere veneer, far more fragile than it seemed, which could collapse back down into a state of savage anarchy and madness at any time – as readers of his novella *Heart of Darkness* will surely know.[7] Given these pessimistic feelings upon Conrad's behalf, Bertrand did well to name his son after him; after all, John Conrad's life itself spelled out an equally unhappy narrative in which, after a bright start, the thin civilised veneer of his own personality began to collapse away, leading to a sad descent down into full-blown schizophrenia.[8] It turned out that Lady Russell's grim prophecy was true after all.

Lord Almighty

A pleasing piece of trivia about John Conrad Russell is that he is sometimes said to have been the only man in Britain to have been barred from voting in a General Election on two grounds – firstly that he was a Peer (by ancient tradition, those who sit in the Lords are not allowed to cast any ballot), and secondly that he was certified insane.[9] Insanity was once no legal grounds for barring actual Membership of the Lords, though, and, following Bertrand Russell's death on 2 February 1970, John Conrad inherited his father's title, becoming the 4th Earl Russell, and being henceforward perfectly entitled to take his rightful place at the heart of our nation's democracy.

In our apathetic age, I suspect there can be few persons outside of politics or the media who have ever actually bothered to buy and read any copies of *Hansard*, the official transcripts of sessions which take place in both the Commons and the Lords. The exception to this rule, however, was an edition containing a particularly memorable speech of Earl Russell's from 1978, which sold out almost as soon as it was printed. So eager were the public to read this particular oration that, in order to satisfy demand, it was later published in full as a separate booklet with the rather long title *The Full and True Text of a Notorious, Remarkable and Visionary Speech Made by John, Viscount Amberley, Earl RUSSELL, on the eighteenth of July 1978 at 9.08pm in the HOUSE OF LORDS*. I have a contemporary advertisement for this unlikely bestseller here before me as I write. It consists of extracts from Russell's speech, illustrated with a scathing cartoon by Ralph Steadman in which the Noble Earl is depicted as an insane and squawking bird wearing a crown and ermine and flapping around his skeletal wings while vomiting out a mixture of feathers, blood and bile onto his fellow 'Parliament of Fowls' clucking away down below.[10]

The picture was odd enough, but the publisher was perhaps even odder; it was not HM Stationery Office, who print off copies of *Hansard* on a regular basis, but an organisation called Open Head Press, who are now, I believe, defunct. Before they folded, though, the company had shown a distinct interest in British politics, in 1979 also issuing an annotated transcript of Lord Clancarty's UFO Debate. This now-rare publication attracted public endorsement from TV's top astronomer Patrick Moore, who called it 'well worth reading', and even *The Anarchist Review*, who accurately opined that 'UFOs attract the bizarre and cranks, and the House of Lords has more of these per square yard than almost anywhere else'.[11]

Open Head Press were, it is safe to say, not your average parliamentary publisher; another of their adverts I have to hand declares that they printed only 'Books that make your Mind Matter!', publications such as *The Fanatic* – 'a paper of passion and conspiratology', apparently – and a pamphlet about Jesus whose title I dare not cite, but which I suspect may not have been blessed with official Church approval. The ad in question also offers for sale 'badges, records, tapes and much more', as well as a large poster, described as being 'white-hot and irradiated', depicting the late Mrs Thatcher engaged in what appears at first glance to be an obscene act, a product you are encouraged to buy and then 'wrap around your head'.[12] Open Head, it should be clear by now, were an example of what was once called 'the alternative Press' – i.e. sellers of 'fringe' books to persons interested in all things counter-culture. But why would such people be interested in printing a mere speech to the Lords? The précis they gave of Earl Russell's 'ecstatic, loony [and] legendary' words in their ad should make it immediately clear:

> The police should be abolished, the Royal Family are all toads, group sex will redeem the economy, and if we want to stop the Third World War we should start communicating with angels.[13]

That's right; the lord had gone loony.

Leave Those Kids Alone!

Russell's rabid rant was nothing if not memorable; it deserves to stand up there with 'We will fight them on the beaches' and 'I have a dream!' in the long annals of truly great political rhetoric. Certainly, it pulled no punches, the Earl being quite happy to ask his fellow-Peers 'What are you? Soulless robots?' before then going on to accuse them all of being nothing but a bunch of 'spiritless Papal bum-boys'. 'Forward, the creative spirit!' he roared, before providing the country with a few very creative solutions to its most pressing problems himself.

In Westminster-speak, Russell's speech was technically classified as being a 'response to an unstarred question' during a debate that was supposed to be about aiding victims of crime, but which ended up being about much, much more. After all, as Earl Russell explained to a bemused House, there was actually no such thing as crime. If Britain was really the civilised nation it pretended to be, he said, then its police force should be merged with the Salvation Army immediately, and its officers retrained so that their only function was to make people cups of tea. If a man tried to steal anything, then that was his perfect right, Russell made clear, giving the example of someone who might walk into a jeweller's shop to snatch a bag of diamonds. If such a thing happened, said the Earl, then surely the only truly humane thing for the jeweller to do would be to *let* him steal them, then give him a second bag as well, for good measure. Prisons, it turned out, should be banned; according to Russell, policemen up and down the land were engaged in a gigantic conspiracy to arrest young men and seduce them in their cells, before then selling them on into lives of gay prostitution in prisons. What way was this to treat the flower of English manhood, he asked? Surely it would be better if the Government just paid them all a fair wage to sit around and do nothing all day in big huts instead of making them become Chief Constables' rent boys?

Earl Russell had some interesting plans for the nation's schoolgirls, too. At the age of twelve, he said, every girl should be considered a woman, and given a free house by the State. Then, 75 per cent of the nation's wealth would be donated to the fairer sex, while the remaining 25 per cent would be used to protect men from the police in their large communal huts, which the girls could then visit in order to choose their husbands – as many as they liked, the men would have no say in the matter. This, he said, would be the true realisation of 'Women's Lib'.

Explaining that 'the habit of arresting young people and raping them in gaol is part of a plot which is designed to destroy the human race', Russell demanded that the nation's youth be put in charge of everything, and encouraged to play outside all day in the nude instead of being treated as mere 'indoor products'. As he said, 'the ancient Greeks fought naked', and so 'naked bathing on beaches or in rivers ought to be universal'. School and work were just yet more Establishment conspiracies aimed at forcing adolescents to stay inside all day instead of romping through fields as nature intended; 'Leisure is the point and working is wrong, being in any case the curse visited by God upon Adam and not to be blessed.' He approved of bored schoolboys burning down their schools, he explained, as it was obvious (to him, at least) that if they were being taught properly by their teachers then the spirit of Sir Isaac Newton would have been reincarnated in one of them by now. Surely we should instead all follow the example of the old cartoon-character 'Little Audrey', who, he said, had 'laughed and laughed because she knew that only God could make a tree'?

Claiming that 'this House is indisputably Marxist and inherits the banner of the Red Army', Russell then laid out his theory that all aristocrats were actually Communists. The upper class, he said, were what the proletariat should aim to be; now that there were machines to do all our work for us, the factories should lie empty and the workers be unchained – automation, he said, 'is a boon, it should be called a boon, it should be used as a boon'. There would be no need for people to go out and earn money, he pointed out, if shops simply gave away all their goods for free or let you steal them, and the State should pay you for being idle anyway. The problem of funding the army could also be solved at a stroke, if only people would say 'You don't exist' to any wars that might arise. As he said, the Cold War was a truly idiotic enterprise, as the then-US and Soviet leaders Jimmy Carter and Leonid Brezhnev were 'really the same person' in disguise. If only the people of Latin America would rise up against their oppressors in the name of the Pope, and 'Euro-Communism' be imposed across the world, peace would reign, and we would all live the pleasant, care-free life of 'Tonga and the South Sea Islands' instead of having to work in the 'satanic mills' of industry. Conveniently, Earl Russell was also most concerned about the contemporary practice of locking up lunatics; I wonder why.

There was indisputable proof that this whole bizarre utopia could be made to work, Russell finally claimed, and it was to be found in a most unexpected quarter, namely the recent restructuring of British Rail, a process which he must have studied in more depth than most observers. His plan could not fail, he said, as, once word of his speech got out, the Old Order would be revealed as being merely a 'fallen boxer' which the populace would immediately assault with 'hammerblow after hammerblow' until 'it cannot get up to defend itself.' The Old Order did then unexpectedly rise up from off the canvas, however, with one Lord Wells-Pestell interrupting Russell in very meek tones, pointing out politely that his speech was a breach of Westminster protocol, because, as he put it, 'I doubt very much that it could be held that what he is saying is relevant to the Question before the House.' Evidently taking exception to this interruption, Russell then left the Chamber, and was prevented from returning by the ushers.[14]

So embarrassing was this episode that a myth has since arisen that it is the only speech ever made in Parliament which was not recorded in *Hansard*.[15] This is not true, but I think I can explain the misunderstanding; Earl Russell had not finished talking when he was forced to give way to Lord Wells-Pestell, and, seeing as the rest of his speech was not actually spoken in the Lords, *Hansard* had no business printing it. This is a shame, however, as, had Russell been allowed to continue, we would have heard that the only true punishment for Cabinet Ministers impeding the wishes of the young was 'the guillotine', and that 'God has not been let into Britain', meaning that 'thunderbolts in Heaven' would eventually be rained down upon 'the Police-Doll that prostitutes people ... the Doll of Love', for its continued abuses. We would also have discovered that the Royal Family were 'pampered, decadent and snobbish' and that such selfish attitudes meant that half of mankind had now been transformed into amphibians; as his most infamous would-be proclamation had it, 'The official rating of the human race in the Northern Hemisphere is ... TOAD!' Russell then planned to end his speech with the surprisingly understated assertion that 'it may be expected that most people will support these proposals, because they are, after all, in everybody's own interest'.[16] In this, as in so much else, I fear he may have been mistaken.

Idle Theories

How did Russell manage to think all this up? The obvious answer is just to invoke his evident mental instability. In fact, however, reading between the lines of his speech, we can see various distinct traces of his illustrious father's own particular worldview. Bertrand Russell, in a 1951 essay about the joys of liberalism, once advised his readers, 'Do not fear to be eccentric in opinion, for every opinion now accepted was once eccentric,' a notion which, ironically, he appears to have stolen from his godfather John Stuart Mill.[17] You certainly cannot accuse Bertrand of failing to practice what he preached upon this issue, however, given that he had a few notably eccentric ideas himself.

While he made genuine contributions to fields as diverse as Logic and Higher Mathematics – i.e. the kinds of things virtually nobody actually reads or understands, including myself – Bertrand Russell was far more familiar to the general public for his media appeals in favour of ideas like pacifism, feminism and democratic socialism. He was prone to making deeply unrealistic statements to the effect that, if only mankind so desired, war, poverty and disease could very easily be abolished within, say, twenty years, and that humanity could 'fill the world with beauty and joy', establishing 'the reign of universal peace' forever.[18] John Conrad Russell apparently thought something very similar – evidently he had been reading daddy's books, specifically his 1932 essay *In Praise of Idleness*.[19] A lot of Earl Russell's notions about abolishing work are clearly twisted developments of the ideas first put forward in this text, which posits that, thanks to the wonders of automation, it should now be possible to institute a four-hour working day for everyone, instead of forcing some employees to work all day while condemning others to unemployment. Seeing as machines had improved efficiency a hundredfold, why not let everyone just share their jobs and enjoy long leisure hours which could be used for the exalted goal of self-development, asked Bertrand?

Even John Conrad's ideas about the workers becoming the new aristocrats were directly anticipated in this treatise; due to having so much time on their hands, said Bertrand, it was the old 'leisure-class' of the nobility who had previously 'contributed nearly the whole of what we call civilisation' to the world, namely literature, the arts, science and philosophy, pulling mankind up out of mere 'barbarism'.[20] It was not that the poor were too stupid to have done such things, wrote Russell, more that they had had neither the time nor the education, due to the insane burden of their work in the fields and factories. In the modern machine-age, however, was it not possible this could all change overnight, if only the Old Order would allow it? Bertrand had little to say about the nefarious 'Police-Doll' allegedly perpetrating homosexual outrages upon young Englishmen in prison, but other than that it seems obvious that John Conrad's famous speech had its essential basis in a rewriting of his father's earlier naive theorising about the world.

Education, Education, Education

It seems almost as if John Conrad had been indoctrinated into holding such views from an early age. Like many aristocrats, Bertrand had been educated by private tutors instead of going away to school, some of whom appear to have been a little mad themselves, one of them having successfully managed to convince some baby chickens that he was their mother, so that they followed him around everywhere he went[21] – so perhaps it is no wonder that, as an adult, Russell had some distinctly odd ideas about education himself. In 1927, in an age long before OFSTED, he set up a Sussex school called Beacon Hill with his wife Dora. Beacon Hill was a place where attendance at lessons was non-compulsory, sex education was given priority, and the pupils were encouraged to lose their inhibitions about nudity and engage in 'healthy' outdoor exercise sessions on a regular basis. One (probably untrue) tale about Beacon Hill has it that a vicar visited one day, saw some naked kids playing in the grounds, and shouted out, 'Oh my God!' at them. One boy stopped playing, and joyously replied 'There is no God!' this being what Russell had been teaching them in class. Perhaps unsurprisingly, Beacon Hill had to close down in 1943, due to the fact that nobody wanted to send their offspring there – nobody, that is, other than Bertrand and Dora Russell, who had forced John Conrad to attend, an experience he found profoundly distressing.[22]

Whatever the source of his odd ideas, Lord Russell continued expounding them in the House of Lords from time to time. In a 1985 debate upon Foreign Policy and Defence, for instance, he rather curiously opined that 'My Lords, I do not think most people believe that either the CIA or the police exist' but that, sadly, they did, both organisations currently being engaged in a sinister plot to make Europe's youth addicted to drugs. 'Fight for your lives, Britain and Europe,' Earl Russell shouted, 'for the CIA are planning to flood Britain with heroin and destroy the younger generation in England as they have in America! The CIA have joined with the police forces of western Europe to enslave the young and make money out of their suffering!' Once again calling for the abolition of prisons, Russell went on to add that the very idea of America itself was naught but a gross and obvious fiction. 'Nobody anywhere in the world thinks that modern Americans are Americans at all. They just think that they are mad monsters!' he declared, no doubt to the delight of John Pilger. By this stage, however, it seems that Russell's fellow Peers had become used to his bizarre ramblings, now having the ability to dismiss them with studied politeness down to a fine art. 'My Lords, I am not sure that I heard every word that the Noble Earl has just said, but I shall read his speech tomorrow in the Official Report with much interest,' said Lord Jenkins of Putney, the next speaker, and quickly moved on to more sensible matters instead.[23]

During a 1986 debate about the Public Order Act, likewise, after Earl Russell had once again interrupted proceedings by saying that Mrs Thatcher's Government 'would not have proposed this Bill if they were not mentally diseased' and that therefore 'we should free [all] prisoners and learn to have fun!', one Lord Inglewood very courteously replied that 'the hour is late' and that, as such, 'the Noble Earl ... probably will not think it discourteous of me if I do not deal with his speech now', as it would 'take quite a time'.[24]

If Earl Russell did find such a blatant brush-off discourteous, however, then he had little chance of gaining any remedy for the fact. It was obvious he was simply being ignored and, in later life, doubtless disappointed by the failure of his calls for a radical reorganisation of Western civilisation, he appears to have more or less retired from public duty, devoting much of his time instead to knitting a large pair of trousers made entirely from string – a task which apparently took him so long to complete because, he said, 'I didn't have a pattern'.[25] As always, the Learned Lord preferred to do things his own way.

A Man of Firm Opinion: Colonel Charles de Laet Waldo Sibthorp, MP (1783–1855)

The most memorable Member of all time, whose lunacy left Queen Victoria feeling most unamused.

Once upon a time, it wasn't only Lords who inherited their Seats, but – in effect, if not in actual law – certain MPs, with many constituencies (or 'Boroughs', as they were then called) habitually returning successive generations of prominent local families to Parliament again and again. Prior to the Reform Acts of 1832, 1867 and 1884, which widened the franchise greatly, very few people could vote in General Elections, this being a privilege extended only to a select few. There were once, for example, such things as 'Rotten Boroughs'; constituencies in which the number of voters was so limited that it was embarrassingly easy for the local landowner to get himself or his proxy returned as the local MP. Many Boroughs could easily have only between 100 and 200 persons propertied and wealthy enough to be allowed to vote, and in such places the local Squire or Earl frequently stood unopposed – after all, such a candidate could generally be relied upon to defend the interests of his fellow wealthy few, so why bother to rock the boat? And, if this didn't work – well, then there was always the option of bribery![1]

I do not think that Colonel Charles de Laet Waldo Sibthorp, the Honourable Member for Lincoln from 1826–1832 and 1835–1855, ever had to bribe his Borough's voters, though – he didn't need to. Like a nineteenth-century Boris Johnson, the good people of

Lincoln probably kept on electing him purely for the purposes of their own amusement. The second of five brothers, Sibthorp's family owned a country estate at Canwick Hall on the southern edge of Lincoln, but their hopes for further social advancement lay firmly with the future Colonel himself, who was named after their distant – but conveniently heirless – relative Charles de Laet, owner of further land and property in Hertfordshire. Sibthorp's parents hoped that this 'touching' (read: calculating) gesture would ensure that his fortune would be passed down to their son by de Laet in his will when he died. This was not to be, however, and de Laet's property and its accompanying acres of parkland didn't actually pass down to the Sibthorps until after the Colonel's death, when his lucky grandson got his hands on the deeds; and so, Colonel Sibthorp had to make his own way in the world.[2]

At first, Sibthorp tried life in the military. A veteran of the 4th Dragoon Guards during the Peninsular War, in 1822, following the death of his elder brother Coningsby, he resigned his post and took to heading up the family estates at Canwick Hall as their new rightful heir, as well as looking after the County Militia. In 1826, at the age of forty-three, the Colonel altered tack and stood for Parliament in Lincoln, where the Sibthorp family was well-known, well-connected and influential – so much so, in fact, that the Borough's previous four MPs had been, respectively, Sibthorp's elder brother, his father, his great-uncle, and that man's own father.[3] He declared himself a Tory, put his name forward, and that was that. The story as it is often told has it that none of Lincoln's privileged electors really knew what Sibthorp's policies or plans were, and that they cared even less. On the day of the poll, when the time came for Sibthorp to get up on the hustings and make a public address, he was promptly knocked unconscious by a brick hurled straight at his head from among the crowd before he even had the chance to lay out his unique political philosophies to the world.[4] 'Just shut up and govern us!' seemed to be the message being passed on to Sibthorp from the good people of Lincoln, and he was soon returned as surely the most interesting and impressive of 1826's new intake to the House of Commons.

But did Lincoln's voters *really* not know what kind of reactionary lunatic they were getting? This was a man who was so opposed to social change of any kind that, in August 1824, he actually went so far as to fight a duel with a local doctor named Edward Charlesworth, purely because of the simple fact that he had expressed certain reformist viewpoints towards him in what

Sibthorp deemed to be an insulting manner at a turnpike. Tragedy was only averted when both men aimed their pistols and missed.[5] I'm sure we all have arguments with people who don't share our politics from time to time – but very few of us then go so far as to try and actually kill them!

The Old Ways Are the Best

Those who were hoping to pass the First Reform Act, then, would find no sympathy from Colonel Sibthorp; what was good enough for his great-grandfather was more than good enough for him, and any attempt whatsoever to meddle with the traditional workings of the world was merely, to use his favourite two insults, either 'humbug' or 'the work of the Devil'. Such was Sibthorp's commitment to the ways of the past that, once he had achieved his Seat in the Commons, he seems to have decided that it would be a good idea to attend its sessions in what was, essentially, a fancy-dress costume. As well as harbouring some bizarre and wholly excessive facial-hair of a type which had probably *never* really been in fashion, Sibthorp would habitually attend Parliament wearing a big white top hat, eighteenth-century frock coat of bottle-green or blue, and wide nankeen trousers pulled up high above his long wellington boots in deliberately archaic Regency fashion, the rough equivalent of an MP today turning up to a Commons debate dressed as Winston Churchill. To further enhance his appearance of oddness, Sibthorp would carry what is sometimes called a 'magnifying glass' tied around his neck with him everywhere he went – although it would in fact appear that this item was actually a huge square gold-rimmed antique quizzing glass, an early predecessor of the monocle.[6]

Just as unusual as the way Sibthorp looked was the way Sibthorp spoke. Charles Dickens, once a parliamentary sketch-writer, described him as:

> [A] ferocious-looking gentleman, with a complexion almost as sallow as his linen, and whose large black moustaches ... give him the appearance of a figure in a hair-dresser's window ... He is ... the most amusing person in the House. Can anything be more exquisitely absurd than the burlesque grandeur of his air, as he strides up to the lobby, his eyes rolling like those of a Turk's head in a cheap Dutch clock?[7]

Sometimes, so abnormal did he look and sound, and so abusive

and bizarre were his speeches, that the House simply mocked poor
Sibthorp, one contemporary observer telling us that:

> 'The moment the Colonel rose, he was saluted with a volley of
> [ironic] cheers, which were repeated at the conclusion of every
> sentence, the interval between being filled up with every variety of
> laughter and schoolboy noise – the cry of an owl and the mewing
> of a cat being, ever and anon, heard from the [public] gallery.' [8]

And, as for what Sibthorp actually talked about in these bombastic,
swivel-eyed speeches of his ... well, if anything, that was even
weirder. Sibthorp's curious dislikes, against which he was ever-happy
to fulminate, included such seemingly harmless things as public
libraries, art galleries, and the 'opera-dancers', as he called them,
who were then appearing on the London stage and singing
loudly at native Englishmen in their ghastly and incomprehensible
foreign tongues. The idea of indoor-plumbing annoyed him even
more, in particular the recent innovation of 'water-closets' – early
versions of what we would now call flushing toilets. What the
Colonel particularly disliked about lavatories, supposedly, was
the incredibly paranoid idea that, one day, gangs of prying snoops
claiming to be sanitary inspectors might go around peering down
into them in the hope of spying upon what private citizens had just
eaten for their dinner. [9]

Sibthorp had a thing about people watching him – once, when he
spied someone up in the Strangers' Gallery using an eye-glass to get
a better view of parliamentary proceedings, he sent up a messenger
to demand this suspicious individual's name, so he could report
him to the Speaker for what he termed 'quizzing' him.[10] Of course,
the Colonel's bizarre appearance was what probably accounted for
the person peering down so closely at him, rather than anything
more sinister – although, seeing as he was always ready to point
out non-existent foreign spies, Jesuit secret agents and international
Jewish bankers lurking around every corner, ready to subvert the
British way of life at the drop of a hat,[11] he appears not to have
realised this fact.

An Absolute Train-Wreck of a Career

Sibthorp's main obsession, however, was with the subject of
railways, a then-novel innovation which he derided contemptuously
as being 'the steam humbug'.[12] Sibthorp's dislike of trains appeared
to stem from the fact that the new London-to-York railroad would

cut straight through some cherished rural spots which contained precious childhood memories for him. In 1846, he gave his utmost support to a petition presented to the Commons by one Lord Grimston, objecting to this line's proposed route. 'I hate the very name of railroad!' Sibthorp stood up and shouted angrily in the Chamber, denouncing the whole thing as being nothing more than a gigantic criminal enterprise, something which led to the satirical magazine *Punch* printing a celebrated cartoon of the crazy Colonel jumping onto a moving train and attempting to perform a citizen's arrest upon it.[13]

Alarmed by the idea that trains would allow the working-classes to move around the country more easily, he denounced them as mere vehicles for sin, calling them a 'degrading mode of transport' which would lead to the immediate death or moral ruin of all those who so much as stepped foot in one.[14] This may sound ridiculous now, but at the time Sibthorp was not alone in fearing the medical and moral consequences of rail travel. Some early critics imagined that the speed at which trains travelled would indeed kill commuters, while an imaginary condition called 'railway spine' was plaguing passengers, who approached doctors claiming that travelling by steam had somehow caused their backs to give way, or worse. The symptoms of this disease were suspiciously varied; everything from blindness to period pains to excessive drooling was blamed upon the railways by sufferers. In fact, it all appears to have been merely a form of passing hysteria, but nonetheless it was taken seriously by some medical authorities at the time and treated with such quack 'cures' as magnets and leeches.[15]

Sibthorp was not alone in thinking trains dangerous novelties, then – but, typically, he took the idea far further than anybody else ever did. So fanatical did Sibthorp become that he actually turned into a sort of early trainspotter himself – but of a very unusual kind. Habitually, he trawled through the newspapers of the day, gleefully seeking out accounts of train crashes and other such accidents, making tallies of how many had died or been maimed and then eagerly reporting back upon his grisly findings to the Commons. Even the very real railway disasters of the time were not enough for Sibthorp, though, and he became the world's first (and probably only) railway conspiracy theorist. He thought that there was a shadowy hidden cabal of evil foreign train-operators and track owners at large somewhere in England, who were deliberately covering up the huge numbers of disasters which, he claimed, were really happening every day, entirely unknown to the general public. Did the Commons not know, he asked, that not one in ten train wrecks was actually declared to the proper authorities, and that the horrendous death-tolls of those that were revealed were deliberately underestimated by sinister Fat Controllers? When the conspiracy was broken and the scandal of thousands of train-mangled corpses finally revealed to the nation, Sibthorp once confidently announced, all the railway companies would immediately become bankrupt and 'the old and happy mode of travelling the turnpike-roads' in horse-drawn carriages and stagecoaches would be restored once more. This was a piece of particularly wishful thinking upon his part, however, seeing as the Victorian railways were so incredibly successful that, by the end of his life, Sibthorp himself had actually taken up travelling in them too, on his way down to London to give his famous speeches claiming that they were the work of Satan![16]

So notorious did Sibthorp's ravings upon this topic become that, in 1868/9, the Russian novelist Fyodor Dostoyevsky – who enjoyed reading reports of British politics – went so far as to base the dubious drunkard Lebedev in his novel *The Idiot* upon Sibthorp.[17] In Part III, Chapter IV of the book, Lebedev is derided by other characters as supposedly believing that the railways were a harbinger of the Apocalypse, these horrible new inventions having been predicted in the Bible under the codename of the infamous 'Great Star Wormwood' which crashes down to earth in the Book of Revelations and poisons all the waters of the world.[18] Lebedev, though, is having none of it. For him, the modern, industrialised world lacks a positive guiding idea to steer people through life; engineering and science have not adequately replaced religion as a comprehensive guide to living, he thinks. The new railways were, to Lebedev, thus merely a *symbol* of forthcoming social disaster and doom, not the literal work of the Devil. Or, as Lebedev himself puts it,

> Show me anything resembling such a power [as religion] in our age of seaminess and railways … Show me an idea that binds the mankind of today with even half the power there was in those [past] centuries. And then you have the effrontery to tell me that the springs of life have not been weakened, been polluted, under this 'Star' [of Wormwood], this net [of railways] that has entangled human beings … The [industrial] wealth is greater, but the [moral] power is less; there is no binding idea left; everything has grown soft, everything has turned to mush! We have all stewed to mush, all, all of us![19]

These are words which could have come straight from Sibthorp's own mouth. Perhaps all 'progress' really is but an illusion, after all – and perhaps it takes someone who is somewhat cracked in the head, like the drunken Lebedev (or the sober Sibthorp) to really be able to perceive this truth.

Foreign Devils

Dostoyevsky's surprisingly nuanced and respectful transformation of Sibthorp into Lebedev might not have been particularly appreciated by the man himself, however, because the great Russian writer represented the one thing Sibthorp hated most, more even than the contemporary Wormwood of the railways – namely, foreigners!

As we all know, foreigners are entirely responsible for anything bad that has ever happened to anyone, ever. War, famine, crime, disease – all have their origin in that nefarious place, 'Abroad'. Or, at least, that was the opinion of Colonel Sibthorp upon the matter, as he never tired of telling anyone who would listen. To the Honourable Member for Lincoln, the only point of an Englishman engaging in foreign travel was to kill Frenchmen. In order to discourage British subjects from journeying to other lands, he suggested that the amount of currency a man could take out of the country with him should be strictly limited, on the seeming grounds that such behaviour was both basically treasonous and bad for the Exchequer. So concerned was he about the idea of coins of the realm falling into the hands of filthy continental-types that he even proposed banning British ambassadors and diplomats abroad from having any salary at all, insisting that such people should be glad to do the Crown's work for free.[20] In spite of all evidence to the contrary, Sibthorp constantly maintained that the country was actually secretly bankrupt – 'there is barely a sixpence in the Treasury', he told the Commons in May 1832 – and, under such circumstances, allowing foreigners to get their hands on British money he thought sheer madness.[21]

The foreigner Sibthorp hated most of all, however, was Prince Albert, whom he objected to purely upon the grounds that he was German. Prior to Albert's marriage to Queen Victoria in February 1840, when the House was due to vote upon giving Albert a £50,000 a year allowance, Sibthorp stood up and objected, demanding that the sum be reduced. Sir Robert Peel, then in Opposition, saw a chance to annoy his political enemies, and supported him; enough of Peel's allies objected to paying Prince Albert his pocket-money for the sum to be reduced down to a 'mere' £30,000 per annum instead. When she heard about this, Queen Victoria was so annoyed that, as long as Sibthorp lived, she refused point-blank to ever set foot in Lincoln again; when, on 27 August 1851, the Royal Family had to pass through the area by train on their way to Scotland, she declined to alight from her carriage when it stopped at Lincoln's railway station. The whole place had been done up with flags and bunting in her honour, but she failed to grace the people with her Royal Presence, leaving her embarrassed PM to go out and greet the cathedral city's Mayor instead.[22]

Getting Prince Albert's allowance reduced was surely Sibthorp's most lasting achievement. After all, most of his other campaigns barely got off the ground; the Emancipation Bills for Jews and Catholics were passed in spite of his opposition to them, as were the 1832 Reform Act and various measures in favour of Free Trade. Other failures included his motions to prevent people from buying French goods, to restrict the sale of beer on the grounds that it would transform every home into a drink-sodden brothel, and to introduce stringent regulations upon hackney cab drivers, seeing as in his view their 'filthy contraptions' were likely to kill their passengers by giving them all cholera. He was also unsuccessful in his campaign to get horse thieves strung up on the spot and their corpses used for dissection in medical schools, and his crusade against deporting convicts to Australia because simply killing them on home soil would be far more economical to the public purse found little support among MPs either.[23] Truly, Sibthorp was the patron saint of lost causes.

People Who Live in Glass Houses ...

Surely Sibthorp's most unhinged campaign, however, was against the famous Great Exhibition of 1851 and, specifically, that 'unwholesome castle of glass' in which it was housed, the Crystal Palace.[24] The pet project of Prince Albert, the Great Exhibition was a huge display of arts and crafts, new inventions, industrial machines and cultural artefacts from around the globe, which was held in London's Hyde Park between May and October 1851, and housed inside a gigantic structure made of glass and cast iron named the Crystal Palace. A sensation at the time, though hugely expensive to build and organise, the venture ended up attracting some six million visits and turning a net profit of £186,000 – about £17,000,000 today – and, just as importantly, acted as a massive propaganda tool for encouraging the development of the new British mantra of Free Trade between all the nations of Europe and their colonies.[25] The general public loved it. Naturally, Colonel Sibthorp detested it.

This utterly harmless endeavour conveniently combined all of Sibthorp's pet hates in one single place; foreigners, science, modernity, Free Trade, new inventions, Prince Albert and, of course, the railways, which people who didn't live in London would inevitably end up having to use in order to get to the evil 'palace of tomfoolery' at all. Sibthorp told some incredible scare-stories about the moral ruin which had supposedly befallen hitherto-innocent country folk who had foolishly stepped onto the wicked 'steam-humbugs' for the first time. Unaware of the price of the fares down to London, he claimed that naive yokels had agreed to pawn their clothes to pay them, ending up wandering totally naked and penniless through the streets, bemoaning the accursed day they had ever agreed to buy a train ticket for the first time.

Foreigners, however, were already inherently corrupt before they had even visited the ticket stations, and Sibthorp actually went so far as to claim that the entire Great Exhibition was simply a sinister plot upon behalf of Prince Albert to destroy the British Empire. Albert's plan, it seemed, had several stages. First, he would cut down large numbers of good, honest, stout English trees in order to build his 'obscene and insanitary structure', a symbolic representation of the devastation soon to come upon our green and pleasant land. Then, Albert would release hordes of Frenchmen and Germans out into the land, an army of utter barbarians who would immediately begin attempting to rape Englishwomen, burgle English houses, spy upon our military defences and start undercutting British trade by selling cheap but faulty merchandise – 'foreign trash' and 'foreign stuff of every description' – to the general populace. 'Take care of your wives and your daughters, take care of your property and your lives!' Sibthorp warned the public, predicting that the residents around Hyde Park would have to lock up their spoons and even their servant girls if they did not wish to see them carried off by a rampaging horde of ne'er-do-wells 'talking all kinds of gibberish' as they went around raping and spreading the plague. Next, all the native criminals in the country would descend upon the Crystal Palace as if to a magnet, robbing everyone in sight like a plague of light-fingered locusts. After this, it would not take long before Christian civilisation itself completely collapsed; the Sabbath would be desecrated, the Government would fall, domestic trade entirely cease, and national bankruptcy inevitably ensue, leaving dirty foreigners free to dominate the globe unopposed – and all because of Prince Albert and his damned Crystal Palace.[26]

So much did Sibthorp hate the glass structure that he even took to praying in public that it would be destroyed by God. Before the Commons on 4 February 1851, the Colonel lambasted the then-PM, Lord John Russell, saying that he 'heartily desired to get rid of the noble Lord', on the grounds that he was little more than a diseased sheep. For Sibthorp, Russell's policy of encouraging international trade instead of supporting the traditional rural way of life was a matter of the utmost concern. *Hansard* recorded his diatribe against Russell's hated palace of Free Trade thus, in its usual third-person style:

> Let them [the Cabinet] go down to the city [Lincoln] he had just left, and they would soon find what was thought there of Free Trade, and of that which he did most strenuously condemn – that fraud upon the public called a 'Glass House' – the 'Crystal Palace' – that accursed building, erected to encourage the foreigner at the expense of the already grievously-distressed English artisan. Would to God – he had often wished it – that a heavy hailstorm or a visitation of lightning would put a stop to the further progress of that work! ... Oh, it would be a beautiful sight![27]

Much to Sibthorp's surprise, of course, the Great Exhibition was in fact a Great Success, and the country did not fall to foreign invasion. Far from it – over the next half century or so, our Empire was to rise to the very heights of its wealth, power and influence. A lot of the life seemed to go out of 'Sibby', as some called him, after his predictions of imminent apocalypse had been proved wrong, and he found few great causes over the remaining four years of his life. The man who so liked to shout 'Humbug!' had, by the end, been exposed as having been something of a humbug himself.

A Truly Honourable Member

Just as with Sibthorp's paranoia about railways, though, Sibthorp's views about the Great Exhibition were not *entirely* without support among the wider public. Many of those who disliked Free Trade also disliked the Exhibition, and numerous unhinged letters of the following kind were sent off to the authorities, predicting doom:

> *Woe* to *England*. All the *French Socialists* it is understood are coming over to the Exhibition!!!! It will be *well* if *London* is not

destroyed by *Fire*!!!! The Pope has successfully thrown the Apple of Discord *among us*!!!![28]

Such letters would seem to prove that the Colonel did have some kind of a public, albeit perhaps a deeply fringe one. In particular, he had a large following back in his constituency of Lincoln, where his independence of mind was greatly respected. At a dinner in Lincoln in 1826, he told the town's voters to 'observe [my] very movements in Parliament, for [I] am no Party man, nor slave to anyone' – fine words, which, as we have seen, were more than true.[29] Even his colleagues in the House acknowledged that, while clearly mad, he was undoubtedly honourable and incorruptible; seeing him walk by one day, Sir Robert Peel himself was heard to remark that 'There goes a man who is always fearlessly and solitarily wrong.' It sounds like an insult – but not at all, if you think about it.[30] In 1826, meanwhile, a broadsheet ballad was printed in Lincoln in which Sibthorp's qualities were further hymned, the Colonel being praised glowingly as 'True to liberty', 'Far above a bribe or fee' and the 'Friend of freedom and the free'.[31]

While he was once burnt in effigy by townsfolk for his opposition to the Reform Act of 1832, and not returned to Parliament between that year and 1835, even when they temporarily threw him out of the House the good folk of Lincoln tried to soften the blow, Christmas 1832 seeing Sibthorp presented with a costly diamond ring by the ladies of the Borough inscribed with the phrase 'The ornament and reward of integrity presented to Charles de Laet Waldo Sibthorp by the grateful people of Lincoln'. The ladies of Lincoln seemed to be rewarding Sibthorp for something else too, however – one account from the time telling us that 'no-one could kiss the girls better than Sibthorp at the last election'.[32] Kissing, though, was not the half of it. In 1828, Sibthorp's wife was granted a separation from him on the grounds that he had been having an affair with one Sarah Ward, 'a lady of low character', for at least two years. This would have come as no surprise to seasoned Sibthorp-watchers; what one source calls his 'notorious appetite for rough sex' was well-known. When one MP, puzzled as to how Sibthorp managed to bag all the best seats in the House for him and his chums every day, asked the doorman about the issue, the lackey is said to have replied that the Colonel slept every night in a 'bawdy house', or brothel, just next to the building, and that he only had to hop out of his hired bed every morning to beat all the other Members there.[33]

As this anecdote implies, however, Sibthorp undoubtedly took his parliamentary duties very seriously, turning up to participate in debates almost every day they were held. Indeed, so assiduous was Sibthorp in his attendance that a myth has since arisen that, during his final speech to the House, he keeled over and died in the middle of giving it, like some early-Victorian Tommy Cooper.[34] In fact, this is not true. His last speech to the Commons was made on 1 May 1855, and he died, of the after-effects of a stroke, at his London house in Eaton Square, on 14 December.

His actual concluding contribution to the life of the Commons was, nonetheless, well worth noting. Characteristically, it was a piece of mischief-making against his old enemy Lord John Russell, a man whom he sometimes seemed to impute was a secret foreign agent trying to destroy the country through his promotion of Free Trade.[35] Russell had just come back from a diplomatic mission to Vienna, and then submitted an expenses claim to Parliament. Sibthorp, however, wanted to know what the bill for Russell's foreign jaunt had been. Observant about the nation's outgoings as always, he noted that some thirty-two persons had gone to Austria along with Lord Russell – including, shockingly, some women! Sibthorp had 'never heard that it was the custom for *ladies* to be sent on foreign missions', he said, perhaps implying that they were being employed for improper purposes. What, precisely, had this free sex holiday cost the British taxpayer, Sibthorp demanded to know?

He received no answer. In reply, Lord Palmerstone, then PM, stood up and politely accused Sibthorp of slander. There would be no public revelation of Lord Russell's expenses bill at all. The Colonel could only conclude from this curt refusal that the Government was 'afraid' to reveal the true cost of the venture, and said that he would 'leave the public to draw their own inferences' about it all. It was, he said, clearly 'an underhand, low piece of business' and declared that he 'washed his hands of it altogether'.[36] MPs fiddling their expenses? We may have no such men as Colonel Sibthorp sitting in the Commons today, but some things, it seems, never change ...

That New Black Magic:
Occult Eccentrics

The ghost-hunters and conspiracy-nuts who ventured less beyond the veil than beyond the pale.

Britain has a long and proud tradition of occultism, with such native dabblers in the Dark Arts as John Dee, Queen Elizabeth I's court-magician, and Aleister Crowley, the self-styled 'Wickedest Man in the World', being legends in their field. The last thing anyone needs right now, however, is yet another potted biography of Crowley or Dee, so it might be more interesting instead to look at some of the ways in which occult subjects – in the broadest sense of that term – have morphed into new shapes in order to continue to keep their relevance in the modern world in which we now live.

For example, the stereotypical image of how it is that a person might try and go about contacting ghosts or spirits revolves around stagy gothic clichés involving magic circles, pentagrams, spell books, animal sacrifices and so forth. Less familiar by far is the idea that items of modern technology might be of some use in contacting the Other World, but this is in fact an avenue which has been explored by several occult eccentrics within our shores. Take, for example, the advent of radio; during the early days of this technology, several persons were struck by the fact that it involved communication across long distances using invisible waves of some kind, something which sounded, superficially at least, not unlike some kind of description of psychic communication. If mediums could pick up vibrations from the spirit world, then might not radio receivers be able to do something similar?

One person who thought that they might was Captain Sir

Quentin A. Craufurd (1875–1957), a former Royal Navy man who, during retirement, developed the unique hobby of attempting to communicate with fairies through a radio set. Craufurd had a long-standing interest in radio, having carried out the first wireless broadcast ever made in Britain from onboard the Royal Navy vessel HMS *Andromeda* in 1907, so, once he had 'swallowed the anchor' as he put it, he set up a kind of radio laboratory in his home with the intention of talking to the fairy folk through it, soon becoming known among his fellow Spiritualists as 'the wireless man'. Pointing some kind of home-made equipment at flowers and plants in his lab one day (fairies supposedly making these things grow, in Craufurd's rather twee opinion), he was pleased and astonished to pick up 'the sound of harps and bells' on his receiver – a noise he immediately recognised as fairy music. Craufurd said something expressive of amazement and joy, and was even more amazed and joyful to receive an immediate spoken response back in return from the denizens of the fairy kingdom. Naturally, Craufurd then began asking his unseen visitors all kinds of questions, claiming to receive information to the effect that the fairy folk were all around us each and every day, but remained unseen and unheard because our minds were not 'tuned' to the right frequency to perceive them – unlike Captain Craufurd's special radio-set! These amiable beings told Craufurd they were a race of marsh fairies, and for five years between 1927 and 1932 nine of them allegedly maintained contact with their new human friend and his Spiritualist colleagues, supposedly giving 'evidence of their mischief and their power' by performing numerous vaguely poltergeist-like little tricks for them. According to Craufurd's own account:

> My tame jackdaw could see them ... Sometimes he would move his head about oddly, following something we could not see at all, and the fairies told us they had been dancing to the music of our wireless. At our request, they danced on the flowers by the cupboard and made them move in time with the music.[1]

By no means was Craufurd the only man to have made occult experiments with a wireless. For example, a man from Hull named Raymond Cass (1921–2002) became convinced that he could talk to the dead using tape-recording equipment tuned in to various radio frequency bands, something now known by enthusiasts as the 'Electronic Voice Phenomenon' (EVP). Cass' interest in this field began while sitting alone in his grandfather's mansion one day at the age of seven reading a book, when he was surprised to hear a male voice calling out his name from a nearby radio-set, which was switched off at the time. Fascinated, Cass began playing with his grandfather's primitive device, seeming to hear random voices coming through it whenever it was in the process of being powered down. Thinking this was something supernatural, in later life Cass joined a local Spiritualist group, where he found to his astonishment that he came from a long line of alleged mediums, most notably a nineteenth-century psychic named Robert Cass who had supposedly once been observed levitating a heavy table up to the ceiling with three men sat on top of it, and who had been the first to introduce the Spiritualist creed to Hull. Following the end of the Second World War, Cass used his knowledge of radio and acoustics to make a good living developing hearing aids – it would be interesting to know if any of his customers ever picked up any unexpected sounds in their ears while using them!

Cass certainly managed to pick up strange sounds on his own radio equipment, using the various devices in his hearing aid R&D laboratory to try communicating with the dead as a nice sideline to his main area of business. According to him, he succeeded, even picking up the voice of Hull's most notable twentieth-century resident, the poet Philip Larkin, following his death in 1985. Cass was certainly picking up *something* on his tapes, though quite what it was is a matter for some debate, with critics claiming that the noises he recorded were simply stray transmissions from aeroplanes, radio stations and ham radio operators, which became garbled on their path through the airwaves. Against this opinion, however, would be the fact that some of the recordings seem to mention Cass himself by name, or contain voices which provide direct answers to questions he had just asked them.

Whatever the 'voices' really were, as his EVP researches continued, Cass developed a new theory about them – that some may not originate from the land of the dead after all, but from outer space. Seeing as some of the voices had a harsh and metallic, almost robotic tone to them, and occasionally said things like 'We are a cosmic race' in a foreign language, Cass theorised that, just perhaps, aliens had sent out robotic probes across the universe, which sprang into life whenever they detected a planet whose inhabitants had reached the stage of being able to emit radio-signals into space. In order not to alarm humanity by suddenly announcing their existence to us all at once, Cass had an idea that instead these aliens might send out radio signals to certain scattered individuals like himself here on Earth, who would then spread the word and thus lay the groundwork for a more gradual introduction of mankind to extraterrestrial life, avoiding mass panic.[2]

The combination of spooks and aliens inherent in Cass' career might seem jarring at first, but actually it simply fits in with a wider pattern of occult development in the post-war world, in which the interest of many persons involved in the field has shifted from the time-honoured tradition of trying to contact ghosts, spirits and demons, around to the more modern-sounding idea of engaging in traffic with extraterrestrials. To some people, the very idea of talking to the fairy folk or inhabitants of the astral plane now sounds unspeakably out of date, the notion of engaging in two-way communication with the inhabitants of orbiting spacecraft seeming much more plausible. Several early UFO groups grew out of or dabbled with Spiritualism, and attempts were made to contact aliens as well as ghosts during séances, as could be seen, for instance, with the 1954 publication of a book called *Venus Speaks*, which purported to be a faithful record of an anonymous British medium's telepathic chats with an alien scientist from Venus. [3]

Some of this shifting happily between the spiritual and the extraterrestrial realms could occasionally produce quite comic results. For example a Nottingham woman named Marjorie T. Johnson (1911–2011), a one-time colleague of Quentin A. Craufurd, was something of a psychic who claimed a variety of strange experiences with elves and nature-spirits, as detailed in her entertaining posthumously published book *Seeing Fairies*. One particular section in this book is of especial interest here, moving as it does from the idea of psychic communication with bees, to the notion of what such insects might look like on other planets. Explaining how she and her sister were frequently being psychically summoned out into their garden by distressed bees which had become entangled in spider's webs, or had collapsed down to the ground due to pollutants in the air, Johnson unexpectedly goes on to explain to her readers how, according to certain occult teachings, bees actually originate from the planet Venus. Then, Johnson provides some truly bizarre accounts from her fellow-Theosophists and other mystics who claimed to have engaged in psychic communication with aliens about the topic. One Venusian, for instance, had supposedly informed a friend of Johnson's that bees flew 'on the humming sound of vibrations just as the spaceships and flying saucers are said to do', while another woman

Johnson knew of had supposedly travelled to Venus herself using her astral body, where she had met a 'mammoth bee ... as large as a small dog' which was being kept by one spaceman as a pet in his back-garden.[4]

The whole nexus which once existed between UFOs and Spiritualism can be well-illustrated by a brief examination of the career of Mollie Thompson, an obscure folk singer who first became interested in flying saucers during the early 1950s and attempted to contact their occupants not over the radio, like Raymond Cass, but, significantly, via a ouija board. Using this occult device, Mollie claimed to have contacted three beings named Ornoor, Lon and Philemon, whom she at first thought were aliens, but then began to think of as being disembodied spirits, a conclusion which puzzled her more literal-minded friends in the Manchester UFO Society. It appears that, in 1965, these spirits (or others like them) surprisingly began making song lyrics appear in Mollie's mind, some of which were about flying saucers, others of which were about more general New Age topics. In 1966 these songs were put together as an LP, 'From Worlds Afar', which was sold to an exclusive audience of fellow UFO buffs at conferences and through small magazines. Some of the songs on this record contained coded references to psychic communications Mollie had been made aware of, speaking of some kind of earth-shattering event involving aliens and nuclear technology which was apparently going to occur on Christmas Day 1967. When it conspicuously didn't, Thompson quickly abandoned the UFO scene and devoted her life instead to psychic studies, showing how easy it can now be to shift between the two fields.[5]

Another way in which occult subjects have metamorphosed to meet the demands and interests of the modern world is through the growing rise in popularity of conspiracy theories, many of which contain their fair share of speculation about paranormal entities and sinister, arcane groups who supposedly practise the Dark Arts in an attempt to control our world. Here, too, Britain has often led the way, through the activities of such figures as Nesta Webster (1876–1960), a well-born member of the idle rich, who was able to spend her vast reserves of money and leisure-time writing books and promoting theories about the so-called 'Illuminati', a supposed secret society made up of powerful individuals who are alleged to manipulate world events from behind the scenes with the ultimate goal of dominating our planet under the aegis of a kind of 'One-World Government'. While Webster was by no means the first to see the ominous hand of this basically non-existent organisation behind many of the great events of world history, she was one of the most influential peddlers of the lie, with her books being read and taken seriously even by Government and Army officials during her 1920s and 30s heyday. Given the ultimate source of Webster's discoveries about the Illuminati, however, this fact seems somewhat surprising.

It all began for Nesta one day while reading an essay about two obscure figures who had lived through the French Revolution. As she scanned through the article, she began to feel that she had once known the people involved, and had in fact lived through the Revolution itself, in a previous life. Now suddenly convinced that she was the reincarnation of a French aristocrat called the Comtesse de Sabran, Webster set out to write a book about this woman's life and times. As she researched and wrote this particular tome, however, it began to strike her that the entire French Revolution itself had been no mere accident of history but, rather, a gigantic conspiracy organised from behind the scenes by persons hitherto unknown – persons whom Nesta Webster wasted no time in identifying as the dreaded Illuminati! These fiends, decided Webster, had carried on with their scheming ever since, fostering such unpleasant developments as the increasing spread of Communism and atheism across our planet. According to her, it was our nation's sacred duty to defeat this Hidden Hand in whatever form it flourished next, whether that be German militarism or Soviet sabre-rattling. By the time she died in 1960, however, Webster's theories had fallen out of favour and she herself had descended down into a state of deep paranoia, rarely answering her door without a revolver clutched in her hand.[6]

Had she lived on for another thirty or forty years, though, then Webster may well have been pleased to see modern variations on her theories come back into fashion, with innumerable websites, books and magazines peddling paranoia about what the Illuminati might be up to these days, whether that be faking terrorist outrages to steal away our rights, or engineering financial crises to impoverish us all. Very rarely, however, is Nesta Webster herself mentioned in relation to all this fevered speculation, with her name almost having vanished from history – why, it's almost as if some shadowy organisation out there doesn't *want* you to have heard of her ...

One modern-day British conspiracy-theorist whom you almost certainly will have heard of, however, is David Icke (b.1952), whose constant stream of books, lectures and videos have brought him literally thousands of fans right across the globe, eager to buy into his own outrageous claims about the secret rulers of our world. I have no idea whether or not Icke has ever read any of Nesta Webster's writings, but he has certainly tapped into that very same seam of paranoia about the supposed activities of the Illuminati which Webster mined – albeit by giving it his own unique and original spin by claiming that our hidden rulers are not human beings at all, but giant, shape-shifting paedophile lizards from another dimension.

Icke's story is a truly remarkable one. A former Coventry City goalkeeper who was forced to retire at the age of twenty-one due to incipient arthritis in his joints, Icke rallied himself from this disappointment to become one of the BBC's main TV sports presenters. However, while flirting with alternative medicine and fringe healing techniques in an attempt to find a cure for his health problems, Icke began to feel a growing attraction towards various New Age philosophies, becoming a prominent spokesman upon environmental issues for the Green Party. Throughout 1989 and 1990, while undergoing a period of considerable personal stress, Icke became convinced that there was some hidden supernatural presence following him around from place to place. Certain of this presence's reality, Icke spoke out loud to it in a hotel room, and asked it to reveal itself. Soon, the entity obliged, Icke claiming to have undergone a bizarre mystical experience in a newsagent's during which he suddenly became paralysed, with his feet feeling as if they were 'held down by magnets'. A voice in his head then apparently told Icke to go and look at a particular section of the shop's shelves. There, he found a book by a Brighton-based 'psychic healer' named Betty Shine, and decided he was being told to pay her a visit. At first, he thought he was being directed towards Shine to seek help with his arthritis, but soon she was passing him on messages, supposedly from the spirit world, telling him on behalf of no less a figure than Socrates that he had been chosen to be a great man who would 'heal the Earth'.

Fascinated, Icke began trying to channel messages from the Other Side himself, supposedly receiving a communication telling him that he was a 'Son of the Godhead', something he announced to the world at a press conference in March 1991. In the meantime, Icke had undergone a profound mystical experience on top of a burial mound in Peru, when a disembodied 'thought-form' had channelled psychic energy into his body, raising his consciousness to a higher level, before then correctly predicting that it was going to rain. After this experience, Icke had been receiving increasing numbers of communications from the spirit-world, telling him of a series of appalling natural disasters which were about to strike the globe, a cavalcade of cataclysms that he kindly enumerated for the watching press; there would be a hurricane in Derry, he said, an earthquake on the Isle of Arran, both New Zealand and the cliffs of Kent would disappear underwater, Los Angeles would become an island and, in 1997, the world itself would come to an end. Naturally, a media feeding-frenzy ensued, and Icke was invited to make his now-infamous appearance on the BBC One chat-show *Wogan* on 21 April, where he turned up wearing a turquoise track-suit in order to channel 'positive energy' into his frame, repeated his predictions of doom and apparently refused to deny that he was the Son of God. When asked by host Terry Wogan why exactly *he* had been chosen from all humanity to heal the Earth, Icke replied, 'People would have said [the same thing] to Jesus.'

Having become a laughing-stock after this interview, with crowds gathering outside his house and chanting things like 'We want the Messiah!' and 'Give us a sign, David!', Icke retreated away from the public eye for a number of years, before returning with a bang in the late 1990s with a new angle on apocalypse – that our world was now doomed because it was in fact being secretly run by giant lizards. Icke's claims, first comprehensively laid out in his 1999 bestseller *The Biggest Secret*, and since added to year on year, are as complex as they are unlikely. Basically, he argues that human beings are an artificial species created by a race of extraterrestrial lizards called the Annunaki, who hail at once from both the Draco constellation and something called the lower fourth dimension. What we see as 'reality' all around us is in fact some kind of artificial construct, being beamed out into our minds from either inside the moon (which is really a gigantic hollow lizard-spaceship) or from the rings of Saturn. In order to keep mankind in line, argues Icke, some of these Annunaki reptiles – who are twelve foot tall and humanoid in form, but also green and scaly, as you might expect – interbred with certain human beings many aeons ago, creating a hybrid human-reptilian bloodline known as the 'Babylonian Brotherhood', whose descendants run all the various societies which presently control our globe, whether secretly or in plain sight, such as the Illuminati, the UN, the CIA and, perhaps worst of all, the London School of Economics.

It would appear that the Annunaki's purpose in creating humanity was to use us to harvest some kind of energy produced by our negative emotions, which allows them to boost their information-processing capacities, speed up their rate of trans-dimensional travel, and shape-shift between human and reptilian form. It is the job of our rulers in the worlds of politics, religion, finance and entertainment – people like the Pope, George W Bush, Tony Blair, Ted Heath, Bob Hope, Kris Kristofferson and Boxcar Willie – to keep the necessary supply of war, poverty and terrorism going, so that their alien masters can continue to feed off the waves of fear, despair, misery and pain they cause. Icke's 'evidence' for these startling assertions stems from many sources, the most sensational of which are what purport to be eyewitness accounts of disturbing blood-sacrifices being perpetrated by the most senior of our lizard-rulers behind closed doors.

Chief among these witnesses was an American lady named Arizona Wilder, who claims to have been trained to preside over human sacrifice rituals for high-up members of the hybrid elite by none other than the former Nazi concentration-camp doctor, Josef Mengele. The point of these ceremonies was to create such distress in the victims – generally children, who were tortured and sexually abused prior to being killed – that the lizard-people were able to replenish their strength by feeding off a special chemical produced by their pain, a substance called adrenalchrome which also gave other Annunaki the power to pass into our world from their own dimension. This, said Icke, explained why Satanists, occultists and witches had supposedly conducted rites of human sacrifice during their black-magic ceremonies down the years; they had thought they were conjuring up demons from the lower astral plane with their actions, but in fact were really summoning up the reptilians from their home in the lower fourth dimension.

Apparently, our very own Royal Family were one of the main perpetrators of such fiendish acts, with Arizona Wilder telling Icke that she had personally witnessed Queen Elizabeth II 'sacrifice people and eat their flesh and drink their blood'. Some of her claims about Her Majesty's supposed behaviour would appear, on the face of things, to be libellous in the first degree:

One time, she got so excited with blood-lust that she didn't cut the victim's throat from left to right in the normal ritual, she just went crazy, stabbing and ripping at the flesh, after she'd shape-shifted into a reptilian. When she shape-shifts, she has a long reptile face, almost like a beak, and she's an off-white colour.

Other claims about the House of Windsor repeated by Icke include that the late Queen Mother was so 'seriously reptilian' that she held the position of 'Chief Toad' of Western Europe (even though toads are in fact amphibians), and that members of the Royal Family 'haven't died for a long time, they have just metamorphised [sic]'. Seeing as Icke is essentially accusing various public-figures, in print, of being half-alien paedophiles, you might expect him to have been sued by some of them by now – and yet (one obscure Canadian lawyer aside), none of them ever have done so. The obvious explanation for this is that Icke's claims are so self-evidently ridiculous that these people see no need to take him to court; however, Icke's view on the matter is somewhat different. The true reason that virtually nobody he has accused of being lizard-people has so far sued him for libel is because they *really are* lizard-people, and so have no legal basis for doing so, he says![7]

While I obviously don't believe a word Icke says, extremely entertaining though it may be, the fact that he has not so far faced any kind of actual prosecution by the authorities in Britain for his allegations is nonetheless something which I actually find to be rather encouraging. It shows that free speech is not yet completely dead here, even if you are using the privilege to say something utterly ludicrous; you would not be able to get away with saying that your nation's leaders are blood-drinking paedophile lizards in a place like North Korea, for instance. In Thailand, you can be charged with the crime of *lèse majesté* (disrespecting royalty) just for placing the King's photograph beneath that of someone else on a website, or wearing black clothing on his birthday.[8] In Britain, you can say that the Queen eats children and not face even so much as a police caution. I like that fact. I think we all should.

Meek, Not Mild:
Joe Meek (1929–1967)

The morbid music producer whose greatest hits were supplied by Buddy Holly – after the plane crash.

In 1966, the Beatles were at the very height of their fame. This was the year that saw them tour the Orient, record such timeless classics as 'Paperback Writer', 'Penny Lane' and 'Strawberry Fields Forever', and in which John Lennon made his infamous boast about the band being 'bigger than Jesus'.[1] And yet, things could so easily have taken a different turn. When their manager Brian Epstein was busily doing the rounds of all the big UK record companies trying (and largely failing) to interest them in the band's demo tapes during the early 1960s, one door he knocked on was that of Joe Meek, then known as the most innovative music producer in the country. Meek, however, was not impressed by the Merseybeat sound; according to him, the Beatles were 'just another bunch of noise, copying other people's music'[2], a harsh judgement, but one which many A&R men at the time obviously shared.

Had Meek agreed to take The Beatles on, however, then, far from touring the East, John, Paul, George and Ringo could well have found themselves embarking instead upon some mental journeys every bit as strange and psychedelic as those they later detailed in their songs 'I Am the Walrus' and 'Lucy in the Sky with Diamonds' – indeed, perhaps far stranger. Not that Joe Meek much cared what the Mersey Mop-Tops were up to at the time, though. After all, on the night of 31 August 1966, Meek had found himself a brand new recording star with a talent far more incredible even than those possessed by Lennon and McCartney. To hear this new discovery's somewhat whining voice on tape for the first time, however, you would be forgiven for not being immediately impressed by it. That is, until you realise that you are listening not to a human being purring words down into the microphone – but to a cat.

Meek had less than a year to live by the time he claimed to have discovered a talking cat and, perhaps ominously, was spending more and more of his spare time wandering around graveyards. His intention was to try and capture the voices of the dead on tape, a task in which he claimed to have succeeded. The talking cat, however, was found by Meek not in a cemetery, but at Warley Lea Farm near Brentwood in Essex, where, local legend has it, a farm bailiff had once hanged himself, his ghost returning to haunt the place in invisible form.[3] Walking through this unquiet location together with a friend that fateful August night in 1966, tape recorder in hand, Meek performed the standard ghost hunting trick of asking out loud whether or not there was anybody there. It turned out that there was. 'Miaow,' the eldritch entity said. Alarm over. It was just a cat. But then – 'Help me,' said the cat. 'Help me, help me, help me!' 'It's an unusual cat,' Joe said into his mike, and I suppose he was right. Profoundly disturbed by this turn of events, Meek could only conclude that the suicidal bailiff's spirit had somehow been reincarnated inside the stray feline's body, and was now begging to be set free.

Or was it? Now, thanks to a 1991 episode of the BBC's upmarket *Arena* documentary-strand, we can judge for ourselves. On this show, over eerie film of Meek's friend the musician Tony Grinham wandering through a darkened churchyard was played sound-footage of the chatty feline talking in what Grinham described as 'half-human tones'.[4] Listening to it, though, it is pretty obvious that the animal was not really speaking English at all, merely making the standard mewing noises, albeit in a somewhat distorted fashion which would allow you to read human words into them if you were predisposed to do so – and Meek was indeed predisposed to do so. While listening to the 1966 song 'Take It That We're Through' by his band the Riot Squad, for example, Meek had managed to convince himself that he could hear a ghost saying 'Hello' to him at the fade-out.[5] In 2012, Meek was given number one spot in an NME article intended to find out who had been the greatest producer in music-history; he could also have been named the oddest.[6]

Mummy's Little Princess
Born in Gloucestershire in 1929, Meek was an outsider from the start. His mother had hoped for a girl, and, unwilling to be

disappointed, had brought her son up like a daughter for the first four years of his life. Presumably this was why, whenever he played with the other children in his street, he always chose to fill the role of 'princess'. Naturally, the other kids thought there was something queer about this – which, in fact, there was. In later life, so eager was Meek to maintain smooth, feminine skin that he shaved himself up to six times per day, and wore face powder and eyeshadow, giving out a clear signal about his sexuality for those who could read it.[7]

Meek needed a retreat from all this childhood mockery, and, like many a harassed male, found it in the shed at the bottom of his garden, which he filled with various pieces of discarded electronic equipment. Meek taught himself to strip this junk down and reassemble it all into circuit-boards, radios and what is sometimes claimed to have been the first working television set in all of Gloucestershire. By the age of thirteen, Meek had made his first valve amplifier, which he put to use as a bird scarer on his father's farm. Leaving school at fourteen with no formal qualifications but plenty of practical talent, Meek found work as an early DJ, lugging his giant, home-made speakers around from pub to pub. For a local am-dram group, meanwhile, Meek provided electronic sound effects for stage productions, apparently specialising in simulating the noise of horrific car-crashes.

During his National Service, Meek worked as a radar technician for the RAF, later finding a job with the Midlands Electricity Board. In 1955 he left for London, hoping to carve out a career in pop. First, he landed a position in the service-department of a TV and radio shop, before being offered a junior role at IBC Studios, then one of Britain's biggest. Moving to Lansdowne Studios in 1957, Meek started secretly using their resources at night in order to make his own private, commercial-quality recordings with obscure bands he had discovered himself. Some of these discs found modest success, enough for him to branch out and set up his own independent production company, Triumph Records, in January 1960 – a decision he was ultimately forced into after being sacked from Lansdowne due to his notoriously quarrelsome nature and habit of throwing cups of tea at any of the 'rotten pigs' working there who happened to disagree with him.

Sadly, this business project was not a success and, barely six months later, Meek dissolved Triumph to enter partnership with one Wilfred Alonzo Banks, a venture capitalist who saw enough talent in Meek to back a new attempt by him to go it alone. This second enterprise was given the name of RGM Sound Ltd, and Banks gave Meek the money to find some premises to serve as his new recording studio. Meek being Meek, of course, he chose the wholly unsuitable location of a three-floor flat hidden away above a leather-goods shop in Islington. After making numerous alterations to the rooms, the address of RGM (renamed Meeksville Sounds Ltd in 1964 following a split with Banks) became legendary. Number 304 Holloway Road was the place where several of the biggest and most fondly remembered hits of the early 60s were to be penned or recorded – a place so full of wonders that, before long, the spirits of Buddy Holly, Al Jolson and even Rameses the Great would end up paying a visit. No wonder that the avid Spiritualist Meek chose to live as well as work there.[8]

Machines Designed for Living In

Given that Meek was such an incredible talent, why was it that Triumph Records folded in less than a year? One reason was that Meek chose to devote a substantial amount of his time and effort to producing a strange and unsellable record intended to help prepare mankind for its first encounter with alien life forms. The resultant LP, 'I Hear a New World', was so non-commercial and weird that it never saw full release until 1991. Made with Ealing skiffle-group The Blue Men, Meek's record – arguably the first true concept album – consists mainly of instrumentals, the main exception being the eponymous first song on the playlist, which features a chorus made up of bizarre high-frequency alien voices sounding not unlike Pinky and Perky.[9] There were supposed to be twelve tracks on the album, but Meek, realising he had a probable flop on his hands, only released it in a limited edition of ninety-nine copies containing four songs, which he marketed direct to hi-fi stores as a demo to help flog stereo sound equipment; what PR material called 'the weird gimmicky outer space sounds' helped demonstrate the possibilities of this new technology perfectly.[10]

This PR description is probably fair, with even Meek himself writing on the sleeve-notes that 'Yes! This is a strange record. I meant it to be.' Intending to create 'a picture in music of what could be up there in outer space', Meek did not simply use ordinary musical instruments to create the sound of life on other planets, but also recorded sounds like water draining out of a sink, milk bottles being banged with spoons, and bubbles being blown into liquid through a straw. This was the start of Meek's peculiar experiments in creating otherworldly sounds on his records; other methods he tried included dropping coins into toilets and dustbins, shorting electrical circuits, placing hot pokers into bathwater to sizzle, and even rigging a piano up with drawing-pins attached to the instrument's hammers so that it made weird sounds when you played it. Sometimes, he recorded people punching doors, kicking bathtubs, winding up clockwork toys, swirling pebbles around on baking trays, and rubbing combs against tables. One some of his recordings you can even hear the neighbours' dog barking if you listen carefully enough!

It has been aptly said of Meek that he was the first person to have used the recording studio itself as one big instrument. Prior to his sonic experiments, the standard practice for cutting a disc was simply to get a band together in the studio and record the entire song straight through a few times until you ended up with a good take. Meek's approach was more akin to audio collage. Typically, he would have musicians record a basic instrumental version of a song, and then layer this over, again and again, with added instruments, vocals, and weird sound effects each time. He would mike up each instrument individually, and sometimes de-tune them slightly in order to produce a stranger version of, say, a guitar riff to overlay and thus distort the ordinary one. After this, he would speed up, slow down or reverse vocals, add a so-called 'heavenly choir' of female harmony singers, and insert reverbs and echoes. He would even force vocalists to sing in his bathroom, claiming that the wall tiles caused it to act as an echo chamber; at other times, he got people to stamp their feet together in rhythm on his staircase as an alternative to drums. 'If it sounds right, it *is* right!' was Meek's watchword, leading him to think of his entire home – toilet, stairs and bathtub included – as being merely one gigantic inhabitable musical instrument.[11]

Has-Bean Heinz

This all made for an amazing sound but one which Meek's acts were often completely unable to replicate live on-stage, leading many to have an exceedingly short shelf life once their heavily doctored hits had fallen out of the charts. Indeed, some say Meek actually *preferred* his acts to be talentless, because then he could better manipulate them in the studio without their objecting.[12] Arguably the most extreme example of this was a former grocery-store worker named Heinz Burt, who may or may not have been Joe Meek's gay lover. Meek himself was definitely a practising homosexual, being arrested for cottaging in 1963, and in 1966 releasing an obscure B-side with his band the Tornados called 'Do You Come Here Often?' in which a couple of men meet up, apparently in a nightclub toilet, and begin saying catty things like 'Mmmmmmm; mine's alright, don't like the look of yours,' to each other in camp voices – an extraordinary gamble, given that such practices were not legalised in Britain until the following year.[13]

Heinz Burt, the Anglo-German bass guitarist of the Tornados, always denied that he had been involved in a gay relationship with Meek, but this did not mean that Meek was not head over heels in love with Heinz himself. Certainly, Heinz lived at 304 Holloway Road with Meek for three years, and, if you believe the testimony of Vernon Hopkins, of Tom Jones' early band the Senators, even shared a bed with him; during a 2009 interview, Hopkins told of how, together with his bandmates, he had found Heinz lying naked in Meek's bed one morning, an incident supposedly followed by Meek attempting to fondle Tom Jones' testicles. The Senators had already been unnerved by Meek's unhinged stunt of firing a pistol at them during a recording session (fortunately it contained only blanks), and when Meek tried to kiss Jones behind a screen, the Welsh Wonder decided he had had enough and left, leading Meek to tear up the Senators' recording-contract in a rage.[14]

If you believe the rumours, though, then Heinz Burt may have been rather more compliant. As a result of his infatuation, Meek decided to withdraw Burt from The Tornados and set him up as a manufactured solo star named simply 'Heinz', forcing his beau to dye his hair with peroxide as a gimmick. Sadly, while Heinz's hair might have been striking, his talent was not – his first release, 'Dreams Do Come True', earned only £15. However, in 1963, Heinz had a smash hit after all with 'Just Like Eddie', a tribute to the American rockstar Eddie Cochran, who had died in a car crash in 1960. Sadly, however, while on the record Heinz sounds like he has an outstanding voice and great guitar skills, once outside of Meek's studio on tour these gifts largely vanished. So poor were Heinz's real-life performances that audiences took to throwing Heinz Baked Beans over him, this being thought much more entertaining than his singing. After later releases like 'Diggin' My Potatoes' and 'Big Fat Spider' failed to set the charts alight, Heinz realised that Meek wasn't going to turn him into the next Elvis after all, and in 1965 turned up at 304 Holloway Road brandishing a surprising new accessory – a girlfriend. Heinz's apparently fake relationship with Meek quickly ended, and, as the years rolled by, Burt ended up drifting into panto and, ultimately, working in a car-assembly plant. Heinz died in 2000 following a stroke, leaving a meagre legacy of £18 and a street named after him in his home town of Eastleigh – 'Heinz Burt Close'. Perhaps appropriately, it is a dead end.[15]

Moon-Struck Meek

I Hear a New World was also something of a dead end for Meek. A genuine space nut, Meek was convinced that mankind's first forays outside our atmosphere would inevitably lead to aliens making contact, and that the human race had to be groomed to accept this fact, ideally through pop music. Meek's most successful attempt at pulling off this trick came with the Tornados' 1962 mega-hit 'Telstar', an instrumental filled with distorted electronic sounds inspired by the launch of Telstar One, the first telecommunications satellite, earlier that year. Despite the Tornados' initial dismissal of the tune as being 'crap', the public disagreed, propelling the track to number one in the charts in both Britain and America.[16] Few of those who bought a copy, however, can have realised that the strange noises heard at the disc's beginning and end were taken directly from 'I Hear a New World', or what the purpose of that original cancelled record had been.

In preparation for its intended release, Meek wrote sleeve notes for the album, which now make fascinating reading. Here, Meek declared his belief that men would soon land on the moon. But what, precisely, would they find up there? Meek, using his amazing powers of mental visualisation, claimed to know: 'I can already see and hear in my imagination from the studies I have made on outer space what wonderful new sights and sounds are in store for us,' he wrote.

So, what were these sights and sounds? Apparently, there were three alien races bobbing around, named the Globbots, the Sarooes and the Dribcots. Meek's album purported to give listeners a sonic representation of how these moon-people lived their lunar lives, and the geographical and cosmic forces with which they interacted. The track 'Magnetic Field', for instance, was about a hitherto-unknown section of the moon that Meek claimed to have discovered mentally, where there was 'a strange lack of gravity' causing all objects to float three feet above the surface, sometimes 'in vigorous motion', at other times with 'everything in rhythm'. 'Globb Waterfall', meanwhile, was intended to 'contradict the belief that there is no water on the moon', Meek's composition trying its best to represent a hypothetical gravitational process whereby 'water rises to form a huge globule on top of a plateau' before falling down with 'a terrific splash' to the ground below. More interesting still were Meek's ideas about our moon's secret inhabitants. First of all, there was 'The Entry of the Globbots', which was structured to convey that the ETs in question were 'happy, jolly little beings' whose 'cheeky blue-coloured faces' could easily be imagined by listeners as they walked by us in parade. The green-skinned Sarooes, by contrast, were 'rather sad people' who lived in a desolate moon-valley where Second World War-style rationing was in place; they never left their deprived home, however, 'for if they did, they would surely die.' Most incredible of all was the insight Meek gave us into advanced alien technology in 'The Dribcots' Space-Boat':

> This [vehicle] looks rather like an egg, and it floats about 100 yards from the surface of the ground. It glides along at about 20 mph and is owned by the Dribcots. It is driven by huge inductance coils ... By varying the polarities and their direction, the space-boat is driven along ... but the big disadvantage, and the reason for [its] drifting 100 yards from the surface, is that if a passing satellite of opposite polarity came by, it would whisk the space-boat, Dribcots and all, away and perhaps into orbit around some other heavenly body![17]

Johnny, Dismember Me

Did Meek intend all this as a joke? Yes and no. Clearly, he did not believe in the literal existence of the Dribcots and their amazing space-boat, or attempt to plot the location of Globb Waterfall on a lunar map. However, these were the basic *kinds* of things that Meek did expect astronauts soon to encounter on other worlds in reality – although, tragically, we are still waiting. But not to worry! Maybe, instead, the space-men would come to us? Fascinated by tales of flying saucers, in October 1963 Meek teamed up with the singer-songwriter Geoff Goddard (1937–2000) to release the now long-forgotten single 'Sky Men', a piece of pro-alien propaganda which addressed a genuine health and safety issue: if you were ever out on a late-night date with your girlfriend and happened to come across a glowing spaceship on your way home from the dancehall, then how, precisely, should a 1960s teenybopper respond to the fact? This was Meek and Goddard's sage advice to the nation's youth:

If you are ever out at night,
You and your darling,

And if you see this flashing light,
You and your darling,
Don't be afraid and run away,
Soon there's going to come the day
When the whole world will hear them [the aliens] *say:*
'Children of the Earth, be not afraid, for we come in peace!'[18]

Another Meek-backed attempt by Goddard to save teenage lives, meanwhile, was 'Lone Rider', released initially as an instrumental by Meek's band the Flee-Rekkers in 1961, and then given lyrics by the heart-throb TV actor and singer John Leyton a year later. Ostensibly, this was part of a maudlin 1950s/60s fad for so-called 'death discs', songs in which tales of tragic teenage car crashes, suicide-pacts and motorcycle accidents were told through the kind of trite lyrics which could only ever really appeal to naive and weepy young schoolgirls. In Britain, these 'death discs' were often banned by the BBC due to their morbid subject matter – which, of course, only made them sell all the better. Soon, singers were trying to outdo each other with ever more bizarre situations appearing in their new releases; Johnny Cymbal's 'The Water is Red', for instance, was about a boy who stabs a shark to death in revenge for its eating his girlfriend, while Jimmy Cross's 'I Want My Baby Back' involves a disturbed young man digging up the coffin of his dead lover and then climbing inside it, intending to spend one last night making love to her dismembered corpse.[19]

With the car-crash deaths of teen idols like film star James Dean making big news during the era, Joe Meek thought he could do with cutting a few death discs too, and Geoff Goddard's unique spin on the genre was to bring ghosts into it. The version of 'Lone Rider' given to John Leyton to sing, for instance, is not simply *about* a dead teen motorcyclist, but is supposed to actually be *sung* by one, the titular 'Lone Rider' being a ghostly biker whose leather-clad spirit travels the highways of the land forever as a kind of spectral warning of the foolishness of not following the Highway Code. 'Lone Rider' may not have been a massive hit, but Goddard's follow-up ghostly death disc, 1961's 'Johnny Remember Me', certainly was. Again performed by John Leyton, it was Joe Meek's first number one as a producer, topping the charts for five weeks and shifting some 500,000 copies.[20] However, perhaps this was no real surprise, seeing as in fact the record hadn't really been written by Geoff Goddard at all – but by the noted (and notably dead) musical genius Buddy Holly.

Ghost-Writer

Goddard was a committed Spiritualist, and on 9 September 1961, an interview with him was splashed all over the front-page of the long-running Spiritualist newspaper *Psychic News*, which carried the long-winded headline 'Does Dead Rock Star Guide Songwriter? 'JOHNNY REMEMBER ME' SENSATION: No 1 disc in hit parade written by Spiritualist!' It turned out that Goddard had awoken one morning with the tune for the song buzzing around fully-formed inside his head, and had immediately crooned it straight into a tape recorder he kept by his bedside. But had this inspiration come from a dream – or from Buddy Holly? Goddard, who claimed to be in regular contact with Holly's ghost via séances, said it was the latter.

If this was true, then it certainly fitted in with the subject-matter of the song itself, a brilliant and eerie composition full of weird echo effects in which a young man walking across a cold, wet and windswept moor suddenly hears the voice of his dead girlfriend singing the words 'Johnny, remember me' from the breeze-blown treetops. It is left ambiguous as to whether the phantom voice (provided by singer Lissa Gray and distorted by Meek to the point where it really does sound like a ghost singing) is real or simply in Johnny's imagination, but the BBC had no doubts – they demanded Leyton's description of the spirit-voice as coming from 'The girl I loved who died a year ago' be changed to the vaguer 'The girl I loved and lost a year ago', so as to lose its tinge of the uncanny. Meek and Goddard complied, but the BBC banned the song anyway, obviously still not understanding how counterproductive this would be. So successful was' Johnny Remember Me' that, in 1962, it even inspired a blatant rip-off record, Johnny Victor's unsuccessful 'Come to Me, Johnny', about a ghostly female who repeatedly beckons her ex-boyfriend to commit suicide so he can join her in the afterlife – advice he immediately follows by driving his car off a mountain.[21]

'Come to Me, Johnny' may not have been all that inspired a composition, but 'Johnny Remember Me' certainly was – the question is, inspired by whom? After all, plenty of non-Spiritualists have woken up in the morning humming a nice new tune too, so Goddard's song need not really have been written by a ghost, merely by his unconscious, dreaming mind. Famously, for instance, Paul McCartney awoke one day with the tune for 'Yesterday' going around and around in his head, and yet he felt no need to blame Buddy Holly for the fact.[22] Joe Meek and Geoff Goddard were different, though. Twice a week, Meek held ouija board sessions at 304 Holloway Road, where one of the most regular disembodied guests – alongside Al Jolson, Rameses the Great, *et al* – was Buddy Holly. Meek valued his advice, asking him whether or not his latest songs were going to be hits; after all, the man behind such best-selling classics as 'Peggy Sue' and 'Oh Boy!' should know. According to Holly, 'Johnny Remember Me' was going to be not only a hit, but a smash-hit – 'See you in the charts!' spelled out Buddy – and, it turned out, the spook was correct.[23]

That'll Be the Day That I Die

The reason why Meek was so receptive towards the idea of Buddy Holly contacting him from beyond the grave lay in a series of uncanny events from early 1958, when Holly was touring England with his band The Crickets. One night in January, Meek had attended a séance together with an Arab mystic called Faud, and the singer Jimmy Miller, of Meek's early band Jimmy Miller and the Barbecues. Faud brought along some tarot cards, and the three men sat in a darkened room holding hands while Faud held his free right hand over a notepad, using a pen to jot down any psychic messages which came through to him during the séance. Once all the cards had been turned over, Meek let out a piercing scream, and the men released one another's grip. Looking down at the paper, they could see a disturbing message spelled out for them. 'February the third,' it read. 'Buddy Holly dies'.

Bizarrely, even though the message had been written down by Faud, it appeared to be in Jimmy Miller's handwriting, something which led Meek to take the warning very seriously. The third day of February came and went without Buddy Holly dying, thankfully, but Meek still felt compelled to seek out a personal meeting with the rock-star when he arrived to tour England later that month. Holly, probably thinking Meek was mad, simply thanked him for his warning and promised to be extra careful on that date from now on, a promise which, apparently, he failed to keep – for, on 3 February 1959, aged only twenty-two, Buddy Holly died in a plane crash in Iowa. When he heard the news, Meek was both distraught and amazed, focusing in on one particular detail; Holly had chosen to take his plane rather than a tour bus partly because he thought it would enable him to save time and get his clothes laundered. Seeing as Meek had been having a series of bizarre nightmares about dirty clothes for some months now, he could only conclude that he was psychic.[24]

If Joe Meek had been interested in the occult prior to 1959, from now on he became simply obsessed. Looking at the hundreds of records Meek released, it is hard not to notice that many had a distinct Gothic flavour to them, bearing titles like 'Night of the Vampire'. One singer much to Meek's liking, for example, was none other than our old friend Screaming Lord Sutch. Sutch's earliest performances took place in a Soho coffee bar, where he would dress up in a crash helmet adorned with buffalo horns and his auntie's torn leopard-skin coat, trying to look like a Viking Tarzan. Under Meek's management, however, Sutch's notorious novelty song 'Jack the Ripper' became the new template for his act, and Sutch began to be repackaged as some kind of cross between Jack and Dracula, dressed in black cape and tall Victorian-style top hat, and brandishing a large knife. His slow-burn 1961 Meek-produced hit "Til the Following Night' (whose original title 'My Big Black Coffin' had been censored by – yes – the BBC) featured numerous spooky sound effects, for instance, and became part of a comical panto-style stage act upon Sutch's behalf in which he was carried on stage in a coffin, chased a pretend prostitute around with a knife and, during one 1966 performance at the Liverpool Empire, swung around on the curtains in a mad frenzy, fighting appalled stage-hands who tried to stop him.[25]

Turn the Other Meek

As this all suggests, Meek always had an eye for a good, if sometimes woefully-misguided, PR stunt. One time, Joe even suggested to Sutch that they buy a naval submarine, sail it down the Thames and threaten to fire torpedoes at Parliament to get their names in the papers – a wildly impractical scheme which may perhaps have been cooked up by Meek while under the influence of the drugs upon which he was increasingly coming to rely.[26]

From 1960 to 1966, Meek produced around 700 recordings, often working eighteen-hour days – a clearly unsustainable pattern. To cope, he took amphetamines, then available legally as slimming pills. In the morning, he swallowed 'uppers' to give him energy, and at night 'downers' to aid sleep. The main effect of this drug-abuse was to fund Meek's already fertile sense of paranoia. Some of this was justified, seeing as several local gangsters – reputedly including the Kray twins – were trying to either blackmail him over his homosexuality or steal his acts, leading him to walk around everywhere disguised in sunglasses, fearing violence. Less reasonably, Meek also thought that rival record companies were hiding bugs inside his wallpaper to steal his ideas. Soon, all important conversations within Meek's studio had to be conducted via writing, as he was convinced his landlady was eavesdropping on him through the chimney. Ominously, Meek came to believe he could control people's minds using high-pitched electronic whistles, and told his acts that he could see what they were getting up to away on tour via supernatural means. Eventually, Meek started thinking that his flat contained poltergeists, that aliens were beaming mind-control rays into his head and manipulating his speech, and that the pictures on his walls were trying to talk to him. Even Buddy Holly turned against him, apparently – from now on, Joe Meek was very much on his own.[27]

Perhaps most damagingly, in 1965 Meek split from his best song-writer, Geoff Goddard, partially over a copyright dispute. This was a far cry from the duo's early days together when Meek had hatched the unlikely plan to launch Goddard as a pop star in his own right as the so-called 'Liberace of Reading, Anton Hollywood', something which failed due to Goddard's unfortunate resemblance to Harpo Marx and weird but apparently uncontrollable habit of stomping his feet and making strange grunting noises at the piano. After leaving Meek, Goddard pursued a most unexpected career-change and joined the catering department of Reading University, his income occasionally supplemented by royalties from his old tracks, including a spoof version of 'Just Like Eddie', re-recorded as 'Just Like Shreddies' for a TV breakfast cereal advert in the 1990s.[28] Compounding his split with Goddard, Meek's money-troubles were soon increased by the rise of bands and singers – like the Beatles – who wrote their own tracks instead of relying on people like him to guide and produce them. Carrying on regardless, Meek's hits dried up and his debts increased; by 1966, Meek was being investigated by the Inland Revenue and had even been forced into stealing food.[29] Something had to give – and, ultimately, it was his mind.

Weird for Sound

Towards the end of his life, Meek began to notice something rather odd about the discs he was recording – namely, that some seemed (to him, at least) to contain disembodied EVP-like voices, presumably from ghosts. Ever eager to contact the dead, in 1965 Meek began wandering around London's Highgate Cemetery late at night, cassette recorder in hand, hoping to capture more such phantom voices on tape. Thinking that he had succeeded, Meek approached a local man named David Farrant (b.1946) and, quite inadvertently, started off a mass panic about vampires.

Farrant was the head of a local occult group, and was impressed by Meek's tapes, interpreting them as containing female voices speaking in 'distant and distorted sentences' from beyond the grave.[30] Farrant soon started wandering through Highgate Cemetery himself in search of ghosts, with some success – in 1969 he claimed to have encountered an unearthly 'grey figure' there, a sighting which, when it found its way into the local press, ultimately became twisted so as to imply that a vampire was on the loose. Eventually, all this media hyperbole led to an unfortunate incident on Friday 13 March 1970, when a gullible mob stormed the cemetery-gates, brushing past police guards in their mad hunt for non-existent vampires. The full saga is too byzantine to go into fully here, but it is worth noting that, in August 1970, the publicity-seeking Lord Sutch appeared on the scene in fancy dress, falsely claiming that he was going to film his own horror movie in Highgate Cemetery, entitled *Daughter of Dracula and Jack the Ripper* (presumably an IVF child, seeing as both monsters were male).[31] Meek's accidental involvement in this whole affair has now largely been forgotten, however – although not by everybody. One of the questions on the FAQ section of David Farrant's website reads 'Did you kill Joe Meek?' to which is appended the one-word answer 'No!'[32] And Farrant is right, too – because Joe Meek, not entirely unpredictably, killed himself.

Who knows what it was that finally pushed Joe Meek fully over the edge? Some relate it to the police finding a suitcase dumped in a Suffolk field which turned out to contain the dismembered body of a young man named Bernard Oliver, who had been known to Meek. Theorising that it was some kind of gay sex crime, in January 1967 the Metropolitan Police announced their intention to interview every man in London with a prior conviction for engaging in homosexual acts – which, of course, would have included Meek.[33] On the morning of his suicide, Meek was acting strangely, but by this stage this was merely par for the course, so when he burned various letters, paintings and documents in his bath-tub and handed a note to his young studio assistant, Patrick Pink, saying 'I'm going now – Goodbye', Pink thought nothing of it. Then, however, Meek sent for his landlady, Violet Shenton, produced a shotgun which had been left behind in his flat by the field sports enthusiast Heinz Burt, and shot her dead before turning the gun on himself. When considering the motives for this appalling act, however, perhaps we should consider one final thing; the date upon which it occurred. Joe Meek committed suicide on 3 February 1967 – precisely eight years to the day since Buddy Holly's plane had crashed.[34] Maybe Meek simply had an appointment to keep with his old friend in the afterlife?

On Another Planet:
Desmond Leslie (1921–2001)

The high-living aristocrat with a hotline straight through to Churchill, the Royal Family – and Venus.

To be a true gentleman, a man needs to be in possession of several things; blue blood flowing through his veins, an aristocrat's natural sense of easy deportment – and, of course, the ability to punch another man in the face with just enough finesse so as not to come across as being too much of a cad in front of others. This final indispensible skill certainly came in handy for Desmond Leslie one Saturday evening in 1963 when, in front of an estimated eleven million TV viewers, he interrupted a live broadcast of the popular BBC satire show *That Was the Week That Was* by emerging from the studio-audience and smacking the show's presenter, Bernard Levin, full-on in the face. Surely this was no way for a relative of the great Winston Churchill himself to behave in public?

In his defence, Leslie would later go on to explain that he was merely defending a lady's honour – and a more impeccably chivalrous motive for violence you could not wish to find. The wronged maiden in question was Leslie's wife, the actress and singer Agnes Bernelle, whose voice had become famous during the War as the voice of Allied propaganda broadcasts. Reputedly, she was chosen to fill this role due to the seductive tenor of her voice – but, if so, then Bernard Levin had proven himself to be wholly immune to the spell of her mellifluous tones. In his part-time role as a theatre critic, Levin had recently penned a somewhat poisonous review of a new stage-play in which Bernelle had appeared called *Savagery and Delight* – a review which, Leslie thought, contained quite a bit of delight in its own savagery itself.

The altercation between the two men is redolent of an earlier and much gentler age. As far from a modern-day lager-fuelled brawl in a pub car-park as could be imagined, it began with the tall and bespectacled Leslie raising decorously from his seat in a well-cut dark suit and walking calmly across to Levin before challenging him to a fight in a manner which could best be described as highly apologetic in its nature. 'One minute, Mr Levin,' he said. 'Before you begin – it won't take a minute. Would you stand up?' Being a well-raised man himself, Levin of course complied. 'Mr Levin,' Leslie went on, scrupulously avoiding the unforgivable faux-pas of presuming to be on first-name terms with a stranger, 'your review of *Savagery and Delight* was not a review, it was a vicious attack.' Levin sheepishly admitted it may well have been, and asked the intruder to sit back down. But Leslie was not to be pacified.

'There's just one tiny thing to be done,' Leslie continued, pulling back his fist and throwing it straight into Levin's face, landing, as *The Times* later put it, 'the most public punch since Sonny Liston took the heavyweight title from Floyd Paterson', before then withdrawing tactfully from the arena. Reasoning that the show must go on, Levin made a vague remark about the values of pacifism, and continued delivering his lines to the camera as if nothing had happened. Except, of course, it had – and the nation was enthralled. Who was this polite pugilist, this latter-day Gentleman Jim of the television age? The following day, the newspapers provided their readers with an answer. It turned out that this striking figure (in both senses of the term) was none other than Desmond Leslie, an artistically-inclined member of the Anglo-Irish aristocracy, whose father was Winston Churchill's cousin.[1] And that, for the vast mass of people, was that; forever afterwards, if Leslie was famous for one thing and one thing only with the average viewer out there in TV-land, then it was for courteously lamping a man in the face on a late-night comedy show. This is something of a shame, however; there was in fact *far* more to Leslie's life than this.

His Father's Son ... Eventually

Born in London in 1921 into an old aristocratic family with branches in England, Scotland and Ireland, Leslie spent his childhood summers at the beautiful country house of Castle Leslie in County Monaghan in what is now the Republic of Ireland. Here, he seems to have been almost purposefully raised to live a life of benign peculiarity. Reputedly, his diplomat father Sir Shane

Leslie (1885–1971) was so distant and detached from his children that, when he happened to come across the four-year-old Desmond sitting on the stairs one day, he looked down at him in a puzzled fashion and asked quizzically 'Hello, who are you?' Apparently, he wasn't joking.[2]

Sir Shane was himself something of a noted eccentric, a poet who had spent time wandering through Russia as a tramp, claiming acquaintance with everyone from Leo Tolstoy to M. R. James. Fascinated by the occult, he collected accounts of spooks for inclusion in his well-received *Ghost Book* of 1955, and maintained that Castle Leslie itself was haunted by the shades of his own ancestors.[3] Perhaps Sir Shane's weirdest alleged experience came in 1904 when, while up at Cambridge, he claimed to have helped exorcise a ghost with no legs from some rooms where a former Fellow named Henry Butts had apparently committed suicide in 1623. Upon hearing that the occupants of these haunted rooms were being bothered by disembodied footsteps (from a ghost with no legs?) and other such phenomena, Sir Shane and two friends, both of whom were training for the priesthood, went over there brandishing a crucifix and Holy Water. The ghost, initially invisible, was supposed to have assaulted one of these would-be clergymen, and hurled him through a bedroom doorway. After this, Sir Shane claimed that 'The Thing', as it was known, then appeared there in that same doorway, forming itself out of a shroud of mist, and began advancing, legless and hideous, towards them as they stood there, paralysed with fear. Then, just as they seemed doomed, a loud crash denoted a big crowd of fellow students barging down the door to the rooms, and bringing in with them a flood of light in which the ghost immediately disappeared. The undergraduates then proceeded to destroy the rooms utterly, ripping off wall panels and smashing cupboards in their search for 'The Thing'. They didn't find it, and the College authorities made sure they never would; annoyed by the damage and fuss caused, they closed the rooms permanently.[4]

Clearly, then, Sir Shane was in possession of a distinct mystical bent – albeit one that was not, as yet, showing through in his sometimes boisterous offspring. Evidently, the children proved to be something of a nuisance to their parents around the 'Big House', a fact that led them to be farmed out to a variety of boarding-schools which, in the words of Leslie's sister Anita, 'performed the same function as kennels did for dogs.' Seeing as the young Leslie spent much of his time playing practical jokes to annoy house guests – once rigging the bedroom door of the visiting French Ambassador so that it caused a hidden car horn to go off every time he used it, for instance – perhaps it was no wonder that Sir Shane wanted time away from his kids in order to ponder the mysteries of the Hidden World.[5]

At the age of thirteen, Leslie was sent away by Sir Shane to board at yet another minor public school in England, this time in Sussex. Here, he finally began to understand his father's interest in matters mystical. The trigger for this dramatic development was an experience he and his school pals had one November night in 1934 when, after 'lights out', a bright green glare suddenly illuminated the boys' dormitory. Yelling in surprise and excitement, Desmond and everyone else leapt out of their beds in time to see what he described as being 'an immense green fireball' which moved slowly across the night sky before then disappearing behind the Sussex Downs.[6] At the time, Leslie did not know what the bright light was – after all, the term 'flying saucer' was not even to be invented for another thirteen years. For now, all he could do was wonder helplessly what it had been; a puzzle to which, as yet, he had no answer.

A Man of Many Parts

Leslie was later to go on to play a major role in introducing the idea of 'saucerology' (as it was then called) to the British public throughout the 1950s, but in the meantime other matters even more important than strange lights in the sky intervened in the young man's life. When war with Germany broke out in 1939, Leslie initially avoided involvement by going away to Trinity College, Dublin, where, appropriately enough for such a seeker of hidden truths, he read Philosophy. Evidently he ultimately decided that he feared taking his examinations rather more than he did the Nazis, however, as after a year he crossed back over to England and joined the RAF.

Leslie had what could be described as a 'Good War'. A brilliant Spitfire pilot, he was also a somewhat independently minded one, reputedly drawing the ire of his superiors for writing swear words in the sky with vapour trails. After nearly giving the top brass a heart attack, however, Leslie soon nearly suffered one himself; a medical revealed he had a weak heart, and he was rapidly invalided out of action and given a desk job, where he spent his spare time writing a best-selling novel called *Careless Lives*, an apt description of his own existence up to this point, perhaps. Spared probable death at the hands of the Luftwaffe, he passed his war dining with Churchill and courting his new lover Agnes Bernelle. Walking through the moonlit grounds of Castle Leslie together while Leslie was on leave, the young sweethearts took charming but unusual delight in pretending to be a pair of fairy-children and dancing hand-in-hand naked around a tree in order to express their love for one another. Once the War had ended, the dashing Leslie married the beautiful Agnes within a few days of the enemy's final surrender, and soon set about thinking what he should do with the rest of his life. With connections like he had, surely the possibilities were endless?[7]

At first he turned his hand to writing, finding success reporting for publications like *Vogue* and *Picture Post*, and penning screenplays for movies, some of which were actually produced, such as 1950s crime-drama *Stranger At My Door* (which also starred his wife Agnes Bernelle, handily enough). Leslie also began some very strange Joe Meek-style musical experiments at around this time, setting out to create a 'music of the future' which would consist not merely of the same old predictable boredom of notes and symphonies being played out in recognisable patterns on real musical instruments, but of random sounds being recorded and then stitched together to make up the kind of tunes you might expect acid-tripping robots to listen to in a darkened nightclub on Mars. With this end in mind, Leslie collected up literally thousands of recordings of bees buzzing, babies crying, horns hooting, bells ringing, and humming tops humming. This may all sound terrible, but the resultant tunes proved surprisingly successful; Leslie's compositions could be heard everywhere from TV ads to early episodes of *Doctor Who*, and he is now known as one of the fathers of modern electronic music.[8] Kraftwerk and other such groups owe him a large debt, it would appear.

Leslie, too, owed huge debts at various points in his life, however; making money from a country estate these days is not easy, although Leslie did his best to try and turn Castle Leslie into a profitable concern once it had passed into his own hands in 1963. His big idea was to open Ireland's first rural nightclub there in 1966, calling it 'Annabel's-on-the-Bog', a slightly unfortunate name which implied that Leslie may not have been entirely familiar with lower-class slang-terms for toilets. Despite this venture's ultimate failure, things did briefly look up for Leslie when Mick Jagger came to visit one day with the idea of renting the Irish Castle in order to escape Labour's punitive 1960s tax regime, but the world's biggest rock star soon abandoned the idea after being chased up a nearby church tower by a gang of hysterical schoolgirls.[9]

The Martians Have Landed (Possibly)

By far Leslie's biggest money-making scheme, however, came from co-writing a 1953 book called *Flying Saucers Have Landed* with a very strange Polish-American man called George Adamski (1891–1965). Adamski claimed to have received a telepathic message one night in November 1952 telling him to go out into the Mojave Desert on the border between California and Arizona, where he would be able to meet a real-life spaceman. This particular occupant of interplanetary craft called himself Orthon and claimed to hail from Venus, no less. Looking suspiciously like a long-haired Scandinavian hippie dressed in a one piece ski suit, he gave Adamski an equally New Age-style message about the urgent need for mankind to abandon all thought of nuclear conflict, which, this being the height of the Cold War, then seemed a very real possibility.[10] When word of this alleged encounter made the newspapers, Leslie, intrigued, wrote off to Adamski requesting more information. Impressed that Leslie was a published author, Adamski wrote back offering to provide him with photographs of actual Venusian spacecraft, if he would only write his whole story up for him. Leslie agreed, and the result was a publishing sensation – *Flying Saucers Have Landed*, published in September 1953, sold over a million copies worldwide, with the reading public simply lapping it up.[11]

The 1950s were, perhaps, the 'golden age' of ufology, when public interest in the then still-new topic reached maybe its greatest peak of popularity. The first saucer sighting had occurred on 24 June 1947 in America, when a private pilot, Kenneth Arnold, famously observed some strange objects which he described as moving through the air over the Cascade Mountains in Washington State with a motion 'like a saucer skipping on water.'[12] Within a few short years, the idea of alien visitors had crossed the pond and become so embedded in British culture, too, that even prominent high-up figures were registering an interest. *The Sunday Dispatch* for 11 June 1954, for instance, carried a full-page article by Air Chief Marshal Sir Hugh Dowding (1882–1970) headlined 'I Believe In Flying Saucers'. Dowding had helped orchestrate the RAF's success during the Battle of Britain, so his words still carried great currency with the public. Therefore, statements like the following would no doubt have disturbed some of the newspaper's readers:

The most important thing ... is to give a warning against attempts to open fire either with guns or aeroplanes on these objects ... such gratuitous folly might well turn natural curiosity into active hostility, and it may be assumed that those who visit us from outer space can well look after themselves.[13]

Adamski-style 'contactees', as such people are known, also began to spring up here, such as the London taxi-driver George King (1919–1997), who said he had been washing dishes in his flat one morning in May 1954 when he suddenly heard a voice shout out 'Prepare yourself! You are to become a voice of Interplanetary Parliament!' Fortunately, King was in fact already well-prepared for just such a supernatural experience – he claimed to have been seeing angels since childhood. Soon, King also professed to be encountering the astral bodies of Yoga masters who materialised in his living room and gave him messages from the cosmos, and hearing the voice of a highly-evolved 3,456-year-old Venusian named Aetherius, who told him to travel to a hilltop in Combe Martin where he would meet a spiritual adept from Mars. Somewhat surprisingly, said King, this adept turned out to be none other than Jesus Christ himself, who flew down from space wearing a glowing bejewelled robe, before firing waves of energy down into the hill on which King stood using a magic wand. This led King to realise that the hill was in fact a gigantic 'spiritual battery' which had been charged up by Jesus, to help mankind. There were various other such colossal batteries disguised as hills scattered throughout Britain, said King, so he founded his own saucer religion, the Aetherius Society, whose members dedicated their weekends to refilling them by climbing assorted peaks and performing slow-motion kung-fu moves on top of them while pronouncing things like 'Blessed are the chosen ones' during their bizarre rituals.[14]

On 7 September 1957, meanwhile, Britain gained its first-ever alien abductee, a man from Runcorn named James Cooke, who claimed to have been taken up in a musical spaceship to the planet Zomdic against his will, where he met a race of bald, bisexual, Nordic aliens who told him to warn the world against the dangers of atomic power. Sadly, nobody listened.[15] Worse, in 1958, for the first time, a British citizen was impregnated by a spaceman – namely, a Birmingham housewife named Cynthia Appleton, who in September was visited in her home by a blonde-haired Venusian who claimed that her womb had been seeded with a 'leader of men' named Matthew for the future good of the planet. When the space-baby arrived in June 1959, however, blonde-haired just like its father, it seemed entirely human. Worse, the man from Venus was a deadbeat dad who, nowadays, would have been on the receiving end of nasty letters from the Child Support Agency. 'He used to pop in regularly every seven or eight weeks,' Mrs Appleton told reporters, forlornly. 'When he left, after forecasting Matthew's birth, he said he would be looking in again soon. But he never returned. I just can't make it out.' Perhaps Mr Appleton had gotten hold of him in the meantime?[16] All of this kind of thing in Britain, for better or for worse, was initially kicked off by Desmond Leslie.

The Lie at Night

Another Brit with an interest in ufology at the time was none other than the beloved TV astronomer and noted eccentric Sir Patrick Moore (1923-2012), whose entire media career had been launched by an appearance on a 1956 BBC *Panorama* episode in which he had interviewed both Leslie and Adamski about their claims. A follow-up programme, *Do Flying Saucers Exist?*, meanwhile, gave Moore an opportunity to expand upon his own views about the subject – facing off against Leslie and Sir Hugh Dowding, he argued firmly against the reality of visiting spacecraft. He had good reason to. Moore had recently written in to his local newspaper describing a fake sighting, only to find that over twenty liars subsequently replied to him, claiming that they had also seen the imaginary thing. Worse, in October 1954, a mere year after *Flying Saucers Have Landed* had been published, an obvious rip-off book called *Flying Saucer from Mars: An Eyewitness Account of the Landing of a Martian* appeared, written by an unknown author named Cedric Allingham. The book told of Allingham's alleged encounter with a Martian in Scotland earlier that year, who had communicated with him via telepathy. Strangely, however, unlike most contactees, Allingham proved reluctant to agree to any media interviews – something probably explained by the fact that 'Allingham' was really Moore himself.[17]

You might have thought that Leslie, if he had known about this hoax, would have been annoyed – but seemingly not. Leslie and Moore became lifelong friends after their BBC appearances, even going so far as to write a spoof book together in 1972, called *How Britain Won the Space Race*. So well did the duo get on that Leslie invited him over to spend a holiday at Castle Leslie, where they made an amateur sci-fi film together, *Them and the Thing*. This featured footage of a fake UFO which Leslie created by dangling an antique Spanish shield down from the end of a fishing rod, then shining mirrors at it to make it sparkle.[18] It is not known whether Moore ever let Leslie know that he was really Cedric Allingham, but, if he had, then Leslie would probably have just laughed. After all, he had been trying to make money out of peddling dubious UFO-related tales himself too, had he not? When Leslie visited Adamski in America in 1954, for instance, he complained to his host that he did not met Orthon or see any saucers there – and yet, while abroad, he wrote his wife Agnes a letter in which he waxed lyrical about having seen 'a beautiful, golden ship' of Venusian origin in the sky, and receiving messages straight from Venus. Agnes fell for all this, produced a credulous article for the *Weekend Mail* headlined 'Flying Saucers Will Land Here Next Year!' based on these fables, and her husband was no doubt left laughing all the way to the bank. Via post, Leslie even claimed to have received 'proof' of Adamski's claims, in the form of a plaster cast of Orthon's footprint, which he took on a lecture tour of Britain, promoting his book further.[19]

Was *all* of Leslie's early championing of the saucers really just a cynical, money-making enterprise upon his behalf, however? Not necessarily. Ever since his encounter with the glowing green light at boarding school, Leslie's interest in the occult had been growing apace, and a manuscript of his which claimed to explain the sudden appearance of flying saucers in light of the teachings of ancient Indian mythology had been doing the rounds of London publishing houses for some time prior to his teaming up with Adamski. Whatever the level of his belief in alien life, his parallel interest in Spiritualism was certainly genuine; and, in 1951, he claimed to have received a message from his dead mother telling him to pay attention to all these stories about the Space Brothers. On the other hand, in private Leslie was heard to confess that he thought Adamski's experiences may simply have been down to schizophrenia.[20]

A Right Royal Scandal

Certainly, there is at least one specific escapade in Leslie's life which has all the hallmarks of him using Adamski purely in order to pull a cunning publicity stunt for his own benefit. One of Leslie's many well-connected friends was General Sir Frederick 'Boy' Browning, a Private Secretary to Her Majesty the Queen. Seeing as in 1959 George Adamski had embarked upon a big European lecture tour, Leslie got Browning to ask the Royals if they would like to meet the

famous contactee. The prospect of them agreeing is not as strange
as it may initially appear, seeing as Prince Philip was a subscriber
to *Flying Saucer Review*, and had secretly been sending out one
of his Equerries, Sir Peter Horsley, to interview UFO witnesses
for some time now. Some of them had even been smuggled back
to the Palace to tell their stories in the Royal presence.[21] Weirdest
of all, towards the end of his time as Philip's Equerry, Horsley
claimed to have met a man from space named 'Mr Janus', who
looked entirely human, but who seemed able to read his mind and
had a suspiciously comprehensive knowledge of Britain's nuclear-
weapons capabilities.[22]

The dangers of the Royals fraternising with contactees, however,
had previously been flagged up by the reaction of the Dutch press
to news that, during his European tour, Adamski had already
been granted an audience with Queen Juliana of the Netherlands.
The Dutch media were outraged, picking up on Adamski's earlier
career as the leader of an esoteric California-based cult, the Royal
Order of Tibet, in order to portray him as a new Rasputin. Thus,
when Adamski made a premature public pronouncement that
Prince Philip wanted to meet him, alarm bells began ringing in
the Royal ears.[23] Even closer to home were some embarrassing
events which occurred at Broadlands, the Hampshire estate of
Lord Mountbatten, Prince Philip's uncle and fellow saucer-fiend,
in February 1955. A bricklayer who turned up late for work there
claimed to have been knocked off his bicycle by an extraterrestrial.
According to the brickie, an aluminium saucer, thirty feet in
diameter, looking like a combination between a humming-top and
a saucepan, but with portholes in the side, had suddenly appeared,
emitting a mysterious force which had made him lose his balance.
Then, a see-through tube had descended down from the saucer,
containing an Adamski-style humanoid, wearing overalls and a
space-helmet. Amazed, Mountbatten went out to the spot of the
alleged encounter to investigate, but could find no evidence of the
UFO ever having been there. Under questioning, it soon became
obvious that the builder had simply been late for the usual reasons,
but, knowing of Mountbatten's interests, had spun the yarn,
hoping to avoid punishment. Hearing of this, Leslie had written
off to Mountbatten, asking his permission to publish details, while
telling acquaintances that it was all a true story – even though he
knew full well that it was not.[24]

Because of his knowledge of such events, when Boy Browning
put the idea to him of meeting Adamski, the Prince turned it down

flat. 'He didn't want to see headlines about him believing in little green men,' Horsley told the *Daily Mail* in 1997, and so Philip sensibly scrawled 'Not on your Nellie!' across an invitational letter from Leslie which Browning had passed on to him.[25] Perhaps astutely, Prince Philip sensed a trap. The sensation that would be caused by the Queen's husband having private talks with a cult leader who claimed to be friends with a long-haired pro-CND campaigner from Venus would have been huge, had it leaked out. Huge enough, you might almost say, to cause a sudden spike in Leslie's book sales ...

Nonetheless, by this time in his life Leslie had certainly made a real name for himself on Britain's lunatic fringe. Evenings at his London flat were constantly being disturbed by telephone calls from strange women asking him to father their children in the hope of creating a race of occult super-beings, or psychics bearing glad tidings from Mars. Eventually, all this took its toll on his marriage to Agnes, who confessed that matters finally came to a head one night when a self-styled 'transfiguration medium' made his way into their flat, collapsed down onto the carpet, and loudly professed that he was about to physically transform himself into what he termed 'a Chinaman' before squirming around on the carpet and pulling funny faces at them. At this point Agnes began to distance herself from her husband's activities, and eventually the couple divorced – although more because of a long-term affair Leslie was conducting with another young Earthwoman than because of his abiding interest in alien life-forms, admittedly.[26]

This interest nonetheless continued to some degree throughout the rest of Leslie's remarkable life, a creditably long innings which finally ended in 2001 in Nice, southern France, where he had relocated in order to take advantage of the warm climate after many years spent looking after Castle Leslie and ensuring that it remained safely in the hands of his family.[27] Nowadays, the ancestral seat is open to paying guests and holiday-makers who can, if they choose, opt to stay in a newly-built extension to the building, called the 'Desmond Leslie Room'.[28] Overnight visitors from the rough vicinity of Venus are made to feel particularly welcome there, it is said.

Loonies of Letters:
Literary and Artistic Eccentrics

The peculiar poets and abnormal artists whose lives provided something really worth writing about.

We have allowed the distinct idea to develop in recent centuries that the artist or the poet is a kind of 'man apart', an inherently different breed from the common herd, prone to strange acts, opinions and beliefs. Ignoring the obvious fact that, like Philip Larkin toiling away in his Hull library, or T. S. Eliot working in a bank, many such people in fact lead the same kind of hum drum lives as the rest of us, our culture prefers instead to imagine our creative types in the guise of adventurous Lord Byron or the ultra-bizarre Salvador Dalí. Sometimes, however, the stereotype really is justified. Possibly Britain's oddest and most otherworldly artist, for example, was William Blake (1757–1827), the engraver and poet, whose foibles are so well-known as to require only the briefest of mentions here. A seer of visions since childhood, Blake claimed to have seen such bizarre apparitions as angels sitting in a tree, the hideous Annunaki-like scaly green ghost of a flea, and even a fairy funeral. Having a liking for the teachings of various great mystics like Emmanuel Swedenborg and Paracelsus, Blake was open to the idea of there being hidden worlds beyond our own, and participated in séances in which he saw – and then sketched – the faces of the famous dead, people like Socrates and Voltaire.[1] It was this visionary faculty, it might be said, which allowed Blake to write his poetry. His poetic 'vision' touched all he saw, something he explained thus:

'What?' [I] will be Questioned, 'when the Sun rises do you not see a round disc of fire somewhat like a guinea?' [Then I will answer:]

'O no, no, I see an Innumerable Company of the Heavenly Host crying "Holy, Holy, Holy is the Lord God Almighty!"' I question not my Corporeal ... Eye any more than I would question a Window concerning a Sight. I look *through* it and not *with* it.[2]

Blake, it seems, was able to see through the prosaic day to day reality most of us inhabit and down to some greater level of imaginative truth which lay beneath, and a surprising number of writers and artists have had some kind of Blakean interest in the occult facility for experiencing visions. Perhaps such eccentricities are a sign of a true artistic or poetic vocation? One man, the writer Colin Wilson (1931–2013), certainly thought so, devoting an entire chapter of his entertaining 1971 bestseller *The Occult* to the subject of what he called 'The Poet as Occultist'. Wilson's basic premise was that there was some kind of hidden power lying latent within the human mind called 'Faculty X', which artistic-types possessed in more abundance than the rest of us. This Faculty X, said Wilson, was nothing less than 'the key to all poetic and mystical experience', a special mode of consciousness which would allow us to reach beyond our present time and location, dissolving away the narrowness of our everyday way of seeing the world and opening up ourselves to the idea of some deeper reality underlying Creation – the same way of seeing the world, in short, which allowed Blake to see the sun as a host of angels, and not merely a big round orange blob in the sky.

To some extent, this Faculty X was coterminous with what most people would label 'psychic powers' and Wilson, in an attempt to prove his theory, sought out various anecdotes about poets undergoing uncanny experiences. He found an account of W. B. Yeats claiming to have projected his astral body to a friend, for instance, and made the Cornish poet A. L. Rowse admit that he had once had a sudden but entirely accurate clairvoyant premonition of catching two men engaged in an embarrassing homosexual embrace in a library. From Robert Graves, meanwhile, he obtained the startling opinion that 'All true poems are written in the fifth dimension', something which accorded with Wilson's own view that the poet in a state of inspiration was like 'a spider in the centre of a web, receiving vibrations from all parts of the universe.' Wilson seemed to think that possession of this poetic Faculty X was to some extent a matter of genetic inheritance, speculating that maybe 5 per cent of people were born with some degree of well-developed psychic powers, corresponding admirably with the then popular idea of there being a 'dominant 5 per cent' in society – the notion that one in twenty of us was cut out to be a leader or innovator of some kind, and the rest of us mere sheep.[3]

The trouble with this kind of thinking, of course, is that it could very easily lead on to the rather unappealing idea of the creative writer as being some kind of *übermensch*, inherently superior to that unfortunate 95 per cent of the population who did not, like Wilson himself, possess some portion of this Faculty X. Wilson's big break came in 1956 at the tender age of twenty-four with his book *The Outsider*, an analysis of existentialist philosophy which he had famously written in the British Museum by day while settling down in a sleeping bag on Hampstead Heath at night due to his lack of money and employment. Promoted by his publisher as some kind of *wunderkind*, Wilson found himself feted in the press, with *The Outsider* selling 25,000 copies in its first six months alone. His book praised 'outsider' figures from world culture, saying that such folk alone had been able to escape from the banal conformities of mass culture and standardised thinking, the clear implication being that Wilson was one of these people himself, too – supposedly, he had been utterly convinced he was a genius since he was nine years old.

It seems that fame only exacerbated such feelings in Wilson, with his proclamations becoming ever more conceited and bizarre; in November 1956, he was loftily pronouncing that Shakespeare had a 'second-rate mind', for instance, while in September he was insisting that people only ever died 'out of laziness' and that, if you had enough willpower like he did, there was no reason why a man couldn't live forever (Wilson died in 2013). Confronted at a lecture by a blameless middle-class housewife who wanted to know what precisely was wrong with the bourgeois values she embodied, Wilson came over all Nietzschean, telling her it was 'appalling you were ever conceived' and that 'Your house is garbage, your garden a midden and a swamp, your husband is Gordon FitzHomo and your children are dung!' These were strong words indeed from a man who claimed to be 'probably the greatest writer of the twentieth century', and in 1957 the Outsider himself suffered a rather painful fall from grace when the parents of his then-girlfriend found one of Wilson's diaries contained what they called 'pornographic content'. Outraged, they broke into Wilson's flat threatening to horsewhip him, a story which inevitably found its way into the papers.

Claiming that the dirty bits were just research for a novel he was planning, Wilson stupidly handed his journals over to the *Daily Mail* to clear his name. Seemingly, their content was not pornographic – but it *was* masturbatory in another sense, Wilson having filled his diary with comically self-aggrandising statements like 'I am ... the most serious man of our age' and 'I must live on, longer than anyone else has [ever] lived ... to be eventually Plato's ideal sage and king.' Regrettably, Wilson had now become a bit of a laughing stock, with the influential literary critic Cyril Connolly, author of one of the most laudatory assessments of *The Outsider*, now admitting he hadn't even read the book before reviewing it, while other critics began to line up and point out that it was full of errors. Wilson's next book, *Religion and the Rebel*, was then subsequently ripped apart, with journalists combing through it to extract out of context statements like 'A man is more alive than a cow' and then reprinting them in their reviews to make Wilson look ridiculous. [4]

This is in some ways a bit of a shame as, while clearly not the greatest man of our times, let alone 'Plato's ideal sage and king', Wilson was a perfectly agreeable and entertaining writer who, at his best, produced some genuinely original and thought-provoking fare (particularly with *The Occult* and its sequels). Wilson was a good writer, but the trouble was the absurdly inflated claims he made for his output, even those elements of it which most would be minded to dismiss as mere hack work – in one 2004 interview, for instance, he confessed to his hope that, in a hundred years time, his *Spiderworld* series of novels would be remembered as masterpieces. [5] Seeing as these are a series of pulp sci-fi books about people in the future fighting a war of survival with a race of giant mutant psychic spiders, however, this outcome seems unlikely, at best.

As a self-confessed 'outsider' convinced of the truth of his own way of seeing the world, Colin Wilson certainly counted as an eccentric, something which could also be said of another writer erroneously certain of his own immortal genius, the infamous Scottish poet William McGonagall (1825–1902). If Wilson was guilty of inflating his talent, then at least he had some talent to inflate, unlike the dire McGonagall, who, despite considering himself to be the greatest poet in the English language with the (possible) exception of Shakespeare, was still able to churn out doggerel like the following, written in the aftermath of an 1882 assassination attempt made upon Queen Victoria by a man named MacLean:

God prosper long our noble Queen,
And long may she reign.
Maclean he tried to shoot her,
But it was all in vain.
For God He turned the ball aside
MacLean aimed at her head,
And he felt very angry
Because he didn't shoot her dead.

Most notorious were his lines upon the new Tay Bridge, opened in 1887:

Beautiful new railway bridge of the silvery Tay,
With your strong brick piers and buttresses in so grand array,
And your thirteen central girders, which seem to my eye
Strong enough all windy storms to defy,
As I gaze upon thee my heart feels gay,
Because thou art the greatest railway bridge of the present day!

Sadly, the Tay Bridge later collapsed in December 1879, leading McGonagall to modify his opinions upon the structure somewhat in a second poem:

I must now conclude my lay
By telling the world fearlessly without the least dismay
That your central girders would not have given way,
At least many sensible men do say,
Has they been supported on each side with buttresses,
At least many sensible men confesses,
For the stronger we our houses do build,
The less chance we have of being killed.

An ex-weaver, McGonagall started out in Dundee, selling sheets of his poems for a penny a piece, and also performing tragic recitals upon the public stage, routines which were so poor he was pelted with rubbish by his audiences, and the theatres where he appeared subjected to official police warnings not to allow him to perform there anymore. Soon, McGonagall was a public joke, being assaulted and jeered at in the street, and was forced to leave town, ending up renting himself out to facetious students in Edinburgh and Glasgow who held him mock dinners in which he was sarcastically acclaimed as the greatest poet of age and, frequently, subjected to beatings – a humiliating procedure which was, by this point, almost his only source of income. A strange-looking, mournful-eyed man with long hair and shabby clothes, his 'fish-belly face' was once uncharitably described by McGonagall's fellow Scottish poet, Hugh MacDiarmid, thus:

> [Like] something half-human struggling out of the aboriginal slime. All the incurable illiteracy, the inaccessibility to the least enlightenment ... are to be seen in the eyes. It is ... a face to make one despair of humanity.

Even more likely to induce despair in humanity was the way McGonagall's countrymen treated him, a relentless chorus of public mockery which seemed to end up driving him half-mad. An account of one of McGonagall's final public performances on the Glasgow stage makes for sad reading indeed.

> He was an old man ... and he appeared to have been shaved the night before. He wore a Highland dress of Rob Roy tartan and boy's size. After reciting some of his own poems, to an accompaniment of whistles and cat-calls, the Bard armed himself with a most dangerous-looking broadsword and strode up and down the platform ... His voice rose to a howl. He thrust and slashed at imaginary foes. A shower of apples and oranges fell on the platform. Almost before they touched it, they were met by the fell edge of McGonagall's claymore and cut to pieces. The Bard was beaded with perspiration and orange-juice. The audience yelled with delight; McGonagall yelled louder still, with a fury which I fancy was not wholly feigned ... I left the hall early, saddened and disgusted ... Was his madness real or feigned?[6]

This is a question which could also be asked of Kim Noble, a modern-day comedian and performance artist for whom the dividing line between art and life seems thin indeed. Having originally tried to make a living selling humorous artworks to galleries, Noble eventually teamed up with his fellow ex-art student Stuart Silver and began performing comedy gigs which were really more video-based performance pieces than normal standup. In 2000, 'Noble and Silver', as they called their double act, won the prestigious Perrier Award at the Edinburgh Festival, and in 2001 got their own series on Channel Four. It was amusing, but didn't exactly meet with mainstream success, with the duo eventually going their own ways and Noble's life and career entering something of a downturn which culminated in him having a breakdown in 2004, being diagnosed with a form of manic depression so severe that his Wikipedia entry currently states that 'as of March 2013, he remains alive', possibly the most pessimistic piece of phrasing there has ever been.

Maybe the web-page's author was wise to think like this, however, seeing as one of Kim Noble's most unusual ideas was to try using threats of suicide as part of his stage act. In 2007, Noble had appeared in the video for the unusual Christmas single *We're All Going to Die*, but in 2009 he went one further by putting on his own acclaimed stage-act, 'Kim Noble Will Die', whose content revolved to a great extent around his professed plan to commit suicide by throwing himself off Waterloo Bridge on 27 May 2009 due to the various depressing turns his life had taken. Was he serious in this intention? In one 2009 interview, he claimed to be, saying that 'When I first did the show, I was like, "Yeah, I'm going to jump" What a great performance spectacle that'll be', while in another he said that, at the time, suicide 'was like an everyday inevitability to me'. It is arguable that Noble really did mean this. Certainly, he managed to successfully convince several audience members that he genuinely meant to kill himself – including an actual psychiatrist, who reported the theatre in which Noble had performed to the police for apparently exploiting a mentally ill person for profit. During performances in Edinburgh, meanwhile, Noble told his audiences that, if they didn't turn up at the city's George IV Bridge at 3 a.m. that night and try and talk him out of it, then he would leap off. A number of people did actually then go there to try and stop him; it seems to be impossible to tell with Noble's act what is real in it and what is not.

In order to be able to convince a watching psychiatrist to call the police, though, Noble must have been doing some pretty extreme things up there on stage, and so it proved. Finding little solace in a self-help book by the TV hypnotist Paul McKenna called *Change Your Life in Seven Days* (it actually took him sixty-two days to read, so banally platitudinous was it), Noble decided to start filming various bizarre acts he felt compelled to perform during his real, day to day life. For one thing, he took to doctoring various products in stores in order to disturb other shoppers. As well as fitting a rape alarm to a chair in IKEA, Noble also bought a copy of Bono's biography and went through it, cutting out pages and replacing them with new ones he had written himself, in which Bono suddenly began to talk endlessly about how great Kim Noble was in bed, then took it back to the shop and replaced it. He even took away DVDs, re-made the movies in question, then returned them to shelves for unsuspecting people to watch, remaking *Ghandi* as a ten-second animated stick-man film in which the great man 'just gets shot', for example. Worse, Noble filmed himself self-harming, playing with himself and being urinated on – and showed all this, live on-stage, for people to laugh at. For good measure, he then handed out cups to his audience, filled with samples of his own semen.

Just as controversial was Noble's stage-show of 2015, 'You're Not Alone', which purported to be a partially filmed record of Noble's attempts to feel closer to other people around him by, for example, drilling holes through his neighbours' walls and recording them having sex, pretending to be a woman and arranging (and actually turning up for) dates with unknown men, calling numbers scrawled on the walls of public toilets, and becoming inappropriately fascinated with a local supermarket check out worker named Keith. Obscenity, too, featured quite prominently, with footage of Noble defecating in a church making an appearance, and him Googling up sick things on a big screen (e.g. a dwarf inserting a milk-bottle up his bum) while the audience entered.

Most notable of all, though, was Noble's bizarre idea of making himself a fake B&Q uniform, then going and working there in a pretend weekend job without the management's knowledge. Apparently, Noble got away with this exploit for several months, secretly filming and photographing himself telling customers he 'didn't give a shit' where the nails were, or dancing with shoppers in the kitchen department. Satisfied with his performance, Noble gave himself an 'Employee of the Month' award, then phoned the Human Resources department and resigned, demanding they hold him a leaving party. After it was discovered that he didn't actually work there, Noble was banned from all branches of B&Q – and even their car-parks – immediately. Judging by an interview Noble gave to *The Sunday Times*, these stunts do not appear to have been faked; the interview in question apparently took place in an unnamed department store where Noble was planning to start secretly living ('I've found a wardrobe that works if I sleep sitting up'), and featured chit-chat about how he was currently stuffing dead pigeons full of shredded copies of another awful Paul McKenna book, *I Can Make You Smarter*, before concluding with him making a series of telephone calls in search of some dead squirrels to place on poles.[7]

Noble's amazing existence seems to embody the idea of a 'Surrealist person' as espoused by that artistic movement's founder, the poet André Breton, whom we met briefly earlier on in this book praising the painter Leonora Carrington for smearing her feet with mustard in a restaurant. For the Surrealists, and their precursors the Dadaists, it was possible to embody the ideals of their artistic movements without actually producing any writings or artworks, simply through the way you lived your life – which, in practice, meant living it extremely strangely, transgressing the normal rules of society and becoming a kind of living work of art. So, for instance, if Leonora Carrington habitually surprised guests at her home by sneaking into their bedrooms, cutting off bits of their hair and then serving it up to them in an omelette for breakfast the next morning,[8] or the New York-based Dadaist Elsa von Freytag-Loringhoven often walked down the street with a coalscuttle on her head and with used postage stamps stuck to her face,[9] then this was just further evidence that each woman was taboo-busting 'Surrealist person', not a mentally ill one.

Surrealism and Dada didn't really catch on in Britain to the extent they did on the Continent, but one native who deserves to be discussed in relation to the idea of living a 'surreal life' would be Tony 'Doc' Shiels (b.1938), described by one authority as having been, at various points in his life, 'a painter, a conjuror, a gun-slinger, a musician, a playwright, a busker ... [and] a self-admitted wizard'. Born in Salford in 1938, Shiels studied, painted and played the blues in 1950s Paris and ran a gallery in Cornwall during the 1960s, before becoming better-known to the wider world in the 1970s through a series of vastly entertaining escapades in which he attempted to raise sea serpents and lake monsters across the world using ritual magic, psychic powers and the efforts of various covens of naked witches. Shiels' efforts culminated in 1977 when he managed to take some remarkable photographs purporting to be of the Loch Ness Monster, which ended up gracing the front page of the *Daily Mirror*. While Shiels is a serious artist, his numerous appearances in the press throughout the 1970s and 80s for his wilfully bizarre and Rabelaisian stage-shows and weird escapades involving spoon-bending, 'ESP cigars' and investigations into alleged sightings of a quasi-humanoid owl-man creature at large in Cornwall, ensured that it was for his surreal life, rather than his Surreal paintings, for which he is now best known.

A 1977 interview with the *Sunday Independent* provided an amusing example of the way in which Shiels liked to play up the more eccentric elements of his existence, claiming to his no-doubt bemused interviewer that, on a recent walk to the pub, he and a friend had been accosted by 'an albino extraterrestrial dressed in a rather neat tailored suit' who introduced himself as being one Norman Crocodilidine, 'the Custodian of the Entire Universe – but not God, who is someone else.' Making a strange clicking sound, said Shiels, Norman made him and his pal a strange proposition: that they take the burden of custodianship away from him. Supposedly, the pair agreed, thus gaining mastery of the entire universe and 'the right to give away stars, twenty-three at a time'. Undoubtedly, Doc Shiels has added greatly to the gaiety of our nation – but it would appear that, in more recent years, he has come to regret some of the time he spent chasing monsters, giving away stars and casting magic, wishing that instead he had spent a little more time focusing on developing his painting. That, I suppose, can be the problem of leading a surreal life; it tends to overshadow appreciation of your actual art or poetry itself, no matter how good it may be.[10]

Another highly eccentric person who probably wishes he had spent more time on his art is Charles Bronson (b.1952), habitually described as 'Britain's most dangerous prisoner'. Bronson, born Michael Peterson in 1952, has been in and out of the tabloids for decades on account of his incredibly strange behaviour while in prison, and has become something of a cult hero as a result, even having a successful biopic, *Bronson*, released in 2008. In his own words, Bronson is 'not mad, but I am a bit disturbed', and reportedly found it difficult to relate to fellow patients during his various enforced spells in secure psychiatric institutions like Broadmoor, one of whom, he said, was so insane he actually tried to eat himself. Originally sentenced to seven years behind bars in 1974 after holding up a post office in Ellesmere Port for a mere £26.18, Bronson's violent prison-based behaviour has seen him remain incarcerated – often in solitary confinement – virtually ever since. Undoubtedly a very strong man, in 2002 Bronson released a fitness book called *Solitary Fitness*, in which he detailed his apparent ability to knock out cattle using a technique he calls the 'Solitary Cow Punch'('A cow's got a jaw; anything with a jaw can be knocked out!! ... Sure, a cow can't hit back! But what's that got to do with [it]?'). Seeing as, during a brief spell of freedom in 1987, Bronson reputedly fought and killed a rottweiler with his bare hands during an illegal prize fight, his claim to be able to floor livestock with a single blow does appear plausible. In his book, Bronson also gave out some other details about his regular regimen, such as that he flosses his nostrils with twine, cleans his stomach by swallowing strips of wet cloth then pulling them out again, and gives himself colonic irrigations by sitting in a bowl and somehow sucking water up through his anus to aid his general well-being.

Seeing as Bronson is so tough, he is not a man you would want to cross, and he has been involved in several hostage situations over the years, some of which have since become legendary. In 1996, for instance, he took two Iraqi hijackers hostage in his cell and demanded that the men address him as 'General' and begin tickling his feet. After hitting one of his prisoners over the head with a metal tray, Bronson felt guilty, handed the tray over to the man and told him to hit him over the head back with it four times himself, to call it quits. When the man refused, Bronson began slashing himself with a razor. The situation seemed difficult to defuse, as Bronson's demands to the authorities were that he be given a helicopter to fly him to Cuba, along with an axe, two Uzi sub-machine guns with 5,000 bullets, a cheese sandwich and some ice cream – if these requests were refused, he said he would eat one of his prisoners. In 1993, meanwhile, during another hostage situation, Bronson had memorably demanded he be provided with a blow-up doll and a cup of tea, before eventually releasing his hostage after he broke wind in front of him! Most recently, after becoming enraged at his most hated football team Arsenal coming back from two goals down to win the 2014 FA Cup Final, Bronson began thinking he could see the ghost of dead gangster Ronnie Kray, urging him on to start a riot. Stripping himself naked and smearing his body with butter to render himself harder to catch, Bronson then attacked a dozen guards dressed in full riot gear, an adventure which got him another two years added on to his life sentence.

Bronson does have his gentler side, though, revealing in a 1999 interview that his best friends in prison were cockroaches, which he lured into his cell with sugar, and spiders, whose backs he tickled to teach them how to jump over matches. Most notably for our present purposes, however, is the fact that for the last fifteen or so years, Bronson has been spending his time inside trying his hand at poetry and art. These pastimes have become genuinely important to Bronson, who has said he once went on a forty-day hunger strike so his guards would give him a pencil to draw cartoons with, and who has recently changed his name to Charles Salvador in honour of his favourite Surrealist painter, Salvador Dalí ('It's now Salvador all the way to Disneyland!' he wrote). He has been acclaimed by some experts as having real talent, too, having some eleven books of poetry and prose published, with titles like *Loonyology*, *My Mad Life* and *More Porridge Than Goldilocks*, and winning several awards from the Koestler Trust charity for his drawings. Mind you, it may not be overly-wise to give Bronson's artworks anything other than fulsome praise, seeing as in 1999 he took a prison art teacher named Phil Danielson hostage for criticising one of his pictures, tying him up with a skipping rope and forcing him to march around his cell after fashioning himself a home-made spear. Perhaps Bronson was so offended by Danielson's critique because, in his own words, 'I've got nothing apart from my poetry, art and cartoons. That's my life.'[11]

A surreal life and a surreal art fused together inseparably in one deeply eccentric figure; you get the distinct impression André Breton would have loved him – at least from a distance.

Not the Bookish Type:
Arthur Cravan (1887–1918)

Oscar Wilde's pugilistic prize-fighting nephew, whose life-story reads like something out of a novel.

For a man who chose to carve out a life as a literary critic, Arthur Cravan had a rather strange attitude towards the written word itself – he seemed to hate nearly every successful writer who had ever put pen to paper, considering much of their work to be tantamount to fraud. 'All literature, it's ta ta ta ta ta ta,' he once wrote – or, in other words, 'blah, blah, blah'. Art, if anything, was even worse: 'Art, what hinges me to Art? [It's all] Shit, in the name of God!'[1] Such was his aversion to bookshops that, when Cravan set up his own literary review, *Maintenant* (*Now!*) in 1912, he refused to allow such appallingly staid, dusty and commercially minded establishments to stock it; instead, he wandered through the streets of Paris selling it from a greengrocer's wheelbarrow, hawking it out loud for twenty-five centimes per copy to passers-by. If any pedestrians took Cravan up on his offer, then they would have discovered a most unusual series of reviews, articles, poems and interviews contained within his little magazine – which, in order to convey his contempt for the creative arts as directly as possible, had been printed on wrapping paper sourced from a butcher's shop.[2]

Perhaps this is why, whenever you open a copy of *Maintenant*, even today, you can still scent the blood. Detesting most successful writers and artists as being little more than stunted sell-outs to the crude whims of the marketplace, Cravan sought to butcher those he most hated in print without mercy. Perhaps his most extreme literary hatchet job was reserved for the celebrated French novelist André Gide. Gide may have been well regarded enough to have subsequently won the Nobel Prize for Literature in 1947, but reputation counted for nothing with Cravan – indeed, the bigger the literary lion, the greater the honour in bagging him.

Cravan managed to secure a meeting with Gide by sending him a note in which he claimed to be Oscar Wilde's nephew – which he was, but only sort of. His father's sister, Constance Mary Lloyd, was Wilde's wife, so the relation was one purely of marriage, not blood. The genius of Oscar Wilde did not actually run through his veins, then, though that did not bother Cravan, who was the very definition of a self-made man – in the sense that he was constantly making up palpably untrue claims about his past. 'Arthur Cravan' was not even his real name. He originally adopted the pseudonym in 1910, taking his surname from his first wife's birthplace, and his forename, seemingly, in honour of the rebellious French poet and gunrunner Arthur Rimbaud. He was actually born Fabian Avenarius Lloyd in Switzerland in 1887, and shared a mixture of Irish and English heritage, his father being a minor Anglo-Irish gentleman named Otho Holland Lloyd, and his mother a former governess named Clara Hutchinson.[3] While he held both British and Swiss passports, Cravan also possessed papers – many of them false or stolen – which would have allowed him to claim any number of nationalities, and considered himself to be essentially a citizen of the world. 'I have twenty countries in my memory,' he once claimed, 'and trail in my soul the colours of one hundred cities.'[4] He also trailed pure havoc behind him everywhere he went.

Wilde Man Blues

When he received Cravan's note, Gide proved receptive to granting the young writer an audience. Gide had met Wilde in Paris in 1891, when he was only twenty-two and Wilde, then as now the more famous figure, was thirty-seven. For several weeks, the two men enjoyed one another's company, Gide basking in the older man's reflected glory, but after Wilde returned to England, Gide began having second thoughts. Rejecting Wilde as a bad influence, and well aware of the rumours then circulating about the great man's homosexual urges – a vice he himself partially shared – Gide started to keep his distance and, following Wilde's death in 1900, saw fit to pen some rather equivocal tributes to the man.[5] These facts appeared to annoy Cravan, who set out to gain his revenge in print.

Cravan's attitude towards his eminent uncle was a complex

one. He seems to have liked the legend of Wilde more than he did his plays, essays and poems – and, certainly, Wilde's celebrated statement (recorded for us by Gide) that 'I have put my genius into my life; I have put only my talent into my works'[6] could just as easily have served as his nephew's own motto. While Cravan did fancy himself as a poet, and even as an occasional painter under an assumed name, his actual lasting artistic achievement was slight indeed. Undeniably, he is remembered more for the sensational nature of his own existence than he is for his writing per se. Those critics who are sceptical about Oscar Wilde's true literary worth might say something similar about him, too; that his biography has more lasting currency than his oeuvre. Yes, his plays are amusing, the argument goes, but ultimately mere entertainment, his children's stories twee and emetic, and *The Picture of Dorian Gray* little more than a flimsy if exciting narrative designed to hang a series of glittering epigrams upon, the nineteenth-century equivalent of Stephen Fry novelising his Twitter account.

A recent book[7] has tried to portray Wilde as having been the first true 'celebrity' of the early media age, the first man to have been more famous simply for being himself than for his actual achievements; when he famously had 'nothing to declare but my genius' at the New York Customs Office in 1882,[8] some people would have it that he was, quite inadvertently, telling the harsh unvarnished truth about himself.[9] Arthur Cravan's best pieces of writing function essentially as publicity stunts too, as extensions of the outrageous man himself, more than as works of literature in and of themselves, and his deliberately ridiculous and distasteful interview with André Gide was no exception. 'He's a millionaire. What a gas it would be to take that old scribbler for a ride!' wrote Cravan in issue two of *Maintenant* – and take him for a ride he certainly did.

Poison Pen

Right from the start, Cravan's write-up of his interview is gratuitously offensive towards Gide, for those who were in the know. Cravan was a notably well built, physically fit and handsome man – a boxer, in fact – and, as soon as he entered Gide's villa, Cravan averred that the illustrious novelist found him to be a physical 'marvel'. 'Already we were running away to Algeria,' wrote Cravan, taunting his host; the reference being to an accidental meeting which had taken place between Wilde and Gide in that country in 1895. Algeria, during the late nineteenth century, was a notorious haunt for European homosexuals who wanted to pick up poor Arab boys for sex. While there, Wilde had apparently managed to tease out from Gide that he desired to do such a thing himself – an admission which, while Cravan evidently knew about it, Gide would obviously not want broadcasting to the wider world.[10]

While in Gide's presence, Cravan claims that his skin-colour suddenly and magically takes on a Middle-Eastern hue, and he begins to hatch a plan to exploit Gide's vast wealth; he will run away to Algeria with him and be his little Arab-boy. 'I dare hope he won't sue me for damages' for writing about this obscene little fantasy, says Cravan, the joke presumably being that, of course, Gide could not do so. The passage in question is written in such a way as to be basically incomprehensible to anyone who doesn't know about Gide's guilty secret, and, if he were to take Cravan to court over the article, then Gide would of course have to reveal what it actually did all mean, thereby leading to his immediate ruin. The situation is, of course, ironically similar to that which Cravan's uncle had once found himself in; after the Marquess of Queensberry had accused Wilde of having a gay relationship with his son, Wilde had unsuccessfully taken the Marquess to court for libel, leading to his own ruination and public disgrace in the eyes of late Victorian society.

However, after realising that in reality he would 'never squeeze ten lousy centimes' out of Gide no matter how desirable or toned his young body, Gide settled instead for making a series of deliberately bizarre pre-prepared statements to his host in order to discombobulate him. His opening gambit, for instance, was to tell Gide that he far preferred boxing to literature. Confused, and possibly thinking that he was being challenged to a fight, Gide replied politely that it was nonetheless on literary grounds that the two men must meet. 'The Bible is the world's biggest bestseller!' Cravan next shouted, before telling Gide that he was 'afraid' to read any of his books, and so knew nothing about them, thereby robbing his host of any expected praise. Cravan then took the opportunity to list the names of some 200 living authors along with insulting dismissals of their work, something which must surely have tested Monsieur Gide's patience. Gide did try to move the conversation on to higher matters, but Cravan deliberately interrupted him with yet more absurd drivel, before abruptly asking him what time it was and telling him he had to go. Back home in his garret, Cravan then scribbled down what is perhaps the most insultingly nonsensical assessment of a great writer's physical appearance ever to have appeared in print:

> Monsieur Gide does not look like a love-child, nor like an elephant ... he looks like an artist ... he could very easily be mistaken for a show-off. There is nothing remarkable about his bone-structure; his hands are those of a do-nothing – very white, my word! Overall, he's a real weakling ... Along with that, the artist has a sickly face, with little flaps of skin, a bit larger than flakes, falling off around the temples ... he is hygienic ... he frequents neither women, nor places of ill repute ... I've described the man, and now I would gladly have described the work, if I could just have avoided repeating myself on even a single point.[11]

Evidently, Cravan thought that Gide's writing was just as weak and puny as he claims Gide himself was; a low valuation which he then seems to prove by offering a handwritten note Gide had sent to him for sale from *Maintenant*'s offices for the princely sum of 0.15 francs – less than a penny. Cravan would probably have maintained that it was overpriced.

Art for Art's Sake

Turning his attention away from literature, in *Maintenant* issue four Cravan made a name for himself as an art critic, too. In his view, there were only 'two or three' genuinely talented painters in the whole of France, so an exhibition of numerous contemporary daubers then being held at the annual Salon des Indépendants seemed to him entirely excessive. Whose work was being exhibited there, in any case? Well, there was the talentless Maurice Denis, for starters, who displayed an alarming inability to paint 'the cheese of feet', a technical failing he managed to hide only by painting pretty pictures of the sky. Even worse was Marc Chagall – 'a man with gas in his anus', apparently. 'He has the ass of a cow!' Cravan wildly proclaimed, before moving on to dismiss Morgan Russell ('I didn't see any quality there'), Per Krohg ('an old con-man'), Alexandre Exler ('one of the worst artists') and Suzanne Valadon ('old whore!'). For other painters, meanwhile, such as 'Tobeen' (Félix Elie Bonnet), Cravan had some valuable, if slightly unorthodox, career advice to impart:

> Ah, ah! Hum ... hum!! My old Tobeen ... Catch yourself a rabbit ... All of your friends are little cretins (the cow, for example).

Give yourself some dignity! Run to the fields, over the plains like
a horse!

A surprising amount of Cravan's criticism was distinctly scatological
in its nature, the work of André Ritter being 'the worst crap', and
one Monsieur Ermein merely 'another asshole', while Ferdinand
Schmalzigang apparently saw nature in the manner of 'a fly that
gravitates towards shit'. The Cubist Jean Metzinger was guilty of
an even worse failing: 'His colours have German accents. It disgusts
me.' Other artists, meanwhile, were subjected to purely personal
insults, quite separate from their work. Alfred Hagin, for example,
was 'sad, sad' and Szaman Mondzain 'a black-out drunk', while
Cravan had only one thing to say to Denys Puech: 'Shut up, you evil
being!' Worse, the 'fat beta' Robert Delauney was abused not only
for his 'big stupid eyes', supposed resemblance to a thistle-eating
donkey and podgy physique – 'he was a squishy cheese' – but also
for having married a Russian woman named Sonia Terk who was,
in Cravan's opinion, worth having sex with only the once. Most
abusive of all, however, was Cravan's assessment of the curiously
lifeless portrait of a female painter named Marie Laurencin, the
lover of the poet Guillaume Apollinaire:

> Now *there's* someone who needs somebody to lift her skirts
> and stick a fat XXXX somewhere to teach her that art isn't just
> little poses in front of a mirror [but] walking, running, drinking,
> eating, sleeping and relieving oneself![12]

What did Cravan mean by all this? Just that 'there is no point in
doubting that a turd is necessary in the formation of a masterpiece'
in the same way that fertiliser is usually necessary to make a flower
grow. Why did so many of the paintings on display have to be so
prim and proper, Cravan wanted to know? Why did they have to be
so pretty, colourful and reserved, so appealing to bourgeois tastes?
Many of these artists presented themselves as being 'rebels', but in
Cravan's eyes they were no such thing, merely fraudulent weaklings.
'It is absolutely necessary that you cram into your head that art is of
the bourgeois and is intended for the bourgeois, a monsieur without
imagination.' Was it really such an offence against art to admit that
'an artist drinks and eats' and goes to the toilet? Looking at the
paintings on display, you would never guess that those who had
produced them had a spleen or a liver, only over-developed brains.
  Where was the sense in these paintings, asked Cravan, that

somewhere outside the gallery lay a more vital world in which people 'swim in Africa with hippopotami', walk through cities 'full of skyscrapers' or meet vibrant, life-filled women with 'strong enough asses to mount horses'? All these boring modern painters, moaned Cravan, 'I want to kick their ass!' Surely 'the first condition of being an artist' was 'to know how to swim', not how to pick up a brush? These talentless morons should abandon their studios and, instead, start playing with skipping ropes again, he demanded, just as they did when they were six years old, 'when you know nothing, and you are closest to foolishness'. Swimming, skipping, defecating, fornicating, consorting with hippopotami, riding horses with hardened bum-cheeks– only by doing such things in order to feel alive again could these moribund, half-dead artists ever hope to put some life back into their miserable little canvases, thought Cravan. If any readers agreed with him in this assessment, he said, then he would be happy for them to send him in some jam, booze or interesting foreign postage stamps as a mark of approval to the usual address.[13]

If not, however ... then why not simply take Cravan at his word and challenge him to a fight? Given that he viewed cultural criticism as a direct extension of the sport of boxing, he would hardly be likely to turn such an offer down – would he? According to Cravan's second wife, Mina Loy, 'the instinct of 'knock-out' dominated [Cravan's] critique',[14] so when the wronged poet Guillame Apollinaire challenged him to a duel on behalf of his insulted lover Marie Laurencin, the wannabe-pugilist had the chance at last to prove it. Seeing as Cravan claimed that he wrote his magazine only 'to anger my colleagues', to gain notoriety and to get money for prostitutes,[15] you may have thought this development would have delighted him. Surprisingly, however, Apollinaire's challenge in fact only led Cravan to issue a rather unexpected and humiliating apology.[16] When it came down to it, was Cravan really so craven, after all?

Boxing Clever

You would not have thought so, given that Cravan claimed to have been crowned the light-heavyweight boxing champion of France in 1910. This *sounds* impressive. However, the way in which this supposed title had been 'achieved' may cast a different light upon the matter. Cravan had genuinely been lined up to fight several opponents in that year, it seems, but had ended up being called the winner by default in each of his match ups without having to throw a single punch. Cravan's first opponent, apparently, got the jitters immediately before the match was due to start, and refused to even enter the ring; two others accidentally went to the wrong venue and thus were disqualified for non-attendance; a third fighter, meanwhile, sprained his ankle while jumping into the ring and was unable to continue.[17] That, at least, is the story – you can believe it or not.

One person who seemingly did believe Cravan's claims, however, was the real-life former heavyweight champion of the world, the American boxer Jack Johnson, who agreed to fight Cravan in front of a baying crowd in Barcelona's Plaza de Toros Monumental bull fighting arena on 23 April 1916. Johnson, the first black champ, was living in exile in Europe at the time, seeing as back home he was facing trumped up charges which, ultimately, were of a racially motivated nature. The so-called 'Galveston Giant' was in need of money, and so was Cravan. Accounts differ as to whether or not Johnson knew Cravan was ultimately a fraud – in his biography, Johnson claims he didn't know who Cravan was before the fight, and attributed his easy victory to the fact that he must have been out of training.[18] However, other sources say that Cravan and Johnson had met previously in the nightclubs of Paris. Seeing as Cravan cast a memorable figure in Paris' night-spots – once dancing the tango in a black shirt with its front cut away to reveal several bleeding tattoos and obscene words scrawled across his chest, for example – it is unlikely that, had Johnson indeed come across the man prior to their fight, he would have forgotten him.[19]

Whatever the level of the two men's prior acquaintance, however, there is no doubt whatsoever that the fight itself was a massive con. According to Cravan himself, prior to the bout starting, 'Johnson laughed and I think I laughed too. I knew I was going to get beaten.'[20] It lasted a measly six rounds, with a heavily inebriated Cravan spending most of his time shadow boxing and generally just acting like an idiot, before Johnson finally laid him out with a few well-aimed punches. It was obvious the whole thing was staged; the crowd booed, and the next day's papers proclaimed the non-event a gigantic swindle. Not that Cravan or Johnson cared about the fact – there was a guaranteed 50,000-peseta purse for them to split whatever the outcome.[21]

Cravan's need for funds was probably even greater than Johnson's. Being a so-called 'citizen of the world' potentially left Cravan open to conscription into any one of several European armies during the First World War, and the enforced discipline of military life was hardly likely to have proved congenial; reputedly, he had already been expelled from an unnamed English military academy for spanking a teacher some years earlier.[22] Seeing as America had not yet entered the conflict at the time of his bout, Cravan saw fleeing to the States as being his best way out of a life in khaki. The fake fight gave Cravan enough cash to travel to New York, on the same steam boat which carried the out-of-favour Russian revolutionary Leon Trotsky off to exile in the New World. According to Trotsky, the craft was full of 'undesirable elements' like Cravan, who apparently told him he was planning to set up a new life for himself as a prize fighter in America, on the grounds that he would 'rather smash a Yankee's face in the noble art of boxing than be done in by a German.'[23] According to Cravan, 'Everything noble has some[thing] thuggish in it and everything thuggish has some nobility in it, because these are the two extremes.'[24] As such, boxing was undoubtedly nobler than meaningless war.

Identity Crisis

Was Cravan a genuine professional boxer, or was he not, then? I suppose the answer is 'yes', but only in a small way. His official record reads as follows: Fought three, Lost two, Drawn one. He achieved no KOs and boxed a total of only eight rounds.[25] However, as always with Cravan, the actual picture is slightly murkier than the official record may suggest. After fleeing to Mexico in 1918, following America's entry into the war, he was employed as a boxing instructor in Mexico City, and seemingly went ten rounds in the ring with the Mexican heavyweight Honorato Castro, losing only on points. The contest may not have had any official status, but, together with his position as boxing instructor, it would seem to show that he did have at least some pugilistic talent.[26] Whatever fighting skills Cravan may have possessed, however, proved entirely secondary to his showmanship, something in which he really was a world champion. Brief newsreel footage of Cravan preparing for his fight with Johnson in Barcelona, for example, does exist. It shows Cravan dawdling around the ring in stripy trunks and taking on a kind of Spanish semi-midget who comes up only to Cravan's chest, into which he runs flailing his fists around like a human Scrappy Doo. It is clear the sparring is being done only for laughs, and serves no serious purpose.[27]

Something else which served no serious purpose other than to entertain were Cravan's deliberately hyperbolic proclamations prior to throwing (or, more often, dodging) his first punch in the ring. Whereas other boxers might declare themselves to be 'the strongest fighter in the world', Cravan preferred instead to introduce himself as being a master of disguise, with a thousand different qualities and absurd identities. According to his pre-match pronouncements, Cravan claimed to be, variously, a hotel thief, chauffeur, draft dodger, butcher, sailor, fruit picker, lumberjack, ailurophile (cat-lover), professor, snake charmer, muleteer, gold prospector, nephew of Oscar Wilde, grandson of Queen Victoria's Chancellor (which he really was!) and, most famously, 'the poet with the shortest hair in the world'.[28] This sense of having no absolute fixed identity was central to Cravan's avant-garde appeal. In his 1916 poem 'Hie!', for instance, he claimed to be, among other things, a chemist, a whore, an acrobat, a child, a millionaire, an industrialist, Don Juan, a pimp, a monkey, a giraffe, and a cactus. 'I am all things, all men and all animals!/What next?' he asked.[29] What next, it turned out, was to become one of the most celebrated heroes of Dada and Surrealism.

We have already examined the ideal of the 'Surrealist person' in relation to such unusual personalities as Leonora Carrington and Doc Shiels. Cravan, though, beat them all to it, his entire life being little more than one gigantic piece of performance art, a performance which people like André Breton absolutely loved. Cravan may have bemoaned what he called his 'fatal plurality' in 'Hie!', but it seems unlikely that he meant it. According to him, he only ever felt at home when 'in voyage', as 'when I stay a long time in the same place, stupidity overwhelms me.'[30] In a way, Cravan became a kind of real-life Fantômas, the pulp-fiction arch-criminal and master of false identities so beloved of Breton and his Surrealists for his shapeshifting qualities.[31] Cravan's appeal for the early Dadaists was similar; adherents of the movement frequently gave themselves false names like 'Dadamax' and 'Oberdada', and the French 'King of Dada' Marcel Duchamp adopted a transvestite alter-ego named Rrose Sélavy, in an attempt to undermine bourgeois society by implying that human identity is not such a fixed thing as most people would like to pretend.[32] Cravan himself had a number of fake alter-egos – the painter 'Edouard Archinard', for instance, was really Cravan in disguise[33] – and he once crossed the border into Canada while dressed in drag,[34] so his appeal to people like Duchamp as a shape-shifter extraordinaire was obvious. His appeal as a provocateur and perpetrator of outrageous pranks was, however, even more marked.

What a Performance!

As well as being a boxer and critic, Arthur Cravan was also available to perform at birthdays, weddings and bar mitzvahs – possibly. At any rate, he certainly liked to put on a good show, advertising 'An Audience With ...' type sessions in Paris' theatres and nightclubs, where the French capital's well-heeled literary types could come along to enjoy an evening of intelligent lectures, demonstrations of modern dance and elegant poetry readings – or, at least, that was what the posters said. In practice, audiences would find themselves being verbally abused by an aggressive drunkard hopping around on one leg and clutching a bottle of absinthe, who would threaten them and, on occasion, fire gunshots over their heads or hurl heavy objects at them while openly praising homosexuals, prostitutes, thieves and madmen. One time, he stepped onstage naked save only for a butcher's apron and, instead of bowing to the attendees as was customary, turned his back, bent over and mooned. Another time, he sold rotten fruit and vegetables outside the entrance for people to pelt him with should they feel the need to do so – which, by all accounts, they did.[35]

Most notorious of all was a 'lecture on art' Cravan had been invited to give at New York's Grand Central Gallery in early 1917 by Marcel Duchamp and his fellow early Dadaist, Francis Picabia. When the time came for Cravan to give his talk, he stumbled onstage drunk, began swearing at the assembled notables and began to strip himself naked, nearly knocking over a valuable picture in the process. The police were called and Cravan ended up being handcuffed and carted off by a group of policemen to spend a night in the cells (though in fact a well-wisher did actually bail him out). 'What an excellent lecture,' said Duchamp, as Cravan was being carried away – as well he might. In fact, Duchamp and Picabia, knowing what Cravan was like, had deliberately plied him with lashings of booze beforehand, anticipating he would cause a scene and thus get their new artistic movement some free column-inches in the press.[36]

Maybe Cravan would have done even more to publicise Dada in America, had he only been given the chance. However, on 6 April 1917, America finally entered into the First World War and, once again, Cravan was forced to flee possible conscription, ending up in Mexico City where, on 25 January 1918, he married his second wife, the English poet Mina Loy, whom he had picked up in New York. Life in Mexico proved hard, however, and Cravan and Loy planned to try their luck in Argentina instead. The couple intended to travel separately, though, seeing as they only had enough money to pay for Loy's journey on a proper passenger ship. In October 1918 Cravan, always eager for adventure, set sail from Salina Cruz out into the treacherous waters of the Gulf of Mexico in a small fishing boat heading for Valparíso in Chile, where it was planned the newly-weds would meet up before heading on to Buenos Aires. He was never seen again.[37]

Life after Death?
Some people have suggested that Cravan's early death at the age of thirty-one was intentional; some kind of 'Dada suicide', the final curtain being pulled down deliberately upon the amazing performance that was his life. Other people, however – including Mina Loy, who thought he was probably languishing in some God-forsaken Mexican prison-cell[38] – have gone one further and suggested that, in fact, Cravan did not die out at sea at all. After all, when it came to faking his own death, Cravan had previous form; he had once hatched the plan of announcing his demise to the newspapers and then having a book published posthumously, in order to garner as much free publicity for it as was possible.[39] While this plan was aborted, upon another occasion Cravan had advertised tickets for people who wanted to see his forthcoming suicide, which he said would take place live on-stage one evening in a Parisian nightclub. When the time came for him to snuff it, however, Cravan simply walked onstage dressed in nothing but his jock-strap – 'for the benefit of the ladies', he said – draped his balls on display across a table and then began remonstrating with his audience, telling them they should be ashamed of themselves for turning up.[40]

If the real-life Fantômas did fake his own death, however, then who did he return disguised as? The simplest answer is – nobody. Realistically, Cravan drowned (or, just possibly, was killed by local pirates).[41] Tales of his survival are probably mere legend. Nonetheless, some refused to let this legend die, one interesting post-death claim being that the pseudonymous Mexican-based novelist 'B Traven', the author of popular adventure-books like *The Treasure of the Sierra Madre*, was simply Cravan in disguise. Certainly, B Traven was not really B Traven; but most authorities now agree that the novelist was in fact the alter-ego of one Ret Maret, an obscure German anarchist and stage actor, who fled Europe for Mexico in around 1924.[42]

More persistent still was the idea that Cravan faked a number of manuscripts supposedly penned by Oscar Wilde and then attempted to sell them under either the entirely false name of 'Dorian Hope' or the merely assumed names of the writers Pierre Loüys – and André Gide. William Figgis, senior director of a Dublin bookshop which traded in literary curiosities, fell for the scam and travelled over to Paris where he actually met 'Dorian Hope'. Hope, said Figgis, was 'a plausible, well-turned out youth of about twenty-five' who turned up for their meeting 'dressed like a Russian Count, with a magnificent fur-lined overcoat' and claimed to be André Gide's personal secretary. However, he was not; when Figgis went to visit Gide seeking further information, an outraged Gide told him he was being duped, and contacted the French police. 'Hope', whoever he really was, fled to London, where he seems to have avoided arrest. But could he really have been Arthur Cravan? The idea was first advanced by the Wildean scholar Owen Dudley Edwards in 1956, and actually had some backup from Wilde's son Vyvyan Holland, who apparently 'always understood that [the forger] was my first cousin Fabian Lloyd'. Certainly, it is easy to imagine Cravan gaining satisfaction from annoying his enemy Gide in this way, but if Hope really was Cravan, then he managed to keep his identity a secret with a suspicious degree of success – although one man who claims to have met Cravan again after this was one Guillot de Saix, another Wilde scholar, who said he found the 'dead' man still busily forging more of his uncle's manuscripts in the backstreets of 1930s Paris.[43] Perhaps, however, this was all simply a case of someone impersonating Arthur Cravan impersonating someone else, in order best to throw people off his trail? Probably the true answer will never be known.

The Wilde Rover
Even more interesting than the idea of Arthur Cravan faking his own death, however, would be the idea of Oscar Wilde having faked his instead – something which, in 1913, Cravan sensationally claimed was in fact the case. Issue three of *Maintenant* carried an arresting headline on its cover, to the effect that 'OSCAR WILDE LIVES!' But did he? According to Cravan, tales of Wilde's death in November 1900 had been greatly exaggerated. Following his release from prison after his trial for gross indecency in 1897, Wilde had sought refuge in France, presenting himself under the pseudonym of 'Sebastian Melmoth', a name partly derived from the title-character of his great-uncle Charles Maturin's 1820 Gothic novel *Melmoth the Wanderer*, who is doomed to wander

the earth in a state of semi-eternal perdition after selling his soul to the Devil. According to Cravan's article, this was not the only way in which his uncle had imitated Melmoth. Finding no refuge from his notoriety, said Cravan, Wilde had pretended to be dead, fled France, and begun wandering through Italy, Greece and Asia, seeking redemption. Cravan knew all this, he said, because, on the night of 23 March 1913, he had opened the door of his flat only to find a most unexpected visitor stood there on the threshold, awaiting admission. At last, Melmoth the Wanderer had returned!

It is not every day that you open your door and find a dead celebrity standing there on the doorstep and, once word about this alleged event got out, it caused a sensation – at least in certain quarters. Literary Parisians, knowing who Cravan was, paid little attention. Across the Atlantic in America, however, Cravan was a complete unknown and was taken at his word, with the *New York Times* sending out a correspondent to check up on these incredible claims. This correspondent, amazingly, fell for the hoax completely. Under the heading 'NO ONE FOUND WHO SAW WILDE DEAD', the *NYT* hack did his best to cook up a mystery where there was none. Saying that he had spent an entire week searching for anyone who had attended Wilde's supposedly faked funeral, the journalist breathlessly wrote that:

> Apparently no one is now in Paris who saw Wilde dead. The doctor, the priest, and the keeper of the hotel where Wilde lived have all disappeared. Even those who attended the funeral service in the Church of Saint Germain de Prés say that they did not see him dead, but merely heard that he was dead and attended the funeral.[44]

The journalist soon commissioned Charles Sibleigh, a translator of poetry and former acquaintance of Wilde's, to seek Cravan out on the newspaper's behalf. When Sibleigh came to call, Cravan must have been delighted, and kept up the whole pretence with a straight face. According to the short-haired poet, Wilde's coffin contained no body, but rather 'a glass jar containing a tragedy and a comedy', two new literary works which were just awaiting someone brave enough to dig them up, an act of sacrilege which Cravan seemed very eager someone should perform immediately; he offered to enter into a $5,000 wager with the French State that, should they exhume Wilde's coffin, Oscar would not be in it. Apparently, Sibleigh found these claims convincing. 'I now almost believe that some day we shall see Wilde back in Paris,' he informed the *NYT* man, upon reporting back from his assignment, and was quoted as such in the newspaper.[45]

The Elephant in the Room

If Charles Sibleigh really did believe this yarn, however, than it can only be presumed that neither he nor the American reporter had actually managed to read the copy of *Maintenant* in question for, if they had, then it would surely have been quite obvious the whole thing was meant as a joke. Cravan's typically mad article begins with him enduring a dark night of the soul in his Parisian garret, thinking all kinds of absurd nonsense to himself: 'I desire a marvellous life of failure', 'I'll eat my money, that will be fun!', 'I thought that science itself had created mammoths', 'Often, I love a pebble', 'My shoes appeared miraculous to me.' Essentially, says Cravan, he was lying fully clothed on his bed in a stupor of seemingly never-ending depression – 'My ennui was frightful.' All of a sudden, however, he was rescued from this frightful malaise by the sound of a bell at his door. Opening it, Cravan comes face to face with 'a huge man' who has 'the magical air of a king or a pigeon'. 'Can your ears hear the unheard?' asked this man, gnomically. Cravan replied that they could. In that case, the pigeon-king had remarkable news to impart: 'I am Sebastian Melmoth.'

If this strange visitor was indeed Oscar Wilde, though, then he didn't really look like him. To Charles Sibleigh, Cravan had tried to present a plausible account of Wilde's changed appearance after nearly fifteen years of wandering; nearly bald, white-bearded and tanned from the foreign climate. In the pages of *Maintenant*, however, while these same basic descriptions were repeated, Wilde nonetheless came across as being a little more unusual in form. For one thing, he had a 'puffy' figure and rotten teeth, littered with gold fillings; 'I noticed that he didn't care about hygiene', commented Cravan, tartly. Even more bizarrely, if you looked at him carefully, then an observant person might be able to notice that Wilde seemed to have magically transformed himself into some kind of elephant:

I began to study him ... In that armchair he seemed like an elephant, his trunk paralleling the shape of the chair ... I adored that he resembled a large beast; I figured he [must] shit like a hippo, and I admired this notion ... He would want to die in the sun ... [In Africa] the flies would make music around [his] mountains of excrement.[46]

In the previous issue of *Maintenant*, we will recall, André Gide had been derided by Cravan for *not* looking like an elephant, so we must presume that this description was actually intended as some kind of compliment. Less complimentary, however, were the insults Cravan claims to have then begun hurling at Wilde after getting drunk; his visitor was a 'next-to-nothing comedian', shouted Cravan, a slug, mere scrapings of horse manure, an 'obese cow' and 'a public urinal filled with piss'. Suddenly suspecting that Wilde may in fact have been his secret father, Cravan soon brings the encounter to a close by telling Wilde that he wants to take him out drinking and then beat him up. Taking the abuse in good spirit – as it was apparently intended – Wilde nonetheless gets up to leave, whereupon Cravan makes a gesture of kicking him. At this point 'the atmosphere became cold' as Melmoth wandered away once more into the dark Parisian night, never to return.[47]

Life Mirrors Art

How on earth should we interpret all this weirdness? Some, like Marcel Duchamp and André Breton, would choose to celebrate it, for reasons already outlined, but others would no doubt prefer to classify Cravan as being much more of a tedious and silly show-off than a proto-Surrealist genius. So, which is he? I think you could make a good argument that he was both at once. In his own words, Cravan once claimed to have

> ... a nature that I could not change without becoming someone else, which, at the same time, always protected me from having proper conduct. It made me sometimes honest, sometimes a cheat, vain and modest, rude as well as distinguished.[48]

With such a quote, we are back, once again, to Cravan's self-professed 'fatal plurality'. Inhabiting, as he did, such a bewildering multiplicity of assumed identities, Cravan appears almost to resemble a mirror more than anything else, a shiny surface, free of any inherent content of its own, which merely reflects images of ourselves back to us whenever we peer into it. If Cravan's life really was a work of art, then this is perhaps the best way to view it. Such a perspective was, no doubt, summed up best of all by Oscar Wilde himself, in the famous 'Preface' to *The Picture of Dorian Gray*, where he used the figure of the hideous man-monster Caliban from Shakespeare's *The Tempest* to sum up the subjective nature of the response to all works of art and literature thus:

The nineteenth-century dislike of Realism is the rage of Caliban seeing his own face in a glass. The nineteenth-century dislike of Romanticism is the rage of Caliban not seeing his own face in a glass.[49]

Or, in other words, whatever it is you think about the life and work of Arthur Cravan – or, indeed, those of Oscar Wilde – probably says more about you than it does about them, in the end. That, I suppose, is just how the mirror of art works.

The Great Offender: Evelyn Waugh (1903–1966)

The literary titan with a pen dipped in acid, who ended up mercilessly parodying even himself.

According to the researches of Dr David Weeks of the Royal Edinburgh Hospital, we may recall, one of the classic telltale signs of eccentricity is the possession of a somewhat extreme sense of humour. If this is so, then the idea of comedy possessed by Evelyn Waugh, one of the twentieth century's greatest writers, qualifies him as having been an eccentric of the first order. Sometimes coming across as P. G. Wodehouse's evil twin, Waugh's brilliant comic novels feature a long parade of jokes about such unsavoury topics as suicide, sexual abuse, murder and dead children, providing a marvellous tonic for those of us who prefer our humour to be as non-PC as possible. But did Waugh sometimes go too far?

Take, for instance, Waugh's incredibly cruel treatment of one of his tutors at Oxford, a blameless (if slightly abrasive) don named C. R. M. F. Cruttwell. The author of such dull but worthy tomes as *The Medieval Administration of the Channel Islands 1199–1399*, it seems safe to say that, were it not for Waugh's intervention, he would by now have been almost entirely forgotten by the world. Thanks to his distinguished student, however, the flame of Cruttwell's fame still burns on a little – although for all the wrong reasons. Going up to Oxford in 1922, the young Waugh clashed with Cruttwell over what the older man saw as being his charge's overly casual attitude towards his studies; a pretty standard kind of undergraduate conflict, you might have thought. Not for Waugh, though, who continued to harbour an undying grudge against his tutor for the rest of his adult life. For one thing, once Waugh had achieved success, he wasted no opportunity to mock his former educator in print. In his 1964 autobiography *A Little Learning*, for instance, Waugh spitefully but expertly skewered Cruttwell as having 'the face of a petulant baby' whose pipe was constantly attached to his horrible 'blubber lips' by a disgusting 'thread of slime.'[1] Just as bad, characters with the name 'Cruttwell' kept on popping up in Waugh's immensely popular comic novels with disarming frequency, beginning with his debut success, 1928's *Decline and Fall*, in which a certain 'Toby Cruttwell', a psychopathic burglar, makes a memorable appearance. A 1935 short story by Waugh concerning the escapades of an escaped mental patient, meanwhile, even saw his arch-enemy achieving the exalted status of title character; it was originally published as *Mr Cruttwell's Little Outing*, though 'Mr Cruttwell' was later discreetly rechristened as 'Mr Loveday'.

All this sounds merely petty – but the way in which Waugh pursued his vendetta against Cruttwell while actually still at Oxford was positively unhinged. His first assaults were made with his favourite weapon, the pen, with an August 1923 edition of *Cherwell*, the university newspaper, carrying a story of Waugh's called *Edward of Unique Achievement*, in which a history student named Edward brutally murders his tutor, a 'Mr Curtis', clearly a fantasy which Waugh had been enacting in his head for some time now. The fact that Cruttwell was easily identifiable as being the murder victim was made even worse by the fact that this character was openly accused in print of engaging in 'the most monstrous' acts of sexual deviancy. Worse, Waugh began to transfer his campaign from off the page and out into the real world; together with a friend, he helped spread the false rumour that Cruttwell enjoyed raping dogs, even going so far as to buy a stuffed canine and leave it outside his tutor's room in the quadrangle, then beginning a craze of going around and barking beneath his opponent's window to humiliate him.[2] Allegedly, Waugh even managed to persuade the female representative of a local animal charity to stand during an election upon the sole platform of preventing Cruttwell from secretly abusing animals in his rooms.[3] Eventually, Cruttwell ended up having a nervous breakdown, and died in a mental institution in 1941 aged only fifty-three – and it has been argued that Waugh's persecution of the poor man may have helped to hasten his decline.

Runcible Goons

Now, it could be argued that this is all rather funny – but, whatever it may be, it is most assuredly *not* normal! Cruttwell was not the only person to find himself being publicly ridiculed in Waugh's novels, however. Indeed, so notorious did these disguised pen portraits become that, in 1930, Waugh actually went so far as to publish a deeply disingenuous article in the *Daily Mail*, entitled *People Who Want to Sue Me*. Here, he made reference to the character of Agatha Runcible – 'a young lady of crazy and rather dissolute habits' – who had recently appeared in his book *Vile Bodies*, a cutting satire of the 'Bright Young Things' of 1920s London High Society. Runcible, quite clearly, was a comic amalgamation of several real-life females from the London party scene of the time. Waugh nevertheless denied that she resembled anybody real at all, feigning confusion about why anyone should say otherwise:

> No one, I should have thought, would see herself in that character without shame. But nearly all the young women of my acquaintance ... claim with apparent gratitude and pride that they were the originals of that sordid character.[4]

Waugh was teasing his readers here. He knew perfectly well that one of the reasons his books sold so well was that people thought the upper-class eccentrics portrayed in them were coded representatives of the real moneyed classes, public guyings whose tone veered wildly between the indulgently affectionate and the outright vindictive. Waugh almost seems to acknowledge this fact at one point in *Vile Bodies* itself when he has a character pen a gossip column for the *Daily Excess* newspaper under the name of 'Mr Chatterbox', in which he exposes the invented foibles of various anonymous mentally ill aristocrats who dress up like Napoleon, make animal noises and claim to have authored the Ten Commandments, a parody of real-life gossip columns of the time which featured similar titillating Society titbits of dubious provenance.[5]

Unlike fraudulent gossip-columnists, though, Waugh had no such need to create all of his characters from scratch. Born in 1903 into a deeply literary family (his father worked for Chapman & Hall, who published Waugh's first novels, and his elder brother Alec was already a novelist of some repute), Waugh was handed an open entrance to the world of the aristocracy by being sent away to public school. He was not actually upper-class himself, but by attending such august institutions as Heath Mount preparatory school and, later, Lancing College, he could certainly mix with some of the children of the upper echelons. Even during his schooldays, it was obvious that Waugh had a flair for writing – and a morbid sense of humour. While at Lancing, for instance, he founded his own society called the 'Corpse Club', whose membership was reserved for those other listless youths who, like him, were already 'weary of life'.[6] Affected teenage avowals of boredom and disillusionment with the world are no mere modern phenomenon, clearly.

Brideshead Reconstituted

The path of Waugh into a position of intimacy with his social betters was already becoming clear; while he may have only been middle class, he was nonetheless 'amusing', and the presence of the boy from Golders Green among the genuinely posh boys at Lancing and Oxford was no doubt tolerated upon this basis. One such aristocratic friend (and probable lover) he made at Oxford was Hugh Lygon, a somewhat ethereal youth whose family pile was Madresfield in Worcestershire. Here, Hugh lived a life of almost unimaginable luxury; the Lygons had a private railway which connected their three houses, thus allowing themselves to shuttle between them without having to share the compartments with any riff-raff. Such were the Lygons' riches that even their footmen were rumoured to have their fingers covered in diamonds as part of their livery. An even odder rumour about the footmen, meanwhile, was that the head of the Lygon family, Earl Beauchamp, used to squeeze their buttocks and feel them up as an essential part of their job interviews. This final rumour, however, happened to be true; in spite of his being married, Earl Beauchamp was nonetheless a predatory homosexual, and whenever his children happened to bring handsome young male friends home, they were advised to lock their doors at night if they didn't want to wake up and find their own buttocks being subjected to a hands-on personal interview, too.

Perhaps due to the humiliation occasioned by this whole embarrassing situation, the Earl's wife Lettice adopted a style of parenting which could best be described as 'harsh'. Upon one occasion, for instance, annoyed by one of her daughters' complaints about getting stung by a jellyfish at the beach, she gathered up a whole bucketful of the creatures and started pelting them at her in order to demonstrate what *real* pain felt like. Maybe the Countess acted this way to get back at her husband, who genuinely adored his offspring (and their young friends' taut posteriors). Eventually, however, Earl Beauchamp ended up fleeing the country to exile abroad after his wife's brother, the Duke of Westminster, exposed his then illegal homosexual activities to the public. 'Dear Bugger-in-Law, You got what you deserved. Yours, Westminster' his enemy later wrote to him, with vindictive delight. [7]

With things like this going on there all the time, it was no wonder that Madresfield acquired the nickname 'Mad' among the children of the family. It was also no wonder that Waugh later ended up immortalising the Lygon family as the eccentric Flyte clan in his 1945 novel *Brideshead Revisited*, 'Brideshead' in fact being a disguised version of Madresfield itself. Waugh may well have included the short note 'I am not I: thou art not he or she, they are not they' at the front of the book, but it is not hard to feel that he might have been protesting too much here. The Flytes were obviously the Lygons – but a wildly exaggerated reinvention of them, their basic personalities mixed up confusingly with those of other well-bred types Waugh had known from Oxford and elsewhere.

Strange Bedfellows

Some other of Waugh's aristocratic acquaintances, however, were quite simply beyond any possible exaggeration whatsoever, most notably the incredible Gerald Hugh Tyrwhitt-Wilson (1883–1950), generally known to students of the well-bred weird as Lord Berners. A talented writer and composer of some note, Berners made his home at Faringdon House in Oxfordshire, and had shown signs of strangeness from an early age; as a child, he had once thrown his mother's pet dog out of the window in a vain attempt to teach it to fly, for example, a test it apparently failed miserably. As an adult, Berners transformed Faringdon into his own personal playground. Famously, he had the feathers of the estate's pigeons dyed bright pastel colours so as to correspond with the hue of his main meal that day, had fake paper flowers planted in the gardens, and displayed various bizarre signs around the place – open up a wardrobe, for instance, and you might find the phrase 'Prepare to meet thy God' painted on the inside of the door, while stray animals were warned off by signs stating that any trespassing cats would be 'whipped' and dogs would be 'shot' (or possibly tossed out of a window instead). His most legendary notice was placed upon a 104-foot viewing tower he had constructed in the grounds, called 'Faringdon Folly'; 'Members of the public committing suicide from this tower do so at their own risk', it cautioned.

Playing silly pranks involving animals were a particular favourite of Berners; he entertained the horse of Penelope Betjemen (daughter of the effete poet John Betjemen, whose teddy bear-carrying habits while at Oxford were also parodied by Waugh in *Brideshead Revisited*) to tea in his dining room, and put cheap Woolworth's pearl necklaces made from pasteboard around his dogs' necks as collars, claiming to visitors that they were the real thing. Berners also liked to travel in style – his own style. He would drive around his estate wearing a pig's-head mask in order to disturb the locals, and, for those occasions when he preferred a chauffeur to take the wheel, had his Rolls Royce fitted with a small clavichord which could be installed in the back seat, allowing him to provide his own music in an era before car radios. When forced to use public transport, meanwhile, Berners would go to great lengths to secure a train compartment for himself. Getting into empty carriages first, he would don a black skullcap and dark sunglasses before leaning out of the window and beckoning sinisterly to strangers on the platform, exhorting them to come and join him for some fun and games on the journey. Those few fools who took him up on the offer were then often treated to Berners producing an absurdly large rectal thermometer and constantly shoving it into his mouth while pulling anguished faces, implying to his fellow passengers that he was dying from some highly contagious tropical disease or other. Needless to say, he usually travelled alone.[8]

If Berners' eccentricity started young, though, then so did something else – namely, his flamboyant homosexuality. At the age of nine, Berners had his first gay experience, with a fellow pupil at Cheam boarding school. It was not successful; Berners ended up vomiting on the poor lad. By 1931, however, Berners had found the love (or lust) of his life – the aptly named 'Mad Boy', or Robert Heber-Percy (1911–1987), according to his birth certificate. Mad Boy was appropriately named; although he did, amazingly, once manage to ride a horse in the Grand National, his main claim to fame was having urinated out of a window onto his headmaster while boarding at Stowe. After meeting Berners, the bisexual Mad Boy was soon installed at Faringdon as 'Estate Manager', whose main duties appeared to take place largely within the bedroom of his boss, who was almost thirty years his senior. Whatever the complexities of this arrangement, it seemed to make Berners happy enough; after all, if a person's presence in his home wasn't welcome, he would soon let them know it by getting down on all fours, donning a lion-skin rug and crawling around in cat form to avoid having to talk to them.[9] This man, incidentally, at one point held a high-ranking position in Britain's Embassy to Rome.

Lord Berners was also, though, an acquaintance through marriage of Evelyn Waugh; Waugh's first wife Evelyn Gardner ('She-Evelyn' to their friends) was the sister of one Alathea Gardner, who later gave birth to Jennifer Fry, Mad Boy's first wife, who lived together at Faringdon with her husband and his lover in some bizarre kind of threesome-type arrangement. This first marriage of Mad Boy's having ended in predictable failure, he then later married the seventy-year-old Dorothy Lygon in 1985, one of Waugh's old pals from Madresfield/Brideshead. While this latter marriage occurred nearly two decades after Waugh's own death, Jennifer Fry's marriage to Lord Berners' toy boy took place in 1943, and Evelyn Waugh did attend Faringdon for dinners, thereby coming to know its occupants. Surprisingly, Waugh didn't seem to make use of either Lord Berners or Mad Boy in any of his fictions, though – perhaps he just thought that nobody would believe it! Waugh's good friend Nancy Mitford, however, did paint an amusingly camp portrait of Berners in her 1945 novel *The Pursuit of Love*, under the false but somehow appropriate name of 'Lord Merlin', so maybe he was just leaving the pleasure free for her.

At Waugh with the World

Of course, merely *knowing* lots of eccentrics doesn't necessarily make you into an eccentric yourself. With Waugh, however, it can sometimes seem as if his proximity to such amiable maniacs eventually ended rubbing off on his own character – albeit in a rather less cheery fashion. Following the end of the Second World War, Waugh became somewhat disillusioned with life. He hated the new 'welfare state culture' which he saw as having been introduced by Clement Attlee's Labour Government of 1945, a development he deplored as being a fundamental assault upon what it meant to be English. In a 1959 article for the *Daily Mail*, 'I See Nothing But Boredom ... Everywhere', in which he claimed to see 'nothing objectionable' in the idea of nuclear holocaust, Waugh explained his thinking thus:

> It may be a good thing or a bad thing to be classless; [but] it is certainly un-British. The most dismal tendency I see is that [together] with our class-system we are fast losing all national character ... [something which] depended for its strength and humour and achievements on variety; variety between one town and another, one county and another; one man different from

another in the same village in knowledge, habits, opinions ... I see nothing ahead but drab uniformity.[10]

Waugh almost began to sound like John Stuart Mill. 'Equality', he thought, was merely a lying synonym for 'mediocrity'. With the dawning of a classless society, there would be no more mad Lord Berners or Earl Beauchamps to brighten up our national life and lend it its customary vigour; together with identical glasses and dentures, identical personalities seemed to be being handed out to people free of charge on the NHS, too. Increasingly, he began making outrageously misanthropic comments. At dinner one evening with Sir William Beveridge, the main architect behind Labour's welfare state, for instance, Waugh asked his fellow diner how he got his main satisfaction in life. 'By trying to leave the world a better place than I found it,' he answered, earnestly. Waugh was unimpressed. 'I get mine from spreading alarm and despondency,' he shot back. 'And I get more satisfaction than you do.'[11]

Given a country house of his own as a wedding present by the bride's grandparents after marrying his second wife Laura in 1937, Waugh clearly felt free to retreat from the world and adopt the public role of faux-aristocratic eccentric himself. Safe in his new Gloucestershire home of Piers Court, and, later, at an equally pleasant manor house in the Somerset village of Combe Florey, Waugh played a strange role in public life from the 1950s onwards, emerging periodically to make increasingly rude and reactionary-sounding statements in magazines and newspapers, and playing a kind of half-real, half-parodic version of himself to the public gallery. Because of this, he gained something of a reputation as being an anachronistic Edwardian Tory relic. In fact, however, his son Auberon wrote after Waugh's death in 1966, Waugh took 'no interest' whatsoever in the subject of politics other than to ridicule it, and, while he did indeed develop a High Tory 'romantic attachment to the aristocratic ideal' and a genuine distaste for socialism, perhaps what attracted him to this way of thinking the most was simply his realisation of how much his opinions annoyed people. [12] Just as, say, Sebastian Flyte in *Brideshead Revisited* was not literally Hugh Lygon, but a blown-up, larger-than-life version of him, so 'Evelyn Waugh' the well-known public commentator and ultra-Tory Squire, was not literally the private Evelyn Waugh, but a comic cartoon pastiche of him. The trouble was that not everybody got the joke.

Radio Daze

In late 1953, for example, some sarcastic young men from the BBC took advantage of Waugh being short of money to trick him into agreeing to do some radio interviews in which they mocked the alleged old fossil by asking him deliberately insulting questions such as 'In what respect do you, as a human being, feel that you have primarily failed?' and enquiring about whether or not he would like to personally hang somebody. Wearily, Waugh decided to mock his interviewers back by giving answers in character, as it were, replying to the question 'Do you find it easy to get on with the man in the street?' with the phrase 'I've never met such a person', and, when asked what moral failings he could most forgive in others, responding with 'Drunkenness – Anger. Lust. Dishonouring their father and mother. Coveting their neighbour's ox, ass, wife. Killing.'[13]

Depressed by these encounters, and having been taking increasingly large amounts of alcohol and prescription drugs into his system for some time now in order to combat his insomnia and rheumatism, early in 1954 Waugh's doctors advised he take a holiday, so he booked himself in on a cruise liner headed for the tropics. Unfortunately, the cocktail of substances he was taking reacted badly with one another, and Waugh ended up with bromide poisoning, something which led him to suffer auditory hallucinations and paranoid sensations of persecution. Convinced that the passengers and crew were out to get him, and that an unholy alliance of existentialists, rogue psychologists and telepathic men from the BBC were broadcasting insults about him and his waning powers over the ship's radio, Waugh essentially went temporarily insane. The alarm was raised when his wife Laura began receiving letters from her husband containing sentences like 'It is rather difficult to write to you because everything I say or think or read is [then] read aloud by the group of psychologists ... the artful creatures can communicate from many hundreds of miles away.'[14] Given the nature and partial cause of Waugh's persecution-complex here, it's only a wonder that he didn't hear C. R. M. F. Cruttwell laughing at him from beyond the grave as well; at least the BBC telepaths didn't claim he was molesting any dogs.

And Waugh's ultimate response to, as he later put it, having gone 'clean off my onion'?[15] Typically, he thought it was funny, and even produced a novel ridiculing the whole affair, 1957's *The Ordeal of Gilbert Pinfold*, his final comic masterpiece. The tale of a successful novelist going completely off his rocker during a pleasure cruise, it might as well have been labelled 'autobiography' rather than 'fiction'. Clearly, the greatest character Evelyn Waugh ever invented was Evelyn Waugh himself.

A Great Family Tradition

After Waugh's unfortunate death while visiting his toilet in 1966, he continued offending others from beyond the grave, with his mordant diary entries being serialised in *The Observer* in 1973, some of which were apparently so shocking that his son Auberon Waugh (1939–2001) claimed to have written a 'fine pompous letter' to the editor on behalf of the entire Waugh family, saying 'how shocked we all were that a respectable newspaper like *The Observer* should publish such filth.' The editor, seemingly not understanding that this was meant to be a joke, allegedly wrote back expressing his puzzlement at the complaint, on the grounds that it was Auberon and his family who had sold the paper the extracts in the first place.[16]

As this curious correspondence implies, welfare state-led mediocrity did not, after all, mean that eccentricity in outlook vanished entirely from these islands with Evelyn Waugh's death. Auberon himself wrote much more than mere letters to *The Observer*, for instance, as people who used to read his marvellously offensive columns in publications like *The Daily Telegraph*, *The Spectator* and *Private Eye* will surely recall. Always happy to cause affront, since Auberon's death in 2001 entire web pages devoted to reprinting the quotes of the man have sprung up online, where fans can retreat to read his common-sense appeals *in favour* of drink-driving, his theories about Nelson Mandela secretly being Chinese, his abuse of the shockingly 'deformed heads' of London cab drivers, and his sensible statements about the splendid 'spectacle of the homeless' being 'necessary to keep the rest of us on the straight and narrow.'[17]

Most infamously, Auberon once made a joke in *The Times* about the comical appearance of certain Muslims' trousers which led to the British Council library in Rawalpindi being burnt down by an outraged mob; he later described the riot as 'the greatest moment of my journalistic career', and declared himself 'naturally proud to have caused such devastation.'[18] Even his father's antics with C. R. M. F. Cruttwell were uncannily echoed in Auberon's 1979 decision to stand for Parliament representing an invented organisation named 'The Dog-Lovers' Party' in an attempt to embarrass the Liberal leader Jeremy Thorpe, whom he had recently accused of having caused someone's pet dog to be shot in the head by an inept hitman.[19] Auberon returned to this self-created political platform from time to time, using it to make various absurd canine-related points, such as his 1987 decree applauding 'the salutary effects of dog mess on the streets of London and our other great cities' on the twin grounds that it 'provides a form of sustenance to urban toddlers which is free and non-fattening' and that the annoyance felt by people when they step in it is 'surely good for their souls' as it 'teaches them humility and an awareness of the fragility of social institutions.'[20]

Perhaps most of Evelyn Waugh's descendents have not yet displayed such commendable levels of public-spirited bile, but there may still be hope; a recent BBC documentary about the Waughs ended with some heartening footage of Auberon's son Alexander proudly watching his own small son disrespecting the grave of Evelyn's hated grandfather in a show of open abuse.[21] I have great expectations of that boy – and so should we all.

Barmy Army: Military Eccentrics

The military madmen who heroically kept this country safe from everyone bar themselves.

You would have thought that, in Britain's Armed Forces, there would be little room for eccentricity; a life dominated by routine, taking orders and myriad petty rules and regulations would seem more than enough to iron out the quirks from even the most ardent of civvy-street nonconformists. However, it is not necessarily so. After all, a wholly excessive love of discipline could in itself be considered a form of peculiarity. Take, for instance, Queen Victoria's father, Edward, Duke of Kent (1767–1820), who was so obsessed with having his men whipped for even the most minor of misdemeanours that he became known as 'The Flogging Duke'. What was particularly eccentric about the Duke's fondness for handing out such cruel and unusual punishments, however, is that he did so largely on account of the fact that he found seeing men be whipped in front of him highly sexually exciting, to the extent that he actually wet himself in pleasure – or, at least, this was how some chose to explain his foibles. Supposedly, a direct correlation thus existed between the Duke's monthly laundry bill and how much he had been enjoying himself lately.[1] Equally bizarre was the tyrannical reign of toilet-based terror instigated by one Admiral Algernon Charles Fieschi Heneage (1833–1915) upon the Royal Navy vessels on which he sailed. The white-gloved and hygiene-obsessed Heneage, known as 'Pompo' to his men, would insist upon inspecting the latrines of officers serving under him after they had used them. If any trace of brown stuff (or anything else, for that matter) remained stubbornly stuck down there, sullying the bowl or the rim, it could have genuine repercussions for that man's future career. [2]

As these cases may suggest, while eccentricity among the rank-and-file was certainly not to be encouraged, once a person had reached officer rank their foibles would be more likely to be indulged. Consider, for example, the bizarre behaviour of Major-General Sir Robert William Norris 'Loony' Hinde (1900–1981), a polo player who graduated from winning silver for Great Britain at Hitler's 1936 Berlin Olympics to later doing his country proud in another important competitive arena: the Second World War. Hinde's military career was every bit as distinguished as his sporting one, but it was for an extraordinary incident during the battle of Villiers-Bocage, following the D-Day landings, that he is best remembered. In the middle of fierce fighting, the insect-collecting Hinde, then a Brigadier, suddenly stopped an important combat briefing with his men when he spotted what he believed to be a rare breed of French caterpillar crawling across the battlefield. 'Anyone got a matchbox?' he demanded to know, in a state of acute excitement, putting all thought of liberating Europe aside for a moment. Surprised, one Lieutenant Colonel Michael Carver pointed out that this was hardly the time to be collecting specimens. This short-sighted response threw Hinde into an uncontrollable fury. 'Don't be such a bloody fool, Mike!' he shouted, angrily. 'You can fight a battle every day of your life, but you might not see a caterpillar like that in fifteen years!'[3]

There were a number of equally strange British NCOs who helped us defeat Nazism, such as the undoubtedly brave Major Angus McCorquodale (1906–1940), who gave his life to keep both Britain free and his uniform neat and tidy. Proud to call himself an 'old-fashioned soldier', McCorquodale despised the new modern uniforms he was forced to wear, and made a few discreet modifications of his own to his kit – including an utterly useless fake helmet made out of papier-mâché, as he felt his standard issue metal one was a bit uncomfortable. He also insisted upon wearing his own favourite green socks and brown shoes on the battlefield, reasoning that 'I don't mind dying for my country, but I'm not going to die dressed like a third-rate chauffeur.' There were, after all, standards to uphold – even in the midst of Hitler's blitzkrieg. One time, after his men had successfully scuppered a German infantry advance, he amazed them by pulling out some vintage sherry, handing out glasses and proposing a toast to 'a very gallant and competent enemy.' Competent or not, however, the Germans ultimately proved less than gallant towards their generous and well-dressed foe – they killed him in action in 1940.[4]

The most influential high-ranking military eccentric of the Second World War, however, was Major-General Orde Wingate (1903–1944), founder of the Chindits, special troops who fought the Japanese behind their own lines in Burma, and one of the fathers of guerrilla warfare. He was also, though, the very model of a mental Major-General – as you could tell immediately just by looking at him. Wingate habitually wore a large oversized pith helmet like a cartoon explorer, and hung raw onions and garlic on a string around his neck, periodically biting into them to bolster his health against the tropical climate and hoping to ward off mosquitoes with the smell of his breath. Another of his health fads, meanwhile, was to strain his tea through his own socks, aiming to weed out impurities. Close observers might also notice that he often wore an alarm clock strapped around his wrist, which he wound up prior to meetings – as soon as the bell rang, that was it, the assembly was over and he was off, even if a colleague was in mid-sentence. Perhaps Wingate was simply fed up wasting time with people asking him why he didn't have any clothes on; he would habitually appear naked in front of his troops and officials, sometimes emerging from the shower in nothing but a bathing cap to issue new orders while washing himself down with a scrubbing brush, or conducting debriefings lying nude across his bed and combing his body hair with a toothbrush. Raised by highly religious parents, Wingate had occasional suicidal thoughts (he stabbed himself in the neck in despair in 1941), which he tried to ward off by endlessly repeating the words 'God is good! God is good!' to himself, over and over again, until the impulse passed. Evidently God wasn't that good to him, however, as he died in a plane crash in 1944.[5]

Arguably Britain's strangest individual combatant of the war against Hitler was John 'Mad Jack' Churchill (1906–1996), a career soldier whose unusual conduct while serving in the Manchester Regiment from 1926 was not overly designed to endear himself to his superiors. There was the time, for instance, that he turned out for parade duty carrying an umbrella. When asked by an appalled officer why on earth he was holding such a thing, he calmly (but logically) replied, 'Because it's raining, sir.' The military during peacetime was not a happy place for Mad Jack, and in 1936, bored by lack of action, he resigned his commission, embarking instead upon a varied career as a male model and minor actor.

During a spell serving abroad, Churchill had learned to play the bag-pipes from a Cameron Highlander, a skill in which he grew proficient enough to land a role in the movie *The Drum*, where he played a piping Scottish soldier, despite the fact that he himself was unmistakably English. Another skill he developed during his time out of khaki was archery, a discipline in which he represented Britain at 1939's Oslo World Championships.

By the time war broke out in September 1939, however, Churchill was ready once more to serve his country, and returned to uniform in time to see action in France during 1940, where he led his men into battle wielding a large claymore on the grounds that, as he had it, 'any officer who goes into action without his sword is improperly dressed.' Churchill also took his longbow with him to France; in May 1940, he famously gave the signal for his men to attack a German unit near the village of L'Épinette by taking the enemy sergeant out with a well-aimed barbed arrow. Another time, while on patrol, he killed two Nazis hiding in a bush – scoring a perfect pair of bullseyes with only two darts. This may all have seemed rather pointless, but it seems that Mad Jack's exploits were actually good for morale; the sight of this extraordinary figure on the rampage was described as 'one of the most reassuring sights' of the conflict in his brigade's official war diary.

Clearly this was a courageous man, and so, when the first commando units were being formed in 1940, Churchill was taken off to Scotland on training exercises without hesitation. In December 1941, Mad Jack undertook his first commando mission, an assault on the German garrison at Vaagso in Norway, where he stood at the front of the landing craft piping a tune before leaping onshore waving his claymore around and screaming blue murder. The assault succeeded, as did an astonishing exploit during the Allied landings in Italy in 1943, which even Mad Jack himself had to admit was 'a bit Errol Flynn-ish'. Surprising two German sentries by appearing from nowhere in the moonlight brandishing a sword and yelling 'Hands up!', Churchill used one Nazi as a hostage and walked around from sentry post to sentry post, forcing his prisoner to speak up and use his familiar voice to ensure free entry, before pointing his sword at the men inside and gaining their surrender, too. In this way, Churchill and a single colleague managed to capture an amazing forty-two German troops, who were taken back behind Allied lines as prisoners. Less successful was an assault on a Yugoslav hilltop in May 1944 when, with all his men either killed or injured, Churchill stood his ground and began defiantly piping away until eventually he was knocked out by a German hand grenade. Awaking in captivity, Mad Jack wasted little time in writing to the German officer in charge, inviting him to have a meal with him and his wife in Britain once the war was over, even giving him his telephone number. Being wrongly considered a relative of Winston Churchill, Mad Jack was chained to the floor in a concentration camp before being transferred to a POW camp in Austria, from which he escaped, crossing over into Italy where he was disappointed to find that the Americans were doing rather well. 'You know,' he once told a friend, wistfully, 'if it hadn't have been for those damned Yanks, we could have kept the war going for another ten years!'

Peace in Europe was an intense disappointment for Churchill, and in 1946 he took a break from the military to play an archer in a Hollywood adaptation of *Ivanhoe*, but was soon putting his life on the line for Britain once again, this time in Palestine. Here, he adopted the risky tactic of attempting to solve violence between Arab and Jew by intervening in potential conflict situations dressed as a comedy Scotsman in kilt, bonnet, red-and-white diced knee-length stockings and white spats, and grinning at terrorists and rebels like a madman, his somewhat hopeful reasoning being that 'people are less likely to shoot at you if you smile at them'. Peace in the Middle East did not ensue, however, and in later life Mad Jack was posted back home to Blighty, where he designed his own surfboard and rode it on the River Severn, before eventually taking up a desk job at the MoD. Finding this role something of an anticlimax, Churchill enlivened his commute home each evening by opening the window of his train carriage and throwing his briefcase out into a back garden by the side of the tracks. His fellow passengers never discovered that the garden was in fact his own, and this was just the way he liked it; obviously, he wanted to continue being thought of as 'Mad Jack' right to the very end.[6]

How to keep the adrenaline flowing following retirement from active service has posed quite a problem for many other ex-soldiers down the years, too. One solution, tried by Colonel Thomas Thornton (1757–1823), former leader of Yorkshire's West Riding Militia, was to take up sporting pursuits. His 1804 account of his hunting exploits, *A Sporting Tour through the Northern Parts of England and a Great Part of the Highlands of Scotland*, was dismissed as incredibly boring by Sir Walter Scott in *The Edinburgh Review*, however, so Colonel Thornton thought he might get a wider audience for tales of his post-militia adventures by shamelessly making them up. Hence, when the conversation among his friends turned to the topic of shooting one day, he explained how he had invented a new method of bagging game with a ramrod (the thin metal stick people used to shove down the barrels of old guns to ram in the gunpowder). By using one of these as a bullet, Thornton explained, he had once killed 'four partridges and a brace of pheasants' with a single shot, his unlikely missile skewering them all through at the same time like some giant feathered kebab.

It was blatantly obvious that Thornton's yarns were falser than those of Baron Münchausen, but that only added to their appeal. Thus, when an acquaintance observed that a man they had both seen fall off his horse would surely be left with a 'broken head', the Colonel scoffed. He himself, he claimed, had once endured a far worse injury, falling from his steed onto a scythe. According to Thornton, he was 'the only man in Europe' to whom this calamity had ever happened, the scythe causing his head to literally split in two right down the middle, each half drooping down over either shoulder 'like a pair of epaulettes'. '*That* was a broken head, if you please, sir!' he exclaimed, turning purple. Clearly, everything someone else had done, Colonel Thornton had done it better. Talk turning to criminal matters one day, Thornton immediately boasted that 'I have been arrested oftener than anyone in England!' When pressed for details, he made up some cock and bull story about being accosted in bed one morning in a lodging house by a fiendish bailiff armed with a red-hot poker who shoved it in under the sheets to make him come quietly. Naturally, Mrs Thornton, being a mere female and thus 'womanlike, as all women', leapt out of bed immediately, but her husband, furious at the man's impertinent conduct, claimed to have remained lying still, enduring the poker's searing thrusts with contemptuous ease, until he observed that the sheets had caught fire. *He* could stand the pain, of course, but if the flames should spread then his fellow lodgers might burn to death, and that would be discourteous. Hence, he gave in, got up and submitted to arrest.

Even while dying, Colonel Thornton could not resist pointlessly embellishing his sufferings by claiming that some miscreant had entered his room during the night and scattered the floor full of sharp pins pointing upwards. Getting out of bed that morning, he said, these objects had immediately stuck into him, causing him, as he rolled around on the floor in agony, to resemble a human hedgehog. So desperate was he for attention that, whenever someone else in his company was the centre of conversation, he would suddenly shout out that everyone was invited to dinner at his place the following evening – invitations which were invariably rescinded the next day, followed by some ridiculous excuse. Drink, it has to be said, may have played a role in all this boasting, but a stranger would still have to be careful about dismissing *all* of Thornton's tales as rank untruths; if, for example, he tried to tell you that his wife was a champion jockey, that he had met Napoleon, or that he had invented a special shotgun with twelve barrels for shooting multiple targets at once with, then he would actually have been speaking the truth![7]

One person who took to civvy-street even more poorly than Colonel Thornton, meanwhile, was Major Peter Labellière (1725–1800), an Anglo-Irish soldier who retired to Dorking in Surrey sometime around 1789 to live off a pension. Perhaps army life had not wholly suited Labellière, however, as by the 1770s he had become a pacifist agitator, urging British troops not to fight against America during the War of Independence. Nowadays, though, the Major is best known on account of a gravestone which stands on the slopes of the noted Surrey beauty spot of Box Hill, whose inscription reads, 'AN ECCENTRIC RESIDENT OF DORKING WAS BURIED HERE HEAD DOWNWARDS, JULY 1800.' This 'eccentric resident' was, of course, the Major and, naturally, such an absurd claim is a complete myth – he was actually buried upside down on Box Hill in *June* 1800, not July.

As his epitaph suggests, during old age Major Labellière became rather odd, neglecting his appearance to such an extent that he earned the soubriquet of 'The Walking Dung-Hill', and keeping a bizarre personal diary, the 'Book of Devotions', which he filled up with strange symbols and reminders for himself to sing a secret anthem of his own creation on certain special days of the year. Still maintaining his political interests, he penned various pamphlets and supposedly once wrote a letter to the king signed in his own blood, asking for the release of some prisoners. A religious man, he practised Christian charity by giving away his own coat and shoes to any beggars he chanced to meet while walking or meditating on his beloved Box Hill, which he saw as being the most beautiful glory of Creation. This love for Box Hill was made all the more remarkable by the fact that, losing his way on it one night during a thunderstorm, he fell straight onto a sharp branch which gouged one of his eyes out. With semi-blindness, though, reputedly came the power of prophecy; apparently, he successfully

predicted the date of his own death in June 1800 (or maybe he had
it down for July 1800, given the mistake on his tombstone?). As
well as requesting that he be buried upside down, Labellière also
asked that, prior to burial, his landlady's children should dance
on his coffin, although only one of them agreed to do so. Perhaps
some of these tales are just myths created in light of Labellière's
weird gravestone, but he does genuinely appear to have been
interred in the ground head first, for reasons unknown. Some
say it was because he thought the world had gone topsy-turvy,
others that he wished in death to imitate the Apostle Peter, who
had been crucified upside down by the Romans. Maybe he didn't
want us to know the truth; Labellière had once solemnly handed
across to a friend a sealed package, with strict instructions not
to open it until his death. Following his demise, the parcel was
quickly unwrapped, and found to contain a notebook ... which
was completely empty.[8]

Conclusive proof that strangeness can be a distinct military asset,
meanwhile, can be found in the life story of Lieutenant Commander
Geoffrey Basil Spicer-Simson (1876–1947), a lifelong Royal Navy
man and scourge of the Kaiser's East African fleet during the First
World War. After joining the Navy aged fourteen, Spicer-Simson
quickly rose up through the ranks and then, just as suddenly,
stopped, stuck for years as a Lieutenant Commander. The top
brass's reluctance to promote him any further was understandable,
given his demonstrable incompetence. There was the time, for
instance, he had nearly sunk a British submarine during a training
exercise, the day he had driven his ship straight onto a beach,
and the occasion he had crashed his destroyer into another naval
vessel, killing a sailor. Just as bad were Spicer-Simson's wilfully
bizarre appearance and manners. Heavily tattooed across his arms
and chest with elaborate images of butterflies and snakes, Spicer-
Simson liked to show these markings off to anyone who wanted to
see them – and to those who didn't. An inveterate show-off who
smoked his own specially made monogrammed cigars, he was
always telling strange but obvious lies and unfunny jokes, claiming
to be an authority on subjects he knew nothing about, even in the
presence of genuine experts, and suddenly bursting into off-key
song at inappropriate moments. By all accounts, he was a deeply
irritating man.

Kept out of the way in a tiny office in Whitehall, Spicer-Simson
looked set for a quiet war, until in 1915 a big-game hunter named
John Lee arrived at the Admiralty with an unlikely plan for taking

out a German mini-fleet patrolling Lake Tanganyika, in what was then German East Africa. The arena of war was an obscure and unimportant one, but that was exactly the point. 'It is both the duty and the tradition of the Royal Navy to engage the enemy wherever there is water to float a ship,' Spicer-Simson was told, but in reality he was being ushered as far away from the corridors of power as was possible. John Lee's plan was doubtful to succeed, at best. Britain's best ships being needed elsewhere, Lee suggested the Admiralty get hold of two small wooden yacht-like vessels, attach a motor and a cannon to each one, and use them as fast gunboats to take on the German flotilla. Then, these boats would be shipped across to Africa and dragged through jungles, over plains and up hills by oxen, before being dropped into the lake to surprise the Germans. This plan certainly did surprise the Germans – when they first saw this pathetic wooden fighting force through their binoculars from the bridge of their massive 220-foot flagship, the *Graf von Götzen*, they fell about laughing. It was Spicer-Simson, however, who would have the last laugh.

The disadvantages Spicer-Simson faced were considerable, and often of his own making. For example, despite the fact his semaphore skills were rusty he still insisted upon waving the flags about himself, spelling out complete nonsense to his men, who thought he was having a fit. Worse, to maintain an appearance of calm during battle, he gave orders with a cigarette holder clenched firmly between his teeth while constantly waving a fly swatter around, with the result that nobody could understand a word he was saying. His men, too, were hardly the cream of the Royal Navy, including, as they did, a former racing driver who didn't understand how an engine worked despite being the expedition's Chief Engineer, a pair of semi-mute, kilt-wearing Scotsmen, and a playboy known as 'Piccadilly Johnny' who sported dyed yellow hair and a monocle and was so addicted to Worcester sauce that he insisted the mission take along two full boxes of the stuff so he could drink some neat before each meal. Nonetheless, Spicer-Simson was proud of his ragtag army, and sewed himself a fake Admiral's flag to fly on a pole above his command post, and took to wearing a skirt his wife had made for him, thinking it well suited to Africa's hot climate. He even adopted a regimental mascot – a captured German goat which he dressed in British uniform to aid morale. The expedition also kept a pet female chimpanzee called Josephine, which was deemed to be an honorary human being, given a bib and her own cup and saucer and allowed to join them for meals. No wonder the whole thing was christened 'Simson's Circus'. It seemed an adventure fit only for clowns.

The thing was – Spicer-Simson won. Thinking they were dealing with an inept madman, the Germans underestimated his tiny wooden gunboats and became careless to the extent that he was able to capture, sink, or otherwise neutralise the entire German mini-fleet. Amazed by his exploits, the local Holoholo tribesmen started worshipping Spicer-Simson as a god. Prior to setting off, the Lieutenant Commander had planned to get the natives onside by bringing them a large supply of free laxatives, but this bizarre bribe was not needed; thinking he had supernatural powers, the Holoholo laid out clay effigies of him along the lakeside, prostrated themselves in his presence and began dubbing him both 'Navyman God' and 'Lord Bellycloth', on account of his skirt. When Belgian reinforcements arrived at Lake Tanganyika after the battle was over, one of their officers summed up the whole incredible escapade thus:

> You English have a genius for amateurism. That's what makes you so dangerous. Who but amateurs could have dreamed up an expedition like this?[9]

The answer is 'nobody' – and that, perhaps, is one reason we have won so many wars.

Grandad's Army: General Sir Walter Walker (1912–2001)

The military hero who tried to save Britain from the Reds, but ended up just playing toy-soldiers.

How precisely does one go about starting a revolution? You would have thought that the process would have to be a clandestine one, at least initially. Secret underground cells would no doubt have to be built up, underground printing presses furtively concealed, and stashes of illegal weaponry hidden away in crates in abandoned warehouses and disused sewer systems, ready for that glorious day when the people finally rise up against their hated oppressors. Or, alternatively, you could just write a quick letter to the *Daily Telegraph*, asking for a few willing volunteers to do the job instead.

This latter method was the one surprisingly preferred by General Sir Walter Walker, KCB, CBE, DSO (two bars), a celebrated war-hero who had successfully led a guerrilla campaign against Japanese forces in Burma and later, in Malaya, had played a central role in stamping out the Communist insurgency which had taken place there throughout the 1950s. Born on a tea plantation in British India in 1912, Walker seemed cut out for a career in khaki right from the start; in his aptly titled 1997 biography *Fighting On*, the adult Walker reminisced fondly about how, while a schoolboy in Devon, he had found his fellow pupils to be 'a motley bunch of idle, unpatriotic, unkempt and 'couldn't-care-less' type of youths', whom he decided to 'straighten out' by bossing them around and providing anyone who dared cross him with 'a straight left to the nose or an uppercut to the jaw' to teach them a very clear lesson about that old-fashioned British quality of having respect for your superiors. So alarmed by this patriotic violence did Walker's teachers become that the headmaster reportedly had to take him aside one day and explain delicately 'the difference between leading and driving' to him. It's a wonder the future General didn't simply punch *him* with a straight left hook on the nose, too.[1]

Walker graduated from Sandhurst in 1933, and went on to have a stellar career in British uniform. Undoubtedly a great soldier and commander of men, in 1969 Walker was promoted to the rank of General and appointed as Commander-in-Chief Allied Forces, Northern Europe, for NATO, where he assumed responsibility for defending Scandinavia and Jutland against any Soviet threat. Here, Walker was gravely disappointed by what he found, and saw it as being his duty to speak out about what he viewed as being the West's lack of adequate preparations in case the Cold War should suddenly turn rather hot. He soon angered his superiors by taking part in an ITV documentary called *A Day in the Life of a General*, in which, sensationally, he implied that if a European war did come any time soon, then the Russians would probably win it. The film was banned from being shown on security grounds, and by February 1972 Walker had basically been pensioned off. If the authorities hoped that he would remain obediently quiet in his retirement, however, then they were wrong.

The Pen is Mightier than the Sword

Readers of the *Daily Telegraph* one morning in July 1974 certainly heard from Walker again. Once they had opened up their favourite paper and turned to the letters page, they would have found printed there a full-on rant from the retired General, in which he fulminated apocalyptically about 'The Communist Trojan Horse … in our midst', and complained of certain unspecified 'fellow-travellers' of Marxism who were busy 'wriggling their maggoty way inside its belly'. Britain was doomed, Walker explained to his fellow *Telegraph*-readers, unless they could find someone willing to provide it with 'dynamic, invigorating, uplifting leadership', a 'true leader' who would put 'love of country before all else', including his career, and who had the 'moral courage to expose and root out those who try to rot us from within'.[2] Stirring stuff. But who, exactly, was this new leader that the then sixty-one-year-old Walker had in mind? Could it possibly have been … himself?

Arguably, this was indeed the case. After all, in the aftermath of the furore that had been caused by his letter, Walker did give a front-page interview to the London *Evening News*, in which he made statements like 'Perhaps the country might choose rule by the gun in preference to anarchy', called for Britain to awake from its 'awful sleeping sickness', and hinted none too subtly that, in spite of his being a pensioner, he 'hope[d] to have some years of activity ahead ...'[3] But then, there are those who prefer to maintain that Walker, always willing to put aside any personal ambitions for the good of the nation, had definite designs upon putting Prince Philip or Enoch Powell in charge of the country rather than taking the reins himself, as such. The Queen's cousin, the sometime host of TV's *Record Breakers*, and a well-loved radio comedian also had strong claims upon being included in General Walker's proposed cabinet, too. What on earth was going on?

To get an answer to this question, we have to remind ourselves of the appalling state that Britain found itself in during the 1970s. The so-called 'sick man of Europe', throughout that tumultuous decade, Britain was faced with runaway inflation, a collapsing currency, civil unrest, IRA bombing campaigns, seemingly daily strikes, rampant union militancy, three-day weeks, mountains of uncollected rubbish and unburied dead and a general sense of doom and irreversible national decline. In such a climate, people felt that they needed someone to blame – and Walter Walker hit upon one particularly likely suspect, namely the Labour Prime Minister, Harold Wilson. The avuncular, pipe-smoking Wilson might have had a benign image with the general public, but to Walker Wilson's genial persona was merely a front, hiding the 'fact' that he was actually a Russian secret agent, being paid by Moscow to hasten national decline and force a beleaguered and bankrupt Britain into the grasping, blood-stained hands of international Marxism.[4]

As may by now have become clear, Walker was a man of very pronounced right-wing views. Quite happy to recount his glorious past campaigns against the 'slant-eyes' in public, to advocate a full-scale military invasion of Northern Ireland, and ever-ready to decry homosexuals as being an appalling breed of people who 'use the main sewer of the human body as a playground',[5] Walker, who had already seen off the Commies in Malaya, fancied himself as being an expert at sniffing out Reds under the bed. In 1974, Walker had joined a shadowy organisation called Unison, which had been set up in 1973 by the former deputy-director of MI6, George Kennedy Young. Young had fantasised about Unison being a 'formidable vigilante group' which would aim to step in and restore law and order should some snivelling little quisling like Harold Wilson ever finally give the order for the threatened Communist takeover to begin. In reality, Unison was far from formidable as a paramilitary force, but, given the credible status of its leader, and the near-ungovernable status of the country at the time, many commentators were willing to take it seriously – especially once it became known that the great General Sir Walter Walker was a member of the body.[6] What happened next is not quite clear, but it appears that Walker was soon setting up a splinter group from Unison, calling itself Civil Assistance.[7]

The People's Army

But what was this organisation of Walker's, precisely? Civil Assistance, said Walker, was nothing less than a means of 'self-defence against national suicide.'[8] To the press, and the general public, this meant one thing only – General Walker was in the process of building up his own private army. But was he? The evidence seems contradictory. On the one hand, Walker was talking about 'rule by the gun' being preferable to anarchy; on the other, he was at pains to stress that his men were not being armed (or, at least, not by *him*!), had no uniforms or anything like that, and were basically just intending to ensure that various essential services, like transport and the electricity supply, continued to run during any Communist-inspired breakdown in public order, or Red-led General Strike. He would leave the real Army to shoot people, he implied, rather than training his personnel up into being some kind of paramilitary force per se.[9]

This is what Walker *said*, but it is not necessarily what the public and the press *heard*; the idea that Civil Assistance was basically an armed citizens' brigade seems to have been what most people thought, presumably including some of those who had actually joined up to it with the misguided aim of gaining easy access to firearms. In any case, to some conspiratorially minded people the British Army itself had by now also pledged allegiance to Sir Walter's command anyhow, making his words about leaving armed intervention to the military highly disingenuous. An address made by Walker to around 100 members of his group in the City of London on 25 February 1975 was infiltrated by representatives from the Communist newspaper *The Morning Star*, who claimed that several serving military high-ups, including a general, nine colonels and six brigadiers, were in attendance to hear Walker give a highly inflammatory speech in which he supposedly accused Labour MPs of being subversives, and claimed that he would soon 'act' against such people, as his group had 'excellent relations with chief constables', thereby implying he had some kind of secret influence over the British police force as well.[10] An unfortunate misplaced comma in the 21 September edition of *The Spectator* which inadvertently made it sound as if Walker was a member of the National Front, meanwhile, probably only made the whole situation worse.[11]

Who exactly was in Civil Assistance, though? In the absence of Sir Walter's membership records being released to the public, this is an issue which still remains rather murky. Walker maintained that, after his July letter had been published in the *Telegraph*, he had been contacted by not only huge quantities of concerned ordinary citizens, but also by a number of high-ranking military officers from the Army, Navy and Air-Force, several ex-MPs, and some rich businessmen who were willing to help fund the creation of Walker's new army of the silent majority. By midway through August, Walker was already claiming to have amassed 100,000 members; two weeks later, he claimed on the BBC that he would have three million men under his command in under a month, and was soon predicting that eventually some 13.5 million volunteers would be ready and willing to rise up and save civilisation, as soon as the long-anticipated 'Red Revolution' finally came.[12]

These are impressive figures indeed, and so serious did Walker's claims seem to some that Labour's Defence Secretary Roy Mason went so far as to interrupt his holiday in order to issue a public condemnation about the dangers of the 'near fascist groundswell' which he saw as sweeping over the country.[13] According to his fellow Unison member Major Alexander Greenwood, so certain was Walker of success in his cause that he even went so far as to pen a speech for the Queen to read out over the radio once he had taken Britain over, in which Her Majesty would advise her remaining non-Communist subjects to put their trust behind the Armed Forces and their new leader. Greenwood claimed to be close friends with the Queen, and to be aware that she 'wasn't very happy with Mr Harold Wilson', implying that she, too, was a tacit supporter of Civil Assistance's aims, although I doubt she ever went so far as to don camouflage gear. Supposedly, the Queen's cousin Lord Louis Mountbatten, former Viceroy of India, even took to calling Walker up over the telephone, cheerily offering his assistance in any way Walker saw fit to use him.[14]

A paramilitary force by Royal Appointment, then – this was fearsome stuff, to be sure. The only problem with General Walker's thirteen-million-man army was that it didn't in any sense actually exist. Several people had indeed written to Walker after seeing his alarmist letter in *The Telegraph*, agreeing with his broad Commie-bashing sentiments, and the General had simply assumed that they would all be willing volunteers in his regiments when the call to arms was finally issued, something which in reality was debatable, at best. Genuine Civil Assistance members did actually exist,[15] but since Walker had arbitrarily commanded each one of them to recruit a further thirty members, and then each of those to rope in another thirty more, and so on and so on *ad infinitum* in some kind of giant right-wing pyramid scheme, it seems as if Britain's elderly leader-in-waiting had gotten rather ahead of himself and just blithely assumed that these future members would all soon sign up to become his troops, which of course they never did. By 1976 it had become clear that Civil Assistance had failed miserably, and in October that same year it was quietly folded up and partially merged with the National Association for Freedom (of which more below).[16]

Dedication's what You Need ...
Walter Walker may not have really had thirteen million followers, then, but this does not mean that he had no followers at all – and some of the men who seemed willing to march on Downing Street under his banner were very well-connected indeed. Quite apart from the unnamed military top brass who had (allegedly) signed up to his cause, Walker did also manage to squeeze money and support out of some high-flying businessmen, such as the chairman of British & Commonwealth Shipping, Lord Cayzer, who apparently handed over a cheque for £10,000 to fund the General's dreamy plans. Shipping magnates seemed to be particularly caught up in the alleged plot; a concerned John Mitchell, the managing director of the Cunard line, reputedly once contacted Harold Wilson to tell him that the secret services had made a confidential request that he lend them the QE2 to act as a floating prison for the Labour Cabinet once the Army had taken control of Downing Street![17] At least Wilson *et al* would have been being kept in the style to which they had no doubt by now become accustomed.

Somewhat more surprising than these shadowy loons and rich free-marketeers, though, was Civil Assistance's rather unexpected 'Showbiz Wing'. The 1970s were an era when several well-known celebrities flirted with Far Right politics, the most astounding example being David Bowie's open calls for Britain to turn fascist, the Thin White Duke telling an interviewer from *Playboy* magazine in 1976 that, in his view, 'Adolf Hitler was one of the first rock stars ... I think he was quite as good as [Mick] Jagger.'[18] Well, he certainly had stage presence. Even the chairman of one of General Walker's rival secret armies, a group of ex-servicemen calling themselves the British Military Volunteer Force, was called Paul Daniels.[19] You *might* have liked this man's vision for a new Britain, I suppose – but not a lot.

Another famous face who was linked with Walker's cause, meanwhile, was Ross McWhirter (1925–1975), the co-founder (with his brother Norris) of *The Guinness Book of Records*, and the amusingly inappropriate co-host of its children's TV-show spin-off *Record Breakers*, an idea almost akin to that of letting Norman Tebbit host *Funhouse*. A one-time Tory parliamentary candidate for Edmonton, McWhirter became a libertarian crusader and prominent advocate for bringing back hanging, who in 1970 had even gone so far as to attempt to sue a TV company for supposedly broadcasting subliminal messages out to the electorate during a parliamentary broadcast on behalf of the Labour Party.[20] In 1975, after putting up a bounty of £50,000 for anyone providing information upon the identity or whereabouts of some IRA bombers then on the loose, the terrorists in question infamously decided to reverse the proposal and shot Ross dead outside his house instead. His twin sibling Norris McWhirter (1925-2004) later claimed to have undergone a mysterious psychic experience at the time, slumping down into his chair as if he had suffered a heart attack at exactly the same moment as Ross was being shot in the chest by a Fenian.[21]

Before his violent death, however, McWhirter had rapidly been turning into much more of a strike breaker than a record breaker. He had sat on the original board of Unison alongside General Walker and George Kennedy Young, and had been heavily involved with various allied activities, such as setting up his own press in order to print newsletters giving useful advice to solid citizens about how to do things like break Communist-motivated strikes and set up your own personal domestic power generators for when society finally collapsed in on itself and people started eating each other.[22] Less than a week after Ross' death, his psychic brother Norris was holding a press conference announcing the launch of the unfortunately named NAFF, or 'National Association for Freedom', in Ross' name, a campaigning organisation which was headed up by yet another ex-soldier named John Gouriet, who, like Walker, had also served with distinction in Malaya during the dying days of Empire.[23] NAFF, of course, was the very same organisation into which General Walker's Civil Assistance was subsumed after it had finally withered on the vine in 1976. Thus, an unlikely sounding link can be drawn between Britain's best-loved dictator-in-waiting, and TV's fabled 'memory man' who always had all the facts and figures ready at his fingertips to answer even the most obscure of queries from the enthusiastically inquisitive children who made up the majority of the *Record Breakers* studio audience. No doubt McWhirter would have served as Minister of Information in Walker's putative national unity government, had it ever come to pass.

By far the biggest sprinkling of stardust in terms of Walker's supporters, though, came in the form of none other than Michael Bentine (1922–1996), one-time co-star of BBC radio's *The Goon Show*, and star or creator of such agreeably demented films and TV programmes as *Potty Time*, *It's a Square World*, *The Bumblies* and *Rentadick*. Bentine had seen Walker's letter in the *Telegraph* too, and had immediately written in offering his own military assistance and expertise to the cause.[24] Something of an eccentric himself, Bentine was also an ardent investigator of paranormal phenomena, a sometime co-presenter of *The Sky at Night* and, in 1968, took part in the first ever hovercraft expedition up the River Amazon. It might be thought that such a person would be of limited use in forming an emergency government – but maybe not, as in fact Michael Bentine is credited in some quarters as having been an influential figure in the creation of the anti-terrorist wing of the SAS!

According to a book published in 1999 by the long-serving ex-SAS officer Ken Connor, Bentine was a crack shot with a pistol who had somehow managed to persuade a high-up SAS man named only as 'The Master' to attend a demonstration of his shooting skills at London's Paddington Green police station in the autumn of 1968. Connor went along too, and was greeted by the incredible sight of Bentine putting on a silly *Goons*-style voice, reaching down into his trousers and shouting out 'I vill now show you all my enormous veapon!' Apparently, the comedian really was armed and dangerous, whipping out not his privates but a loaded .44 magnum and beginning a rapid-fire demonstration of his shooting skills before then going on to explain solemnly to 'The Master' how the greatest coming threat to Britain was from within, with extremist groups and armed drug dealers necessitating the rapid formation of a new counter terrorism wing within the SAS, trained to deal with delicate hostage-taking situations and the like. The Master agreed and such a unit did indeed soon come into being.[25] Having worked in military intelligence during the War, under the direct command of the famous Colditz escapee Airey Neave – another man whose name pops up frequently in terms of alleged 1970s plots to overthrow the British state – perhaps Bentine had the right kind of connections to be able to play a bizarrely prominent role in Walker's new administration, should he have wished to do so.

General Ridicule

If the idea of one of *The Goons* being made Minister for Defence sounds a comic one to ears today, however, then it seemed equally so to some at the time, too. Most notoriously, General Walker was made fun of in David Nobbs' hit 1976 BBC sit-com *The Fall and Rise of Reginald Perrin*, in which the character of Jimmy Adamson, played by Geoffrey Palmer, was presented as a nutty ex-Army man who kept a cache of guns hidden in his bedroom ready for an apocalyptic final battle with, as he put it, the 'forces of anarchy' and 'wreckers of law and order'. In Jimmy's view, these massed enemies of the state included not just Communists and militant union leaders, but also such nefarious foes as 'long-haired weirdos', 'atheists', 'foreign surgeons', 'football supporters', 'namby-pamby probation officers' and the prominent Labour Minister for Energy, Anthony Wedgwood Benn. Worse, said Jimmy, the Chinese restaurants then springing up all across the country were really secret vehicles for hidden Maoist cells – 'Why do you think Windsor Castle is ringed with Chinese restaurants?' he once asked, in typically paranoid style.[26] So successful was this parody of Walker's ways that, in 1984, a re-jigged version of the Jimmy Adamson character, now renamed Harry Kitchener Wellington Truscott for copyright reasons, popped up in a new sitcom by David Nobbs on Channel Four, entitled *Fairly Secret Army*, in which he was now the main character and an object of open derision.[27] Far from his plans being taken seriously, General Sir Walter Walker had now become a long-standing national joke.

How could serious people, some of them in positions of actual power and responsibility, ever have come to take the idea of a coup by Colonel Blimp and his well-bred showbiz chums seriously? In his own recent discussion of the failed plans of General Walker, the *Private Eye* journalist Francis Wheen came up with a plausible answer. The mad fantasy of Walker's coup was simply one that he and 'many other despairing Englishmen of a certain age and attitude found so consoling that they clung to it rather as one sometimes clings to a dream on waking, reluctant to be parted from the delicious delusion.'[28] How else could such persons have been expected to endure the dog days of British decline during the 1970s, than by fantasising about taking the whole place over by force and then sorting everything out themselves, like they once had done in places like Malaya and Burma?

In any case, as it turned out, General Walker and his ilk didn't need to bother; on 3 May 1979, Margaret Thatcher and her new Conservative Government gained the keys to Number 10 Downing Street, and someone prepared finally to face up to the sinister 'forces of anarchy' lurking within the country's Chinese restaurants gained power by democratic means, without the need for any military coup at all. Indeed, in his farewell letter to Civil Assistance members, sent out in late 1976 after the organisation's demise, Walker referred openly to Mrs Thatcher, then the newly elected leader of the Conservative Party, as 'the salvation of this country', leading some fringe commentators to whisper darkly about their possible secret links behind the scenes. It has even been suggested that Sir Walter was deliberately conned by the security services into believing that he had his own private army, in order to smooth the path to power for Thatcher somehow, unlikely though this may seem.[29]

In the 1980s, following a pair of unsuccessful hip operations, General Walker's health began to decline, and he ended up all-but retiring from public life. While he could still be relied upon to supply the occasional drily amusing quote to the newspapers – 'Britain has invented a new weapon. It's called the Civil Servant; it doesn't work, and it can't be fired!' being his most famous effort[30]– General Walker was forced at last to leave the Good Fight to others. He was finally called up to report to that great Parade Ground in the sky and present arms to God in August 2001, aged eighty-eight. General Sir Walter Walker may not have achieved his ultimate aim of overthrowing the supposedly 'Communist' Labour Government of Harold Wilson and Anthony Wedgwood Benn, but at least he provided a lasting model for the rest of us of how to keep yourself busy during a long retirement.

Mr Freeze: Geoffrey Nathaniel Pyke (1893–1948)

The insane inventor who planned to freeze Hitler in his tracks by building battleships out of ice.

Had you been a Luftwaffe pilot during the Second World War, then, during your night-time bombing-raids over Britain, you would have had to face numerous dangers, from ack-ack guns to barrage balloons – but, if one man had had his way, then there would have been another, rather stranger, obstacle lying in your path as well. In 1942, the idea was seriously floated that large chunks be hewn off from icebergs and towed out into the English Channel, with big neon signs saying 'BOMB ME – I'M A DUMMY!' placed on top in an attempt to fool Heinkel and Dornier pilots into wasting their payloads on shattering these useless objects down into ice cubes, rather than using their bombs to blitz our ports and cities with.[1] The idea was either a cunning psychological ploy devised by a genius, a double bluff brazen enough to outrank all others, or else an insane and pointless proposal put forward by a madman, depending upon who you spoke to. After all, it had been suggested by none other than Geoffrey Pyke, perhaps the most divisive British scientist of the entire war – a man who undoubtedly had the ear of both PM Winston Churchill and Chief of Combined Operations Lord Louis Mountbatten, but of few others.

The years 1939–1945 were a curious time for science. Whatever the evils of a state of total warfare existing between developed nations, there is little doubt that it acts as the greatest spur possible to industrial innovation; it has to, otherwise your side will lose. All sides involved in the conflict enjoyed their amazing scientific breakthroughs, from Germany's V-2 ballistic rockets to

America's atom bomb, but in 1940, when Britain stood alone, her need for help from the men in white lab coats was perhaps the most acute of all. Hopelessly outnumbered by Japanese, Nazi and Soviet manpower and industrial might, Britain could not hope to defeat the Axis powers through conventional means only. It was during this point in our history, surely, that John Stuart Mill's old adage about the level of eccentricity tolerated among a country's population being a reliable indicator of its level of 'genius, mental vigour and moral courage' was put to its ultimate test.

There is no doubt that, whatever the reality, in subsequent years the idea has arisen that we won the war largely because of a superior degree of lateral thinking of the kind so often engaged in by eccentrics. In films like *The Dam Busters* and *The Imitation Game*, it is the contribution of unconventional lone visionaries like Barnes Wallis and Alan Turing that is presented as having helped turn the tide against Germany, with their seemingly loony ideas for bouncing bombs and giant code-crunching computers, an image in distinct contrast to American and Russian mythologising of the war against fascism, where qualities like superior might and a willingness to sacrifice lives for the motherland come more to the fore. This is, of course, a rather exaggerated picture – but not wholly. As noted in this book's introduction, Churchill himself was something of an eccentric, and it was a good thing for people like Wallis, Turing and Pyke that he was, as it meant he was open to taking some very bizarre ideas seriously. A fan of H. G. Wells' science-fiction fantasies, during his earlier incarnation as a journalist Churchill had put his name to fanciful speculative newspaper articles with titles like 'Death-Rays' and 'Are There Men On the Moon?' and, in a 1924 piece for *The Pall Mall Gazette*, had speculated about the coming of nuclear warfare, asking whether 'a bomb no bigger than an orange' might one day be found to possess 'a secret power' enabling it to 'blast a township at a stroke'.[2]

Most famously, there was Churchill's formation of the so-called 'Landships Committee' in February 1915, while serving as First Lord of the Admiralty during the First World War. 'Landships' were the early name given by Churchill to tanks, a name – and an idea – he derived from a 1903 short-story by H. G. Wells called *The Land Ironclads*. An 'Ironclad' was a type of early steam-powered battleship, and in his story Wells imagined the military potential of creating giant armour-plated battleships which could move across land, simply crushing any opposition underfoot. Churchill liked to imagine the military potential of such an idea too, and, after much effort, finally managed to put in motion Britain's development and deployment of the first ever tank – as the landships came to be called – at the Somme in September 1916. While Welles did not invent the tank, exactly, in October 1916 Churchill nonetheless wrote a letter to his literary hero, saying that he must have been pleased to have seen his machine escape from the page and onto the real-life battlefield at last.[3]

As this interest in gleaning ideas for potential wonder-weapons from sci-fi indicates, Churchill, though undeniably visionary, was not scientifically literate as such. *How* a weapon worked was immaterial to him; it was whether it *did* work or not that was important. Look back, for instance, at Churchill's supposed prediction of the atom bomb; he merely imagines that such a device will contain a 'secret power', without making any real attempt to explain what precisely this secret power might be (although he did have a vague idea) or how it might be unleashed. The reason for this, obviously, was that he didn't really know – as with H. G. Wells' 'Land Ironclads', he just liked the sound of Britain having access to such a device. It was no wonder that Churchill dubbed the Second World War the 'Wizard War'; a child of the 1870s, many of the contraptions produced by its most able scientists must have seemed to him almost akin to magic.

The Misappliance of Science

Indeed, magicians did play a small part in the war effort. Jasper Maskelyne (1902–1973) for instance, a prominent stage illusionist, put his skills to work in Egypt, making a fake version of Alexandria's harbour for German planes to attack by recreating its lighting-pattern in the desert after dark. He tried a similar trick with airfields, strewing real ones with false rubble by day to make it appear that nocturnal enemy bombing raids had already put them out of action – a ruse eventually rumbled by the Italian Air-Marshal Italo Balbo, who jokingly had his planes drop harmless wooden 'bombs' onto British positions in retaliation. So advanced were Maskelyne's illusions that he even boasted he could project a giant image of Hitler sitting on a toilet a thousand feet into the sky to undermine German morale – an offer he unaccountably failed to be taken up on. Famously, he also helped devise the cunning ploy of hiding explosives in dead rats and then depositing them near coal heaps in Germany in the hope that workmen would shovel them into boilers and furnaces – with explosive results.[4]

Almost any idea would be considered if it might help win the war. Impractical suggestions like dropping plane-loads of glue on German positions to stick their troops to the ground were proposed, along with slightly more more sensible ones like the idea of developing 'sticky bombs', a variety of hand grenades which could be stuck onto the side of tanks (when they didn't stick to British soldiers' uniforms by mistake). Surely most bizarre of all, though, was the secret Allied plan to make Hitler grow breasts. Amazingly, this proposal was actually put into action; noting that Hitler's younger sister Paula, who worked as a secretary, was somewhat more docile than her more famous relative, American and British secret agents bribed Hitler's gardener to inject the Führer's carrots with oestrogen to bring out his feminine side. The hope was that he would become less aggressive, lose his moustache, grow breasts and develop a squeaky voice, in order to destroy his credibility among the German people – a plan which ultimately failed, possibly because the gardener in question is alleged to have simply pocketed his money and thrown the oestrogen away.[5]

How, though, to weed the good ideas out from the bad? Churchill's solution was to appoint Britain's first ever Chief Scientific Advisor to his War Cabinet, the Oxford physicist Frederick Lindemann. The problem, however, was that many other top-ranking types were rather less receptive than Churchill was to the outlandish ideas of those who wore white lab coats instead of khaki. Arthur 'Bomber' Harris, for instance, Commander-in-Chief of Bomber Command, did not take kindly to being offered statistical guidance from the zoologist and primate specialist Solly Zuckerman about where precisely he should drop his explosives; he contemptuously dismissed Zuckerman's plans as a mere 'panacea' devised by 'a civilian professor whose forte is the sexual aberrations of apes'.[6] Given his attitude, Harris should be grateful that he worked for the RAF and not the Admiralty; for there, he would have had to deal not only with tedious ape-botherers like Solly Zuckerman, but with the strangest wartime inventor of them all – Geoffrey Nathaniel Pyke.

Imperfect Pyke in All Parts
The first biography of Pyke to appear was somewhat misleading in title – written in 1959 by David Lampe, it was entitled *Pyke the Unknown Genius*. And yet, as Solly Zuckerman himself wrote in a contemporary review in *The Spectator*, 'If Geoffrey Pyke truly deserved the description 'genius', then he certainly did not deserve the qualification 'unknown'.' After all, due to his bizarre and

eccentric ways, Pyke was never forgotten by those who met him – and those who did meet him included many of the most celebrated politicians, soldiers and scientists of the day. Zuckerman takes a quote from Lampe's book – 'Pyke was the sort of man who would have invented the wheel' – and says it is true, with one important qualification:

> If he had invented the wheel, one has a suspicion that he would have discovered, to his dismay and fury, that somebody else had developed a slightly different, possibly even better, wheel just before; or that the need which had stimulated the idea of a wheel had vanished.[7]

Pyke was a man full of bright ideas – but bright ideas which were continually being thwarted at the last step. Like many a frustrated inventor, he complained that everything he suggested, no matter how wild, was perfectly practical, and the only reason he ever failed was because the eternal motto of those who held the public purse strings was that 'nothing should ever be done for the first time'.[8] Another reason most of his schemes failed, though, was because of his insistence upon living entirely within his own head whenever he was at work on a new one, neglecting the usual norms of human behaviour to such an extent that many who encountered him simply thought he was mad. For instance, in need of somewhere to stay while performing his vital war work for Churchill, he broke into his friend Cyril Ray's house, claimed part of it as his own, and declared that he now lived there. Worse, he wanted to rearrange the place; as he paced around the floor a lot while thinking, he proposed to Ray that all the furniture should be suspended from the ceiling with wires and only lowered down when needed, seeing as otherwise he just kept on bumping into it. Cyril Ray, however, was not convinced. 'I don't think it would be very attractive,' he protested, and the idea ended there.[9] Another thing that was not very attractive about Pyke, meanwhile, were his living habits; in order to save valuable thinking time, he frequently called official meetings to his borrowed bedside, where he presided over discussions dressed in his pyjamas and surrounded by empty bottles which he would suddenly pick up and urinate into in the name of efficiency. Time spent getting up and going to the lavatory, it seemed, was time which could have been far better spent devising new ways to defeat the Third Reich.[10]

Pyke was quite simply unforgettable and, as Zuckerman pointed out, had actually achieved fame on several separate occasions throughout his life, each time in quite different fields. After the war had ended, for instance, Pyke was a regular campaigning presence in the British media. In 1946 and 1947, he was even commissioned to write official reports into how best to staff the forthcoming NHS, so it is not as if he had no public recognition; it is just that, increasingly, it was the erratic side of his nature which came to capture the public's real attention.[11] For example, in August 1945 Pyke appeared in *The Manchester Guardian* (a national newspaper, in spite of its name), writing anguished articles about what he called 'Europe's coal-famine'.[12] In the aftermath of Allied victory, mainland Europe lay in ruins, and starvation lurked in wait for its huddled masses; due to the widespread destruction of industry, there was not enough coal to go around to heat homes, power factories, or allow trains to run, meaning that scarce food supplies were simply not being distributed properly. Pyke's solution to this looming famine was simple – pedal power!

In the pages of *The Manchester Guardian*, and in an *Economist* article entitled 'The Mobilisation of Muscle', Pyke laid out the details of an amazing new invention, the Cyclo-Tractor. In essence, these proposed vehicles were giant, four-wheeled bicycles designed to seat twenty to thirty men, who would pedal along in unison attached to trains, pulling them along the tracks. Rather than wasting tons of coal fuelling vehicles, would it not be far more efficient to simply force captured Nazis to become human horses in this way, thereby helping feed the starving millions?[13] While these articles were left unsigned, Pyke had earlier attempted to persuade the Loyalist faction to convert their own trains to pedal power during the Spanish Civil War, so it was easily deduced that the idea was his.[14]

Pipe Dreams

Pyke's proposed Cyclo-Tractors were a classic example of the fatally flawed nature of his brilliance. *Technically*, the scheme would have worked – but only in an impossibly ideal world. It hinged upon the fact that the victorious Allies had access to plenty of sugar supplies, but far less oil, coal and petrol. Therefore, Pyke calculated the calorific content of a certain amount of sugar, and how much energy output this would amount to in terms of the leg muscles' ability to pedal a giant bike when that sugar was eaten by a prisoner. Essentially, the German or Italian POW became the train's new engine, with each unit of sugar equating to a lump of coal, keeping that engine stoked. Pyke was very careful to lay out the mathematical proof that feeding Europe's defeated soldiers sugar in this way would save twelve million tons of coal per year from being consumed in train boiler rooms, but there were any number of issues he didn't consider. How and where would these Cyclo-Tractors be made? Would all be POWs be in a fit state to man them? Wouldn't some try and escape? Where would the manpower to monitor them in this task come from? Pyke provided no solutions.[15]

People laughed at Pyke's human-powered trains, and they laughed even more when, in 1951, three years after his death, another article appeared in *The Manchester Guardian*, entitled 'Men in Pipeline: The Idea That Was Never Carried Out'.[16] Here was detailed Pyke's insane 1943 proposal that troops be shot directly across Europe to wherever they were needed through a network of giant pipes, like a real-life version of *Super Mario Bros*. Again, Pyke's idea was technically-sound, but woefully unworkable in actual real-world conditions. Did Pyke not realise that all these pipes would have to be laid and manufactured at massive cost, and that the Luftwaffe would only have to bomb one individual section of any pipeline to render the entire thing unusable? It seems he did not. Initially, Pyke's idea was to attach long pipes to supply-ships, and then, using jets of high-pressured water, shoot food and ammunition down them onto French beach-heads quickly and easily. Then, once territory had been gained, the pipelines could be extended ever-further inland, keeping advancing Allied armies well-supplied with kit. It was only later that Pyke came up with the proposal to flush men through the pipe-network too; it would be particularly useful for shooting soldiers across swamps and over mountains, he decided. Aware that the experience of being flushed down a giant pipe by a jet of super-pressured water would probably be an unpleasant one, Pyke proposed that troops be drugged up beforehand, and that they travel in pairs for company. After all, Pyke said nonchalantly, the whole experience should be 'far less unpleasant, and take very much less time to become used to, than ... being bombed'.[17]

Another plan of Pyke's hovering on the borderline between brilliance and madness was his idea to sabotage the vital Nazi oil refinery in Ploesti, Romania. Fire bombing Ploesti was the obvious option, but the Nazis had anticipated this, and had fire crews on hand to handle any potential blaze. Pyke's solution was ingenious. Together with fire bombs, why not drop some parachutists who could hijack the Romanian fire engines, steal their crews' clothing, and rush to the scene of the fire? Then, waved through by German guards, the fake firemen could substitute gasoline for water, or else seed it with fused incendiary bombs, so that, as they fought the flames, they only made them blaze more brightly. Pyke's superiors thought this was a much better idea than his earlier plans to flood the area with friendly dogs carrying bottles of brandy to make the guards drunk, or women of loose morals to seduce and immobilise them, and serious thought was given to putting it into action – though, once again, ultimately it was not. Maybe it should have been. In later years, the scheme was tried as a military 'war-game' exercise, in which commandos disguised as firemen succeeded in capturing an RAF base from its unsuspecting guards. Pyke had been right after all![18]

When word of his ideas began to get out into the post-war world, however, people laughed at Geoffrey Pyke, and he became a figure of fun, openly mocked in the press. Becoming ever more pessimistic about the future of the human race, on the evening of Saturday 21 February 1948, Pyke shaved off his beard, put a 'Do Not Disturb' sign on his door, took to his bed and opened a bottle of sleeping pills. His landlady found him lying dead beneath the sheets that Monday morning. Far from being the 'forgotten' genius of Lampe's book-title, however, Geoffrey Pyke received an adulatory obituary in *The Times*, where he was praised as being a 'fearless innovator'.[19]

The Great Escape

Pyke merited his *Times* obituary partially on account of the early success of his 1916 book *To Ruhleben and Back*, a stirring account of his escape from the German POW camp of that name, where he had been interned as a spy during the First World War while working as an undercover reporter for the *Daily Chronicle*. Kept initially in solitary confinement prior to his transfer to Ruhleben, Pyke kept himself sane by singing, reciting poetry and whistling – something he received special dispensation to do from the director of the prison. Once actually in Ruhleben, Pyke soon began making plans to escape. In his book's first edition, Pyke did not reveal precisely how he had eventually managed to do so, however, on account of the fact that he was forever sending in food parcels to his former fellow internees, fitted with false bottoms containing instructions for how to get out of the place; instructions nobody else ever actually bothered to follow.

So, how did Pyke escape? Later editions spill the beans. Initially, he gathered data upon all previous failed attempts, and subjected them to statistical analysis in order to determine what the common factors were. Then, together with another prisoner named Edward Falk, he noticed that there was a store hut in Ruhleben through which the sun shone in such a way at a certain time in the afternoon that its glare would get right in the eyes of any guards who might peer in through the window, checking over the area. Pyke and Falk crouched down beneath some tennis nets in the hut at this precise time one day, and their theory was proved right; the blinded guard did not see them. Then, they waited until dark and crept outside, climbing over various fences and making their way across country towards the Dutch border, where they found sanctuary.[20]

When Pyke returned to England, he found his daring exploits had made him famous, yet his response was typically quixotic; told by his editor at the *Chronicle* to write some articles about his escape, he refused and quit his job to try a new direction, setting to work on his bestseller and giving lectures about his adventures. One of these took place at his old alma mater, Wellington College, where he told the boys that, even during his lowest points in captivity, when he thought he was going to be shot, he was never as miserable as when he had been a pupil at Wellington.[21] This was no joke; despite his obvious intelligence, Pyke was not a great student, finding the rigid structure of school life uncongenial. It seemed to him that Britain's entire educational system was geared more towards smoothing a path to the top for the elite than anything else, a suspicion confirmed for him one day while standing idly around near London's Stock Exchange, watching the public school-educated traders walk by. In Pyke's damning words, 'all of them appeared ineffably stupid and many of them were my relatives', twin facts which led him to conclude that, if he put his mind to it, he could outdo them in their work and make a fortune – which he promptly did. Using complex statistical methods of his own creation, before long Pyke was raking in the money from his investments, to the point where, allegedly, he owned one-third of the world's entire tin supply.[22] Idealistic as always, Pyke used this money to set up his own school where children could be nurtured, not abused. He called this curious establishment Malting House School, and it could surely rank alongside Bertrand Russell's ill-fated Beacon Hill as one of the oddest schools in English history.

Mess-Up in a Brewery

Malting House was set up in 1924 in an old converted brewery in semi-rural Cambridge, and the advert Pyke placed in the press seeking a teacher made it clear this was to be no ordinary school. For a start, the ad appeared in the *New Statesman* and *Nature*, not the local paper, and asked for someone who would be willing to conduct teaching duties 'as a piece of scientific ... research' rather than as a job, per se. As such, Pyke explained, he did not really want a qualified teacher to fill the role. While 'previous educational experience is not considered a bar', the advert said, what Pyke really wanted was a recent female university graduate 'who has hitherto considered themselves too good for teaching' and who was, ideally, an atheist.[23] Another advert, meanwhile, which appeared in 1927, didn't specifically ask for a teacher at all, but 'A scientist of the first order ... to investigate ... young children'.[24] As this suggests, Malting House was considered essentially as a giant laboratory, with the children cast as 'co-investigators' of the world around them, not pupils needing instruction. This is why, if you look at plans of Malting House, you can see balconies from which stenographers were supposed to be employed in the task of recording all the children's words and behaviour – the 'teachers' were really human zoologists, making notes on the natural conduct of how children acted in the wild.[25]

Such Stasi-like methods were a far cry from the rarefied atmosphere promised in advertisements, however, where parents who were 'dissatisfied with the overworked ignorance of the majority of our schools' and yet 'at the same time anxious to avoid the emotionally determined efforts of cranks' were, for the price of £115 per year, offered the chance to bundle off their offspring to Malting House, where amazing new equipment such as 'animals which breed' and 'double-handed saws which compel co-operation' were on offer.[26] Allowing small children access to saws may have sounded dangerous, but Pyke saw nothing wrong with allowing kids aged three to ten free and ready access to things like test-tubes, Bunsen-burners, cooking-ranges, dissection-labs for cutting up dead dogs, and even an industrial lathe.[27] For Pyke, it was much better for a child to find out how to do things for themselves than to explicitly instruct them. After all, he had taught himself how to drive a car by looking at a Ford owner's manual, not by paying for lessons, and thought that all education should work similarly.[28] Therefore, there were to be no formal classes at Malting House, and teachers were not allowed to answer children's questions with the correct information, instead being obliged to parrot the response 'Let's find out, shall we?'

The example Pyke liked to give in adverts of this supposedly benign principle in action was Malting House's garden, which was filled with plants for the children to tend. However, said the press ads, if the child-scientists wished to do so, these plants could 'without taboo be dug up every day to see how they are getting on', something which would of course kill the flowers, teaching the baby professors a valuable lesson about the need for patience – or so Pyke hoped.[29] In fact, it just gave them a taste for digging up other things, too, like the corpses of the 'breeding animals' which wandered the school grounds, in order to find out whether dead rabbits had gone up 'in the sky' to animal heaven. It turned out they had not.[30] Eventually, Malting House closed down in 1929, not because of parental complaints about their children being exposed to the horrors of rotting animal flesh, but because Pyke's metals investments finally failed in 1927, leaving him bankrupt.[31]

Don't Tell Him, Pyke!
Pyke next resurfaced just prior to the Second World War, when he hit upon the notion of employing secret agents to infiltrate Nazi Germany dressed as golfers and conduct a massive opinion survey which he then intended to present directly to Adolf Hitler, in order to prove to him scientifically that his people did not really want war. It was a noble effort, but seeing as Hitler invaded Poland before the survey could be written up properly, Pyke was forced to abandon his plans.[32]

If Hitler wouldn't listen to reason, however, then Pyke had no option but to try and defeat him by other, less polite, means. For the first few years of the war, Pyke was ignored, but in 1941, when Louis Mountbatten was made Chief of Combined Operations, he was on the lookout for unusual thinkers, and Pyke was certainly one of those. Pyke's first scheme, submitted to Mountbatten in 1942, was for a mini-invasion of Norway, using new snow weapons of his own devising in order to destroy Nazi armaments factories and power plants. His main idea was for a family of mechanised sledges or snow ploughs, screw-propelled vehicles which would drill through the snow at top speed, towing along smaller sledges with torpedoes and explosives attached. The idea was that, if being pursued uphill, these torpedoes could be fired off at enemy troops, or the mini-sledges themselves released to slide back down and explode. While this idea was, as usual, rejected, it was nonetheless mechanically sound; similar screw-propelled vehicles were successfully used by Arctic explorers during the 1950s. The problem was not physics, but practicality; how could these machines be landed and concealed in Occupied Norway prior to the attack? Pyke's idea was to hide them in the open by attaching signs claiming they were secret Gestapo death ray machines, which were not to be touched. For added effect, said Pyke, some large animals could be killed and left lying around nearby, so it looked as if the device worked. Alternatively, Pyke asked, why not simply put canvas tents over the top of them together with notices saying they were field toilets intended only for the use of top-ranking Nazis? Seeing as German troops were notorious for 'only obeying orders', they would surely be unwilling to go inside the tents themselves, thus leaving the vehicles safe in plain sight – presuming Himmler didn't turn up, needing a dump.[33]

Pyke had a real interest in matters of ice and snow, as proven by his most famous scheme, the idea to create a series of gigantic aircraft-carriers made out of ice reinforced with wood pulp, a substance he did not invent, but which was named 'pykrete' in his honour. The benefit of adding sawdust to the ice was that it would make it stronger, and greatly increase the time it took to melt. By adding a series of pipes circulating compressed, refrigerated air, Pyke thought he could construct a vessel which would be indestructible; walls of ice, thirty feet thick, would render the ship impervious to torpedoes which, it was calculated, would create holes only twenty inches deep in the hull – holes which could, of course, be repaired simply by pouring sawdust-laced water into them to freeze over again. Pykrete was as strong as concrete, but could float, creating, in essence, giant movable islands. These massive ice carriers could end up being 2,000 feet long, Pyke calculated, and carry 200 Spitfires. They could even be equipped, he hoped, with special gun turrets to fire super-cooled water out over enemy positions, freezing their artillery and tanks, and turning soldiers into human statues. He envisioned smaller ice battleships forcing their way into enemy ports, and freezing up the enemy's fleet with their ice guns. Once the port had been captured, huge blocks of pykrete would be rolled ashore to build a defensive wall, transforming the area into an unassailable ice fortress. Then, to prevent Nazi reinforcements arriving, special teams of ice warriors would be sent out to fire super-cooled water into surrounding railway tunnels, transforming them into giant impassable ice lollies.[34]

From Nice Bath to Ice Bath

While these latter ideas were just mad fantasies, top-secret experiments in manufacturing pykrete were carried out in the refrigerated basement of a fake Smithfield Market butcher's shop; the 'shop assistants' were really disguised commandos, with the pykrete lab concealed behind rows of frozen animal carcasses to avoid suspicion. Famously, once samples of pykrete had successfully been made, Lord Mountbatten is said to have taken a slab to Chequers, the PM's country retreat, where he was told that Churchill was having a hot bath. 'Good,' said Mountbatten, 'that's exactly where I want him to be!' He then ran up the stairs and threw the pykrete into Churchill's steaming bathwater. It did not melt, and Churchill is supposed to have been sold on the project immediately – at least according to an after-dinner speech given by Mountbatten following the war.[35]

Another colourful story involving pykrete was told about a demonstration of the new wonder-substance at a secret meeting of the Allied Chiefs of Staff in Quebec during 1943 when Mountbatten produced two blocks, one of ordinary ice and one of pykrete, laid them out on the floor and shot his pistol at them. The ordinary ice block shattered instantly, but the bullet pinged off the pykrete one and buzzed 'like an angry bee' around the room at leg-level, grazing the trouser-leg of Fleet Admiral Ernest King. However, another version of this story has it taking place at Lord Mountbatten's Combined Operations HQ back in Britain, has a Lieutenant Commander Douglas Grant firing the gun, and has the bullet hitting Chief of the Imperial Staff Sir Alan Brooke square on the shoulder instead.[36] Could such a similar thing really happen twice?

Some of the stories told about Pyke's inventions may perhaps have been somewhat fictional, then, but his actual ice ships themselves certainly were not. Given the codename 'Project Habbakuk',[37] a prototype, sixty feet long and weighing 1,000 tons, was actually built on a Canadian lake, and it seemed to work. Lord Mountbatten visited, and tried to blast a hole in the battleship's side using a shotgun; it barely even scratched it. And yet, in the end, giant ice battleships were never built. Their cost was enormous, supplies of pykrete were scarce, and the problem of how to steer vessels so vast was never really solved. In any case, aircraft carriers were of more use fighting the Japanese in the Pacific than the Nazis in Europe, and America had begun capturing various Pacific islands to use as airbases, greatly lessening the need for them. By the time the first atom bomb was dropped on Hiroshima on 11 August 1945, the need for giant ice ships had evaporated completely.[38] As usual, Geoffrey Pyke's dreams had melted away into nothing.

The Human Zoo:
Zoological Eccentrics

The prize specimens who were experts on the strangest creatures on earth – themselves.

The British are famous for their love of animals – but sometimes this love can go a little too far. For instance, we must all be familiar with the phenomenon of the so-called 'Cat Lady', a term used to describe some mentally unbalanced individual (generally female) who, for whatever reason, gets it into their head to begin hoarding stupidly large numbers of domestic animals within their home, in woefully unsuitable conditions. For instance, one Mary Elizabeth Dear, known as the 'Cat Woman of Rottingdean', made headlines during the 1860s when news of her bizarre domestic arrangements seeped out to the world at large.

This 'Cat Woman' was quite definitely mentally unsound; she thought she was a great artist, and decided to specialise in animal portraits, like George Stubbs and Edwin Landseer. To this end, Miss Dear set about collecting a wide variety of pets to keep as artist's models. She ended up amassing quite a collection – and not always via legal means. Her neighbours in the seaside village of Rottingdean, near Brighton, had several times caught her invading their yards and gardens, seemingly in search of cats and dogs to kidnap. When one local, a Mr Moody, found three of his own felines were missing in February 1866, he drew an obvious conclusion and called the police. Miss Dear's house being searched, a bizarre and disturbing scene was discovered. Somehow, she had managed to accumulate some 150 pet cats – together with fifty dead ones, six of which were busily rotting in their mistress' bedroom, where they kept her company at night. In addition, she was also found to be harbouring fifteen dogs and a tame fox. Needless to say, the stench was indescribable and, seeing a clear public health hazard, a magistrate ordered the madwoman's lover (yes, she actually had one!) to clean the place up. However, this proved an impossible task; by May 1867, the appalling odour had returned, and an 'Inspector of Nuisances' was despatched to investigate. This time, he found over a hundred cats wandering the property, together with a fox, a goat, and large numbers of turkeys, geese and other fowl – all of them unwashed and caked in layers of their own faeces. Had Mary Elizabeth Dear really been a talented painter, then any portraits she may have been inspired to produce by these particular brown-coated animals may not have turned out as appealing to the public as she might have hoped.[1]

Another such sad case was that of Celestina Collins (1733–1803) an elderly miser who died in her house in Canterbury aged seventy, all alone in the world – except, that is, for the dozens of pet chickens which she allowed free reign of her abode, letting them sleep in her bed or nestle down in the oven. According to one contemporary report, the filth these fowl created was so bad that their excrement 'defiled not only her bed, and every article of her furniture, but even the plate out of which she ate.' Her two favourite animal companions were one particularly old and abnormally large cockerel, with spurs three inches long, and a massive rat of equally gargantuan proportions with which she used to take meals at her table – until, that is, the giant rat took a bite out of the bird one day, leading Ms Collins to strike it an almighty blow in chastisement. Sadly, the whack was so hard the rat died, leaving its mistress to enter mourning; maybe she died of a broken heart? Whatever caused her death, Collins certainly had a thing for rodents. When the dead woman's home was entered and her sheets pulled back, it was found she had been letting a nest of mice share her bed with her each night, enjoying her body warmth.[2]

We hear such stories and cringe, thinking Mary Elizabeth Dear and Celestina Collins to be mere lunatics. We might also be expected to think the same thing of a man who, while renting an Italian villa during his continental travels, decided to keep himself company there by installing his own personal menagerie on the premises, consisting of ten horses, eight dogs, three monkeys, five cats, an eagle, a crow and a falcon – and yet, seeing as this man was none other than the great Romantic poet Lord Byron (1788–1824), we would probably be minded to reconsider our assessment and class him as an admirable eccentric rather than an outright madman. The stories about Byron's excessive love of animals are well known; the marble monument he had erected to his favourite dog after its death, the trio of geese he rescued from the cooking pot and donated to his bemused banker for safekeeping, and the tale of how, while up at Cambridge, he got around his College's 'No Dogs' rule by installing a tame bear in his rooms instead, there being no specific prohibition against owning such a beast in the university statute books. Byron loved his animals; we know this and we laugh, people did not, as with the neighbours of the Cat Woman of Rottingdean, call in the services of the local Inspector of Nuisances to put an end to his zoological whims. Why is this? We are back, I suppose, to the privileges of wealth – Mary Elizabeth Dear could not afford to feed her animals properly, leaving many of them in a truly pitiful state. Lord Byron, however, heir to the stately home of Newstead Abbey, could afford to spend £20 per year on the food for one of his pet dogs alone – at a time when a housemaid's wages and lodging costs combined would have cost him £30. As a result, Byron's own animal army was rather better-groomed than that of Misses Dear and Collins.[3]

Likewise, when Miss Dear wanted to express her grief about her dead cats, she did so by retaining several of their decaying corpses in her bedroom. When one of the pets of Sir Thomas Barrett-Lennard (1826–1918) died, however, then he could afford to give them a rather grander send-off. His estate of Belhus, in Essex, contained special plots where he had his cats, dogs and horses buried, their corpses being placed within specially constructed animal coffins and then carried to the graveside in solemn procession by a troop of footmen decked out in full livery. Once laid within the ground, Barrett-Lennard then had the local vicar preside over a full formal burial service for the departed animal, against all usual custom. The Baronet's love for the Lord's creatures even extended to the household rats; he expressly forbade any of his staff to kill them and, instead of putting down poison, had bowls of fresh water prepared for them to drink from. The end result was that the rats grew as big as cats and overran the barns and corridors; they were so huge they could actually push furniture around the place. And yet – no Inspector of Nuisances ever came to call. No policeman came to intervene, either, the day Barrett-Lennard beat up a man he had observed being unkind to a pony, nor the time he was caught laying false trails for the hounds of the local Hunt (of which, bizarrely, he was Master) in order to allow the foxes to escape. As the High Sheriff of Essex, clearly he was considered to be above the law. Neither did mad doctors cause Sir Thomas any bother; they couldn't, as he was Chairman of the local Asylums Committee! [4]

It seems that the rich and privileged can (or could once) get away with treating animals in a way which, if replicated among us lesser mortals, would cause indignation. Take, for instance, the recent case of a Cambridge resident named Paul Dutton, who made the papers in 2013 due to his unusual habit of dressing his pet dog up as Adolf Hitler. Described at the time as a jobless father-of-six, Mr Dutton spent weeks creating a sheepskin brown-shirt uniform for his Chinese Crested dog Albert, adorned with a large swastika and an SS symbol on the buckle, as well as arranging the animal's hair so as to resemble the Führer's famous comb-over. The swastika-tattooed Mr Dutton had previously made unpleasant headlines for his habit of attending his local ASDA store dressed as an SS man, and seemed proud of his behaviour, telling reporters his dog was simply a member of the 'Woof-Waffe' – the canine equivalent of the Luftwaffe, presumably. Images of Dutton, clad in Nazi armband, taking 'Heel Hitler' for a walk are certainly striking, but in a purely negative way. Predictably, reports did not portray Mr Dutton as an agreeable eccentric but, rather, as an object of public disapproval. The *Daily Mail* called him 'a shameless Hitler fanatic', for instance, not a 'lovable rogue', and carried quotes from outraged locals who found his behaviour offensive. [5]

Undoubtedly, Mr Dutton's behaviour was highly odd. Far, far odder, however, were the animal-dressing antics of Francis Henry Egerton, 8th Earl of Bridgewater (1756–1829), who was famous for kitting his numerous pet dogs up in human clothing and allowing them to dine with him – just so long as their table manners were good. If they were not, then he would order his human underlings to have them measured by a tailor and fitted out with his servants' livery of yellow coats and knee breeches before banishing them to dine in an ante-room for eight days, thus depriving them of the honour of their master's company. If his dogs proved to have good etiquette, though, then they were treated well; after inheriting a then massive £40,000 a year and moving to Paris during middle age, he decked out his canine pals in silver collars and scaled-down versions of the very latest human fashions, right down to specially-made tiny shoes, and gave them a chair each at his dining table. There, they were waited on by flunkies – one to each animal – who tied napkins around their necks and laid out dishes of tasty treats on monogrammed plates. His dogs (and the household cats) were also given use of a specially prepared carriage filled with silk cushions so they could accompany Egerton on his Parisian run-arounds. When nature called, meanwhile, the Earl's servants were on hand to hold parasols above the dogs' heads while they urinated in the street. Egerton also dressed somewhat extravagantly himself, incidentally; he seems never to have worn any footwear more than once while in Paris, and to have catalogued each day's apparel by lining his shoes into long rows which he used as a makeshift calendar, counting back the days through each discarded pair. Again, however, the Earl's eccentricities, both zoological and sartorial, were tolerated and celebrated, not condemned – he was the rich son of the Bishop of Durham, after all, and a noted Fellow of the Royal Society, not some jobless, tattooed Führer-fan from Cambridge.[6]

Excessive love of animals is not all pure whimsy, though, and there have been some well-heeled zoological eccentrics who have made a real contribution towards the store of human knowledge, men such as John Victor Aspinall (1926-2000), a controversial figure who, though from middle-class roots, made huge sums running gambling dens, and used most of this money to fund his own zoo in the grounds of his country estate, Howletts in Kent. The first indication of Aspinall's animal-hoarding instincts came when, while occupying a London flat in 1956, he built a shed in the backyard and installed a capuchin monkey and two Himalayan brown bears inside there, at the same time buying a nine-week-old tigress named Tara which he allowed to share his bed. Noticing the neighbours were becoming rather disturbed by all this, Aspinall moved out, bought the mansion at Howletts, and promptly began filling its grounds with gorillas. His zoo-keeping methods were unorthodox, though, to say the least; Aspinall delighted to play with his apes, saying they should be treated as honoured guests, not prisoners on display, giving them Sunday dinners of roast meat and chocolate bars for dessert. Such methods undoubtedly provided some notable successes – Aspinall bred over fifty gorillas in captivity, for instance, and hundreds of tigers – but they were not without their cost, with several of his keepers being mauled, trampled or killed.

You might wonder, however, quite how much Aspinall would have cared. A distinctly misanthropic individual, he held the bizarre view (apparently inspired by a reading of an H. Rider Haggard novel) that there had once been some kind of 'Golden Age' in the long and distant past, during which animals and man had lived together in perfect harmony as equals, but that humans had since betrayed their former animal-friends, and begun waging war against them. Considering humanity itself to be a kind of plague, he is supposed to have been overjoyed to hear news of any natural disasters, and once said he would have been quite happy to kill himself if only he could take another 250 million people out with him – suicide by atom bomb may have been the best solution. Malaria, too, he positively encouraged; if only it could be allowed to spread further, killing off, say, another two billion of the lower orders. He also cheerfully admitted he would be willing to kill his own children if it would save an endangered species from extinction.

Animals, he was adamant, were simply *better* than people; of his thirty best friends, Aspinall once said, at least half could be classified as fauna. It was wrong, he explained, to view animals as inherently different to humans, as they had distinct individual personalities just like we did. He claimed to know some remarkably honest tigers, for instance, and once rather ungallantly described his then-wife as 'the perfect example of the primate female, ready to serve the dominant male and make his life agreeable'. Most notoriously, in 1993 he explained why he was quite happy to allow his infant grand-daughter to play with his live exhibits, saying that 'I'd rather leave [her] with gorillas than with a social worker.' As these quotes might suggest, John Aspinall was somewhat right-wing, politically. Not only did he stand for Parliament in 1997 upon behalf of the anti-EU Referendum Party, he was on record as thinking Hitler had a point when it came to eugenics. 'Broadly speaking, the higher-income groups tend to have a better genetic inheritance [than the poor],' he pronounced, and once gave a speech at a friend's funeral in which he spoke disparagingly of a certain 'genetic flaw' in the man, earning him a punch on the jaw after the service. Aspinall died of cancer in 2000, a disease he faced with some bravery – at one point, he seriously considered ending his treatment and going out in a blaze of glory by feeding himself alive to one of his own tigers instead![7]

Aspinall's obvious misanthropy, however, gives rise to one possible thought about why it might be that some people become so overly fond of animals – namely, due to some deep-seated personality-flaw which means they hate most of the human race. Lady Anne Isabella Byron, for example, once wrote of her estranged husband that

The reason why some tyrannical characters have been fond of animals, and humane to them, is because they [the animals] have no exercise of reason and could not condemn the wickedness of their master.[8]

This certainly appears to have been the case with Hastings William Sackville Russell, 12th Duke of Bedford (1888–1953), one of the coldest fish the aristocracy has ever produced. Like some grotesque miser straight out of Dickens, Russell liked the silent company of his pets so much that he treated them better than his own neglected children. The son of a former President of the Zoological Society, in 1906 Hastings led an expedition to China to collect specimens for the British Museum, later becoming an acknowledged expert on parrots, being appointed President of the Foreign Bird League and penning a noteworthy book on the subject, *Parrots and Parrot-Like Birds*. At one point, he had a collection of some 400 exotic birds in his home, to which he fed chocolates – items which his half-starved children were reduced to stealing themselves through hunger. Another of the 12th Duke's pets which seems to have been fed better than his own offspring was a favourite spider, to which, reputedly, he would regularly feed portions of roast beef and Yorkshire pudding.

In 1959, Russell's eldest son, John Ian Russell, published a deeply hostile memoir, *A Silver-Plated Spoon*, in which he called his father 'the loneliest man I ever knew, incapable of giving or receiving love, utterly self-centred and opinionated'. No wonder he preferred the company of animals. According to John, his father had been relentlessly bullied at Eton and denied any love from his father Herbrand, the 11th Duke, who had been a recluse, 'a selfish, forbidding man', living 'a cold, aloof existence isolated from the outside world by a mass of servants, sycophants and an eleven-mile wall.' Apparently, Hastings didn't speak to Herbrand for the final twenty years of his father's life, a rift which suited both men equally. A man of few words, Hastings was so uncommunicative towards his children that, as a boy, John didn't even realise he was heir to the dukedom – his dad simply never bothered to tell him. Having had an unhappy childhood himself, Hastings was determined to hand down his misery to the next generation; once John did finally find some joy in his life, marrying his lover in 1939, his father wasted no time in attempting to disinherit him.

Word of Hastings' extreme misanthropy soon began to spread – to the extent that, during the Second World War, he was investigated by MI5 as a potential traitor due to his apparent Nazi sympathies. He spent the war years calling for peace with Hitler, pumping out a series of pamphlets with titles like *Propaganda for Proper Geese*, and making speeches in the House of Lords in which he blamed Britain for starting the war in the first place, insisting that Hitler was a perfectly nice man who could be trusted to keep his word about anything. In 1940, he even made a trip across to neutral Ireland to meet with the German Ambassador in Dublin and attempt to negotiate peace with the Nazis himself. Maybe it was no wonder that Hastings had a bit of a thing for the Führer; after all, Hitler too was an animal lover, and was also reputedly a vegetarian, just like the 12th Duke, who earned the disparaging nick-name 'Spinach Tavistock' on account of his lettuce-chomping ways. MI5's investigation into Hastings concluded that he was 'a sexual pervert, physical coward and a rebel against all authority', who would most likely be appointed leader of a Nazi puppet government, should Hitler's planned invasion ever succeed. As soon as any German landing took place, he was earmarked for immediate arrest – but such a landing never did take place, and in 1953 he died of a self-inflicted gunshot wound on one of his estates in Devon. The coroner recorded a verdict of 'accidental death', but there was strong suspicion it had been suicide. It was a shame he didn't live on a little longer so as to be able to meet John Victor Aspinall – perhaps then he might have found a kindred spirit in life at last.[9]

Nowadays, of course, Britain has strict animal-protection laws, and the exploits of many of the zoological eccentrics detailed in this chapter would no longer be even remotely possible to pursue legally. One pair of zoological eccentrics whose antics would now be frowned upon, for instance, were the father-and-son team of William Buckland (1784–1856) and Frank Buckland (1826–1880). As well as being a respected theologian and Dean of Westminster, William Buckland was also the first person to successfully excavate and properly describe a dinosaur skeleton, and the first to realise that certain hitherto-mysterious fossils were in fact prehistoric dinosaur turds, a discovery which so pleased him he later had his table inlaid with several representative examples. During his time as a lecturer at Oxford, Buckland became known for his strange talks, where he would prance around on stage imitating the gait and movements of various extinct animals before producing a large blue bag filled with exotic items like animal skulls, fossil teeth and his beloved lumps of dino excrement. During one particularly memorable lecture, Buckland pulled out a hyena skull, rushed up to some unfortunate undergraduate, thrust it in his face and demanded to know 'What rules the world?' The student had to admit he did not know. 'The stomach, sir!' shouted Buckland. 'The stomach rules the world! The great ones eat the less, the less the lesser still!'

The stomach certainly ruled William Buckland's world. It was his bizarre lifelong ambition to eat his way through the entire animal-kingdom, initiating a brief craze for a practice known as 'zoöphagy', or the eating of unusual animals. At his dinners, guests would be served cooked crocodiles, panthers, hedgehogs and puppies, a particular speciality of the house being mice on toast. Buckland enjoyed the flavour of most of these creatures, but thought two in particular tasted absolutely vile – the humble mole and, worst of all, the common household bluebottle. When you consider what such insects usually feed on, perhaps this fact is not too surprising! Buckland's desire to taste strange fruit supposedly even extended to humanity itself. Visiting a cathedral one day, upon being pointed towards a strange reddish stain on the floor and told the legend that it was the miraculously preserved blood of some old martyred saint, Buckland is alleged to have got down and started licking it. Disappointed, he told his host that the stain was not blood at all – merely bat's urine, a substance which apparently he knew the taste of. Another tale, perhaps exaggerated, has it that when visiting the Archbishop of York Buckland was shown a curious relic, the preserved heart of King Louis XIV, kept for posterity in a silver casket. Unable to resist, Buckland is said to have immediately seized the valuable item and swallowed it, keen to see what royalty tasted like.

William's son Frank, born in 1826, was just as bad, if not worse; rather than pursuing zoöphagy as a mere hobby, he attempted to practise it in a semi-professional capacity. A surgeon, popular author and, later, holder of the august post of Her Majesty's Inspector of Salmon Fisheries, due to his childhood experiences at his father's dining table Frank Buckland was a natural choice to be invited to a strange meal held in London in 1859, dubbed the 'Eland Dinner'. An eland is a breed of African antelope, and the dinner was designed to see if its flesh was at all palatable, with the ultimate aim of introducing such exotic beasts (and others, like kangaroos and ostriches) to England to be bred in captivity, thus adding variety to the national diet. In 1860, Frank Buckland took matters onto an official footing and helped found an organisation called The Acclimatisation Society, which was wholly devoted to this mission. However, Buckland himself was perhaps not in it *entirely* for philanthropic purposes. While at school and university,

Frank had annoyed locals and teachers by catching field mice and cooking them over a fire al fresco, as well as hunting various other inappropriate creatures, pulping their bodies and scoffing them just like daddy. Several of his culinary experiments during adulthood also seemed unlikely to catch on. There was little prospect of his recipe for elephant's-trunk soup or rhinoceros pie becoming popular, for instance, and his rushing off to London Zoo after he had heard that there had been a fire in the giraffe house just so he could see what these animals tasted like when roasted was pure opportunism, nothing more.[10]

Some zoological eccentrics have been rather kinder to poor, dumb beasts, however, such as James 'Jemmy' Hirst (1738–1829), a farmer from Rawcliffe in Yorkshire who first showed signs of oddness while still a schoolboy, when he somehow managed to train a pet hedgehog to follow him around like a faithful slave. Supposedly, Hirst's nuttiness truly began in earnest, though, after his fiancé had died from smallpox, whereupon he retired to bed and contracted what was termed a 'brain-fever'. Upon recovering, Hirst took his hobby of taming wild beasts to ever more extreme lengths, most notably with a bull named Jupiter that he trained to pull his carriage instead of horses. Reputedly, Hirst once rode Jupiter during a fox-hunt, using a pack of specially trained pigs as hunting dogs, though this may be a mere fable. Seemingly true, though, is that he kept a veritable zoo's-worth of tamed creatures living inside his house and garden with him, including a fox, a pack of dogs, several mules, an otter and (so some sources say) a large bear called Nicholas. Word of this private collection even reached the ears of King George III, who invited Jemmy down to London to meet him – an invitation which he initially declined, on the grounds that he far was too busy teaching an otter to fish.

Hirst's dress was just as remarkable as his menagerie. When out hunting, he would wear a yellow woollen hat with a 10-foot brim, a bright red hunting coat with blue sleeves and red-and-white striped stockings. When attending the Doncaster races, meanwhile, he preferred to don a lambskin hat whose brim was a mere nine feet in length, and a shiny waistcoat made from duck feathers. This final item had several capacious pockets which were filled with bundles of special bank notes Hirst had made himself, bearing a hand-written promise to pay five-and-a-half pence to anybody who took one, and with which he tried to make bets. If Jemmy looked strange while actually at the races, meanwhile, he looked even stranger on his way there in his bull-drawn wicker carriage, a remarkable contraption which apparently resembled a giant upside-down lampshade to which were fitted four huge wheels, and which was said to include a wine cellar and double bed hidden away somewhere inside it. This may or may not have been true, but Hirst definitely did have the vehicle fitted with an innovative contraption of his own invention which caused a bell to ring whenever the carriage had travelled a mile, thus allowing him to know how far he had gone. When Jupiter the bull was feeling tired, Hirst is said to have tried fitting his coach with sails to catch the wind as a labour-saving device, but this just led to Jupiter losing control during a high breeze and crashing the vehicle through a shop window in Pontefract.

It seems that Jemmy Hirst was eccentric in every facet of his life, not just those relating to animals. For example, when he got married, he allegedly insisted upon wearing a toga and having the entire ceremony conducted in some form of sign language. His farm prospering, Hirst soon grew generous to man as well as beast, regularly summoning the poor and elderly to his home for a free meal by standing outside and blowing on a hunting horn. Once these charity cases had ventured inside, however, a strange scene awaited them. Hirst had hung his walls with chains, pieces of rope and various rust-eaten farming implements, and had already bought his own coffin, which served prior to his death as a kind of drinks cabinet. This strange item was built for comfort; it reputedly had windows and shelves built in, and Hirst charged curious visitors a fee to lie in it. When Jemmy finally needed this coffin for himself, aged ninety, the bottles of drink were removed and replaced with his lifeless corpse, which was to be carried away to the graveside by twelve young female virgins. Sadly, come the funeral these persons proved impossible to source, but two old widows bravely stepped into the breach and helped bear the casket along instead. His other wish for the funeral also failed; he had left instructions for musicians to follow the cortege playing happy songs, but the vicar forbade it. He couldn't, however, prevent Hirst from making out a will which left his accountant a piece of rope to 'go hang himself with'.[11]

Animals are all God's creatures, of course, a position certainly entertained by the Reverend Robert Stephen Hawker (1803–1875), who was firmly of the opinion that Heaven was not a place reserved simply for the souls of human beings, but for all creatures great and small, too. Hawker, the vicar of the remote Cornish parish of Morwenstow from 1834 until his death forty years later,

was a truly remarkable figure who, had there been space for a
section about religious eccentrics in this book, would have received
a chapter all of his own. A practical joker in his youth – when he
had painted a horse in stripes to disguise it as a zebra and falsely
arranged for coffins to be delivered to people's doors to spook
them – during adulthood Hawker developed into something of a
mystic. While during his wayward youth he had sat at the end of
a breakwater in Bude draped in seaweed, combing his hair and
singing mournful songs at night in an attempt to convince locals
he was a mermaid, in later life he was claiming to have seen *real*
mermaids himself, swimming in the waters below his clifftop hut
at Morwenstow, where he retreated away to smoke opium, write
poetry and commune with fairies, spirits and saints.

As these facts suggest, Hawker, though living in Victorian times,
had a mind which belonged more to the medieval period, it not being
unknown for him to interpret storms and crop failures as trials sent
by demons, devilish beings which he also blamed for revealing the
despicable secrets of gas, electricity and steam-power to mankind.
A very strange dresser, Hawker despised the usual black garb of a
clergyman, preferring to wear a velvet-cuffed cassock of what he
called 'blushing brown' on the grounds that (in his view, at least) it
was the same colour as the Virgin Mary's hair, combining this with
a variety of strange hats, including a natty pink fez-like number,
and eschewing the standard issue dog-collar for a soft white cravat.
The ensemble was completed by a pair of knee-length sea-boots,
which he felt appropriate to existence in a coastal parish. In later
life, he took the symbolism of his costume even further by dressing
in a purple or claret coat which he always left unbuttoned to show
off a blue fisherman's jersey, indicating that, just like Jesus, Hawker
too was 'a fisher of men'. This jersey had a small red cross sewn
in the side, corresponding to the spot on Christ's torso which had
been pierced by a spear, while various items of strange jewellery
dangled down from his person too, including medallions to ward
off evil spirits and a carpenter's pencil, symbolising Jesus' earthly
trade. As if this wasn't enough, Hawker also sometimes used to add
a yellow poncho to his outfit, as well as a pair of scarlet gloves, and
would carry a walking stick shaped like a sword in case he should
encounter the Devil. He must have made quite a sight when holding
his services in Morwenstow's parish church – particularly seeing as
he would habitually take his favourite cat into the pulpit with him
and, at certain points during the ceremony, throw himself down
on the floor with his arms outstretched and his legs pulled together

in the form of a human cross. This was when Hawker, who was anxious about public speaking, wasn't fainting in the middle of Mass, or running out of the building with a sudden fit of nervous diarrhoea.

A man of very odd ideas – such as the belief that Jesus (like himself) had no earlobes – Hawker nonetheless has a good claim to have invented the Harvest Festival, and also wrote the ballad *The Song of the Western Men*, now considered virtually the Cornish national anthem. It was his unique attitude towards animals, though, which earns him a place here. During his early career, Hawker kept a pet pig called Gyp which he considered so 'well-groomed and intelligent' that he took it out on house calls. When his sister objected to having this hog brought into her home one day, Hawker asked why, pointing out that 'he's as well-behaved as any of your family'. At Morwenstow, he kept nine cats (one of which he is dubiously claimed to have excommunicated after it caught a mouse on a Sunday) several large dogs and two deer, one of which supposedly assaulted a visiting Bishop and attempted to eat his apron. Many of these pets he would allow into church, something he thought permissible as 'there were dogs in the Ark'. He also developed the curious belief that the local bees, sick of being blown away in high winds, had cleverly begun picking up pebbles with their legs to act as ballast, dropping them when they reached the safety of the hive.

His special love, though, was for birds, to which creatures, like St Francis of Assisi, he claimed to be able to talk. Hawker's basic idea, similar to that of the old medieval bestiaries, was that animals were essentially living symbols sent down from Heaven into the world of man – or 'the attributes of God visibly roaming the earth', as he put it. His views were inconsistent, but he appeared to believe that birds indicated the presence of angels or demons in the area, according to their species and behaviour, once becoming convinced that a robin which sat in a churchyard tree while he was burying a dead child was really an angel because it seemed to chirp and sing at appropriate points during the funeral – 'We said the Service together, that bird and I.' So close did Hawker come to the local birds that he gave many names like Tommy or Jacky, and each would come to him to be fed crumbs when he called them by name, apparently following his verbal instructions. When a scarecrow was erected nearby, dressed in some of Hawker's old clothes, it had quite the opposite effect to that intended, with flocks gathering round it expecting to be fed. Such was Hawker's love for his animals, however, that in later life he stopped keeping so many, on account of the appalling grief he suffered whenever one died – his only comfort at such times, presumably, being that one day he would meet them all again in the Afterlife.[12]

Another person who thought animals might enter Heaven, meanwhile, was the long-forgotten Victorian psychiatrist Dr William Lauder Lindsay (1829–1880). Born in Edinburgh in 1829, in 1854 Lindsay began work at the Murray Royal Institution for the Insane in Perth, where he stayed until his retirement in 1879. Also an expert on botany, in 1857 Lindsay was offered the unlikely post of Official Lichenologist to the Canadian Government, but turned it down and in 1859 married a fellow Scot named Elizabeth Reid. In 1860, he suffered a nervous breakdown, and took a two-year trip to New Zealand to recover; less than a year after returning to Scotland, however, he suffered a nervous shock of another kind when Elizabeth died. Many people, after losing a spouse, have quite reasonably sought solace in some hobby to try and while away the lonely hours. Lindsay was no different; it is just that, instead of taking up gardening or cookery, he decided to try and prove that animals could become mentally ill, just like his human patients (and, arguably, he himself) were.

To this end, Lindsay spent seven years combing through newspapers, books, magazines and obscure journals in search of as many accounts of animals acting like humans as he could possibly find. The result was a 1,200-page book, *Mind in the Lower Animals in Health and Disease*, published in 1879 in two volumes, the first of which dealt with how animals acted when sane, the second with their behaviour when insane. Lindsay was lucky to be writing at a time when, due to the rapid expansion of the popular press, tales of bizarre animal behaviour which would once have remained unwritten were beginning to be picked up and distributed to a wider audience for entertainment purposes. Many of these tales could be interpreted as providing evidence that animals could go insane, if viewed through Lindsay's eyes. In 1880, for example, it was reported that a monkey named 'Jocko' had hanged itself with a clothes line in a barn in North Carolina, after being repeatedly taken to see public executions taking place by its irresponsible owner, one Rockwell Syrock. The monkey's suicide was represented as a form of 'monkey-see, monkey-do' play gone horribly wrong, but perhaps its exposure to so much death and suffering at the gallows had simply driven the poor beast loopy? Another simian suicide, meanwhile, is meant to have taken place near Barnsley in 1890 when a monkey belonging to a miner named John Hines got hold of his master's razor and tried to shave his two children's faces with it. However, Daddy-Monkey proved less than skilful with his blade, and chopped his kids' heads off by mistake. Woebegone, the ape then turned the razor on himself.[13]

Dubious stories like this were pure cat nip to Lindsay, who came to believe that animals could display religious impulses, demonstrate love and affection, and were aware of concepts such as justice, claiming to have found evidence that Barbary apes sometimes held public trials of misbehaving monkeys, complete with simian lawyers. He was not above ranking species according to their presumed moral worth, either, claiming that lobsters were more sophisticated, loving and appreciative of classical music than their hard-shelled cousins the crabs were, and praising cattle for having developed a sophisticated class system, saying admiringly that 'every cow knows her place and keeps it'. Just as strangely, Lindsay claimed to have identified which specific medical disorders which species of animal were particularly prone to, accusing bees of being habitual kleptomaniacs on the presumable grounds that they kept on stealing nectar from flowers. As Lindsay put it:

> There is an air of roguery about the thieving bee, which to the expert is as characteristic as are the motions of a pick-pocket to the skilful policeman. Its sneaking look and nervous, guilty agitation, once seen, can never be mistaken.

There was another, darker, side to Lindsay's anthropomorphic theorising, however, as it ultimately led him to feel that animals were in many respects far superior beings to all forms of humanity bar that single sector of it which really mattered – namely, middle-class white Europeans. He seemed to feel that many non-whites were quite literally lower than monkeys, and derided even certain lower-class elements of white British society – such as the 'women-kickers of the Black Country' – as being somehow less truly human than some animals were. So ingrained did this misanthropic prejudice become that, by the 1870s, Lindsay was publishing 'scientific' papers in which he claimed that rabies didn't really exist, being merely a rumour that had been put about by drunkards, children and 'illiterate Irishmen'. Just as odd, it seems that towards the end of his life Lindsay, perhaps influenced by the late-Victorian craze for Spiritualism, was planning a book proving that animals had immortal souls. His own death in 1880 put paid to this, but did lead to a marvellously arch assessment of his legacy appearing in *The Edinburgh Medical Journal*. Lindsay's books were so pro-animal and so anti-human, said his anonymous obituarist, that 'one would think ... he expected them to become extensive purchasers'.[14]

Another eccentric anthropomorphic theoriser was James Burnett, better known as Lord Monboddo (1714–1799) a once-famous Scottish judge and philosopher. A brilliant youth, with so great a reputation for Classical learning that he claimed to be the only man alive able to pronounce the Ancient Greek tongue correctly, Burnett's abilities as a lawyer were quickly recognised and he was promoted to be a Judge of Session and given the title 'Lord Monboddo', after the Kincardineshire mansion, Monboddo House, where he had been born in 1714. Fame and fortune allowed Monboddo to indulge his love of the classical world, which he thought far superior to modernity to the extent that he indulged in several Ancient Greek health fads to keep himself in shape, such as bathing in the open air at six every morning in a tub filled with cold water taken from a stream. Like Cincinnatus, the ancient Roman who retired from public life to tend his farm, Monboddo frequently shed his judge's robes, donned rustic gear, and ploughed his own lands using oxen instead of horses, Roman-style. Refusing to use a carriage, such things not having existed in antiquity, he went everywhere on horseback, reading his copy of Homer. It was his view that mankind during his own day was undergoing a sad decline, and that the world would soon end. The Ancient Greeks had been superhuman giants, he calculated, some fourteen feet tall. Humans during the eighteenth century, however, had since shrunk to be literally less than half the men they used to be.

The main trouble with Monboddo's love of all things ancient, though, was that he trusted the books of Classical authors like Pliny so much that he thought their word gospel – even when they were spouting nonsense about far-off regions of the globe supposedly containing such aberrant sub species of humanity as mermaids and dog-headed men. Thinking these tales meant that humans could come in all shapes and sizes, Monboddo began theorising that perhaps the world's various monkey-species were really just different, if hitherto-unrecognised, primitive sub types of human beings too – particularly orang-utans, which he described as living in their own 'nation'. While he admitted apes didn't have speech, Monboddo, not unlike William Lauder Lindsay, set out to prove they were just like humans in every other conceivable way, collecting as many anecdotes about monkeys acting like men as he could. Some of the stories he amassed were as remarkable as they were dubious; he found alleged eyewitness accounts of apes raping humans, monkeys who had learned to play musical instruments, orang-utans who were embarrassed to be seen naked, and details of supposed 'chimpanzee-villages' governed over by idle but honoured monkey kings. Beavers, too, were just as advanced, he thought, owning slaves and conducting wars.

In Monboddo's view, the whole of Creation had a kind of substratum of psychic consciousness present within it, which was constantly striving to arrive at the kind of self-aware rational state of mind currently possessed only by man; monkeys and beavers were close to achieving this, he thought, but other forms of existence rather less so. Apples, for example, were morons; magnets, too, were rather dim, while stones and pebbles were positively retarded. Nonetheless, when an apple fell to ground, a magnet attracted filings or a stone rolled downhill, Monboddo felt that this was because, however vaguely, they *desired* to do so. All talk of such alleged forces as 'gravity' or 'magnetism' was basically bunkum; *mind* was the only true motivating force in the universe. Confirmation of these theories was provided during a vision Monboddo had in 1778, when a beautiful spirit-maiden appeared before him and gave a philosophy lecture in French, in which she agreed with his every word.

Despite his odd ways, Monboddo was a highly respected figure of the Scottish Enlightenment, mixing with fellow philosophers like David Hume, and even with royalty. His downfall finally came, however, after he came across a passage in an obscure book by a seventeenth-century Swedish sailor who claimed to have encountered a savage tribe on one of the Nicobar Islands, who had captured and eaten some of his crew. The strange thing about these cannibals, however, was that they allegedly had tails! Astounded by this account, Monboddo went public with a new theory proposing that nearly all human beings, as cousins of the monkey tribe, were actually born with tails, but that an international conspiracy of midwives was at work to cut them off at birth so nobody would ever know. While it has been suggested that Monboddo only said this to gain publicity and stimulate debate, if it really was some kind of early PR-stunt then it back fired as he was widely ridiculed, depicted in cartoons as a sort of ape-man himself and labelled a lunatic.

By 1773, Monboddo had retracted his opinion, but it was too late. While a sympathetic reading of Monboddo's works would reveal that, among all the madness, he had actually quite independently reached some of the same basic conclusions later arrived at by Charles Darwin and Sir Francis Galton, if he was remembered at all after his death in 1799, then it was, essentially, as a monkey-mad nutter. For instance, Thomas Love Peacock's 1817 novel *Melincourt*, in which an orang-utan adopts the false name Sir Oran Haut-Ton, dresses as an aristocrat and stands as an MP, was intended as one long mockery of Monboddo's ideas. Footnotes in the novel actually direct the reader towards quotations from Monboddo's books, providing jokey 'scientific justification' that each new plot point really could happen.[15] No doubt some eccentrics would happily believe it!

A Most Unnatural History: Charles Waterton (1782–1865)

The acrobatic explorer who invented the nature reserve, but lacked any reserve whatsoever himself.

There are some books you just know are going to be good right from the moment you open them, one such tome being Dr Richard Hobson's amazing 1867 biography *Charles Waterton: His Home, Habits and Handiwork*.[1] As has been pointed out before,[2] the contents pages alone of this valuable work are an absolute delight. As a personal long-time friend of Charles Waterton, the Squire of Walton Hall near Wakefield in Yorkshire, Dr Hobson, a local physician, had a close-up view of one of the strangest people of all time – and he wastes no time in letting us know. His chapter headings include the following: 'The Author suspects that the Squire had a foreknowledge of the trees' suicidal termination when he trained them', 'The Ape searching the Squire's head reminds him of a Cambridge anecdote', 'Capricious Freak of a Duck', 'Mr Waterton 'fairly floored' by Mr Salvin's clever imitation of a Pig', 'An allusion to a stench from a Dead Herring near the Grotto induces the Squire to relate an incident regarding Dead Letters', 'The Squire filled the Author's pockets and carriage-box frequently with Nuts', 'Explanation why the Squire was able to make his Elbows meet', 'Ludicrous circumstance associated with the Death of a Mallard' and, of course, 'An Oxe-Eye Titmouse builds her nest in the trunk of a tree prepared for Owls, but declines occupying it in future years because a Squirrel had used it'.[3]

If, as soon as you opened the covers of Hobson's book, you knew you were in for an odd time, then exactly the same could be said about opening the gates of Walton Hall. Coming as he did from an old Catholic family, Waterton could trace his lineage back through several illustrious ancestors, no less than seven of whom had been canonised saints, the most famous being Sir Thomas More.[4] While there was a definite strain of saintliness to the Squire's character, however, the first impression of any first-time visitor to Walton Hall might well have been that its chief occupant was much more of a Holy Fool than a Blessed Saint.

First of all, the unprepared visitor might wonder what exactly was going on there to necessitate the construction of a nine-foot wall right the way around the estate boundaries, a distance of some three miles. The answer was simple; it was there to keep the poachers out. While the term did not really exist during Waterton's day, Walton Hall under his benign stewardship was the first true nature-reserve in history, and a paradise on earth for bird life in particular. No gun was to be fired within its 300 acres, nor hunting dog given free access, nor boat allowed to cross its lake between September and May, lest the environment be disturbed.[5] If any poachers did gain access, though, then they would surely be fooled by the fake wooden pheasants which Squire Waterton had placed in his trees to make them waste their bullets.[6] The saintly Squire seems also to have been the man who invented the idea of a nesting box for birds,[7] deliberately creating holes in trees, sometimes fitting them with tiny doors, then filling them with various things useful to bird life. To him, bird cages were essentially prisons, and animals always best studied in their natural environment, through either close observation or a telescope.[8]

These were enlightened attitudes indeed for Waterton's day, and he was one of the first to warn mankind about the dangers of pollution from the new industries which were then springing up across Europe, perceiving early on that the smoke and noxious vapours from a factory did not affect only its immediate locality, but could be carried on the wind far and wide.[9] When a soapworks opened near his home in 1839 and its fumes began killing his trees, Waterton took its owners to court, becoming probably the first man in England to gain an injunction against a company upon environmental grounds.[10] It is appropriate, then, that today the largest memorial which exists to the Squire of Walton Hall is another, much larger, nature reserve – Waterton Lakes National Park in Canada, all 195 square miles of it. Waterton never actually visited the area, but a lake there was named after him by a Royal Artillery officer named Thomas Blakiston, who surveyed it in the 1850s.[11] Evidently Blakiston was a fan, but that was no terribly unusual thing; other people to have cited Waterton as an inspiration were the co-formulators of the theory of evolution, Charles Darwin and Alfred Russell Wallace.[12]

The Book of Nature

This nature reserve Squire Waterton liked to fill not only with the usual wonders of nature, but with as many bizarre freaks as he could lay his hands on. No doubt the hundred lunatics from Wakefield Asylum whom he allowed to wander, dance and picnic through the grounds loved to come across them.[13] Perhaps the lapse of nature he coveted the most was a truly peculiar duck born in the nearby village of Bingley in 1857 which, in the words of Dr Hobson, had been

> ... hatched with its head reversed, having its bill ... appearing and indeed actually situated immediately above its tail, so that when food was placed on the ground, behind its tail, this duck always had to seize it by turning a somersault.[14]

What a pet that would have been! Sadly, when Dr Hobson sent down to Bingley for the bird, it transpired that the superstitious villagers, thinking it a work of Satan, had killed it, together with all but one of its siblings, the entire brood having been born with a diverse range of interesting deformities. This last surviving duck being brought to Dr Hobson, it was discovered to have webless toes, a quality which earned it a new home on Squire Waterton's lake, the bird being christened 'Dr Hobson' after its discoverer. Maybe, if you were visiting, you would pass by this curious specimen on your way – as a farm worker did one day in 1860, finding it lying still on the banks of a dam. 'If you please, Squire, Dr Hobson is dead' said the saturnine-faced yokel, hat in hand, as he went up to the Hall to pay his condolences. Naturally, Waterton got the wrong idea and prepared to enter mourning until, finding the embarrassing yet thoroughly heartening nature of his error, he made preparations instead to get hold of the dead duck and have it mounted before presenting it to the real Dr Hobson as a kind of *memento mori* illustrating the ultimate way of all flesh, whether human or mallard.[15]

Waterton termed such freaks *lusus naturae*, or 'sports of nature', and revelled in finding them, not only for their intrinsic curiosity-value, but also because he liked to discover hidden symbolic meanings in them. For example, an old mill stone had at some point been dumped in an orchard on his land and, by chance, a seed had blown into the circular hole in the middle of the stone, a filbert tree growing up through it from the soil beneath. Seeing a natural allegory at work, instead of moving the stone away, Waterton left it where it was. As the tree flourished ever higher, it took the mill stone up with it, bearing its weight, though only precariously; it looked as though it could collapse at any minute. This phenomenon Waterton took to be a valuable warning from God upon the disastrous potential consequences of excessive government spending, christening the arboreal *lusus naturae* 'John Bull and the National Debt', this outstanding cheque being viewed by him as an even bigger mill stone hanging around the nation's neck.[16] It seemed that, to Charles Waterton, nature really was one giant book just waiting to be read.

A Weird Welcome

After passing by these amazing displays, you may then have been lucky enough to encounter Squire Waterton himself. Maybe you would catch him by the lake, hunting pike or water rats with a bow and arrow,[17] or else you might find him wandering about trailed by a long line of birds of all descriptions, who had become attached to the Squire on account of his habit of walking everywhere with his pockets stuffed full of bread.[18] If he ever forgot to pack such titbits on his person, Waterton would begin to feel guilty, going out of his way to avoid the social embarrassment occasioned by facing his favourite goose, which waited for him on a particular bridge every night, empty-handed; according to one eyewitness account, 'If he could not find a bit of food for it, he would wait at a distance till the bird went away, rather than give it nothing when it raised its bill'.[19] So excessive was his love for animals of all kinds that, in the words of another of Waterton's friends, Father J. Wood, he

> had no idea that he was doing anything out of the general course of things if he asked a visitor to accompany him to the top of a lofty tree to look at a hawk's nest, or if he built his stables so that the horses might converse with each other, or his kennel so that his hounds should be able to see what was going on.[20]

Possibly, if you were well known to him and well liked, then, regardless of the weather, he would rush out and start dancing down the driveway, kicking up his feet and propelling his slippers above his head in sheer joy at your company. Kicking off his footwear in all directions was, it seemed, a particular hobby of the Squire, one he facilitated by the means of always wearing shoes which were deliberately too wide and too loose, so that he could shed them at any moment. Please him with your conversation, and he would end up barefoot in no time.[21]

If the master of the house did not see you coming, however, then you would have to knock on his door, provided you could work out how to do so. Squire Waterton had two metal door knockers which, according to Dr Hobson, were 'ludicrously strange-looking appendages' cast 'in the similitude of human faces of a very extraordinary character ... one representing mirth, and the other misery'. It seems that the mirthful face was so amused because it was stuck immovably to the door, meaning unwary visitors would be unable to rap with it no matter how hard they tried, leaving them stood there feeling foolish. The miserable knocker would prove more functional, but nonetheless came with a catch, as when used 'this rapper appears to scowl upon you as if suffering intense agony from the blows you have just given it.'[22] If you actually made it past these curious knockers and into the Hall itself, then another obstacle may well have awaited you, in the form of the mansion's butler. He was a strange chap; sometimes, when a stranger arrived, this faithful servant would answer the door bearing a brush and a coal scuttle, and cause disappointment by denying them entrance. Then, however, he would jab them in the ribs with his brush before giving them a hearty handshake and shedding his disguise – for the 'butler' was in fact none other than Charles Waterton himself, done up in fancy dress.[23]

An even worse fate than encountering Waterton in disguise, meanwhile, was to come upon the savage beast that lived beneath the coat table kept in the front entrance hall for visitors. This was covered by a large cloth which hung down to the floor, giving the unseen monster a place to hide. Get too close, and a loud growling would be heard, followed by your legs being gripped by the paws and teeth of what seemed at first like some foul fiend – but which in fact was only Squire Waterton himself, crouched down on all fours and pretending to be a guard dog. Dr Hobson suffered this fate several times until, heartily sick of being bitten on the ankles by his friend, he pointed out that being on the receiving end of such sudden shocks had more than once been enough to send a man insane. Waterton immediately apologised and vowed to act the savage beast no more; if he ever did, he promised, he would give Hobson a whip and allow him to violently assault him.[24] The

Squire was as good as his word. From now on, he would play a different trick upon his friend instead; during Hobson's many visits, Waterton would now somehow contrive to fill his visitor's discarded coat full of nuts. Going out to his carriage, as often as not Dr Hobson would find it packed with eggs or pieces of fruit, too; acts of kindness, strangely expressed.[25]

I've Created a Monster!

Other strange creatures lurked within the walls of Walton Hall too, though, for Charles Waterton was also an expert taxidermist. Feeling the usual methods of preserving dead animals to be somewhat inadequate, Waterton devised his own technique, scraping away most of his specimens' internal layers of skin and then treating the remaining hide with a solution of mercuric chloride to harden it up. Then, he would adjust and pose the animal's position until it was to his liking. Unusually, his trophies were all hollow, rather than stuffed – as he would demonstrate to visitors by twisting their heads off and inviting them to peer inside. 'Allow me to inform you that there are no *stuffed* animals in this house,' he proudly told a guest in 1856, and he was telling the truth. However, while Waterton's method does appear to have produced superior results to any others available at the time, it was seldom copied as it was difficult to master and slow to complete.[26]

There were other reasons why Waterton's methods were rarely copied, too – for, alongside all the specimens preserved for purely scientific purposes, were a few freaks of the Squire's own devising. These wholly unnatural *lusus naturae* generally consisted of two or more corpses stitched together to form hideous mutants which embodied some kind of allegorical message of Waterton's own choosing. This was appropriate, as the very word 'monster' comes from the Latin term *monere* meaning 'to warn'. With his love of Classical learning, Waterton would certainly have known this, which is why his preserved monsters came with symbolic titles like (once again) 'John Bull and the National Debt' attached. This particular eyesore was formed from a porcupine whose face had been manipulated to look human-like, and whose back was encased within a large tortoise shell. On top of this were two big money bags, one of which bore the phrase 'National Debt – Eight Hundred Millions'. Also perched upon John Bull's shell was a grinning dragon, formed from a baby caiman with bird claws attached as spines and horns. Just as bad, a further five such evil creatures surrounded John, ranging from inexplicably toothed toads to angler fish spliced with snakes. The message was clear; Britain was being weighed down and assaulted by the twin demonic burdens of the deficit and the consequent excessive governmental taxation.[27]

As this particular *lusus naturae* suggests, Waterton's politics were distinctly conservative in nature, though he always steadfastly refused to vote, considering the House of Commons a mere snake pit.[28] The National Debt was, undoubtedly, one of the Squire's main political concerns, though; he could never understand why it had been allowed to develop, distrusting the machinations of modern finance so much that he held even cheques and paper money to be the Devil's work, preferring always to pay for things in the 'solid tin' of coin, even when the sum was absurdly large. When he decided upon having the massive wall built around his estate, for instance, Waterton delayed construction until he had saved up and hidden around his house the thousands of gold sovereigns needed to pay for the structure. The builders might not have been used to getting their wages in gold, but that is what happened; otherwise, the Squire feared, a 'drunken mason' might accidentally choose to light his pipe with a banknote, thus acting to 'deprive his family of sustenance for the next month'. Waterton claimed he did not fear his hoard being stolen, as 'according to the political aspect of the times in which we live and are so unmercifully taxed, the money is quite as safe in my favourite drawer as it would be in the Bank of England.'[29]

Another of Waterton's *lusus naturae* which embodied the evils of taxation was 'The Nondescript', a striking-looking red howler monkey whose head and shoulders Waterton had mounted like a Classical bust, and whose facial features he manipulated to make it look almost human. Indeed, some people thought it *really was* human and, when it was placed on display and engravings made public, some morons said what a disgrace it was that Waterton had been allowed to kill some poor foreigner purely in order to demonstrate his skills in taxidermy. There was even talk of taking Waterton to court, forcing him to clarify that the thing was merely a monkey after all. Those who examined the head of this creation particularly closely, however, might have noticed that the monkey man bore an uncanny resemblance to one human being in particular – namely, one J. R. Lushington, Secretary to the Treasury, who had told Waterton that he could only receive his howler monkey through Customs upon payment of the correct duty-fee. When Dr Hobson put this theory to his friend, Waterton simply smiled and replied, 'Let those who think the cap fits put it on.'[30]

As a good Catholic, Waterton's other main bugbear in life was the idea that everything in England had gone rapidly downhill since Protestantism had been embraced as the State religion. As such, one of his especial hobbies was creating tableaux of various lizards in human-like poses and labelling them with the names of influential Protestants of the past – thus anticipating David Icke by some 150 years. The most insulting of all these pro-Papist creations was undoubtedly 'Martin Luther After His Fall', which cast a female gorilla called Jenny as the titular father of Protestantism. It crouches down with its arms folded in a comical fashion, and comes complete with two large horns attached to its head, thus implying that Luther was really Satan in disguise.[31] Mounted in pride of place at the top of his main staircase, meanwhile, were Waterton's two most famous trophies, a huge alligator and a massive boa constrictor. Waterton enjoyed trying to explain this latter beast's presence in his home by claiming that he had shot the Devil[32] – but how did it really get there?

Waterton's Wanderings

The simple answer is that Charles Waterton brought these corpses back himself from his various adventures abroad, particularly in South America, where he played the role of intrepid explorer to a tee. He first got the travel bug – literally – in Malaga, Spain, in 1802, where he experienced an epidemic outbreak of some obscure plague known locally as the 'black vomit', which killed Waterton's uncle, but not himself. Charles did catch the disease, but, unlike thousands of weaker mortals, his constitution was strong enough to pull him through.[33] Having escaped from the jaws of death this once, Waterton seems to have had little fear of anything afterwards, setting out to what is now Guyana in 1804 to take charge of another uncle's estates, and between 1812 and 1824 making several lone expeditions into the then largely unexplored South American rainforest. Was Waterton scared of the dangers he may have faced? Not at all; in 1825, he published an account of his adventures, *Wanderings in South America*, where he wrote the following rather blasé account of jungle-perils:

> Snakes in these wilds are certainly an annoyance, though perhaps more in imagination than reality ... Tigers [i.e. jaguars, etc] are too few, and too apt to fly before the noble face of man, to require

a moment of your attention. The bite of the most noxious of the insects, at the very worst, only causes a transient fever, with [only] a degree of pain, more or less.[34]

Indeed, in the teetotal and highly moral Waterton's view, a night out drinking and whoring in the theatres and flesh pits of London was far more dangerous than penetrating the virgin jungle.

The youth who incautiously reels into the lobby of Drury Lane, after leaving the table sacred to the god of wine, is exposed to more certain ruin, sickness and decay than he who wanders a whole year in the wilds of [Guyana].[35]

It is easy to feel that Waterton was being overly modest here; during his explorations, he swam across alligator-infested rivers, caught a near fatal fever, and was nearly killed by a rattlesnake.[36] More famously, he fought with a giant boa-constrictor, some fourteen feet long, and a large caiman, ten-and-a-half feet in length. The boa he dug out from its lair in the ground, only finally vanquishing it when he removed his braces and used them to tie the snake's mouth up with. He then bundled the serpent into a bag and spent a night sleeping in the same room with it, being kept awake by its irritatingly loud hissing. In the morning, doubtless tetchy from lack of sleep, Waterton slit its throat, curious to see what the monster's teeth were like. Apparently, the Squire found them to be something of a disappointment.[37]

Less disappointing was the giant caiman (South American alligator) which Waterton vanquished one day by the simple method of riding it bareback to the point of the reptile's utter exhaustion. After the caiman had been caught by a group of Indians on a rope, Waterton ordered them to pull it out of the water and onto dry land. Waterton's account of this feat is exciting indeed:

This was an interesting moment ... I instantly ... sprang up and jumped on his back, turning half round [in the air] as I vaulted, so that I gained my seat with my face in a right position. I immediately seized his fore-legs, and by main force twisted them onto his back; thus they served me for a bridle. He now seemed to have recovered from his surprise, and, probably fancying himself in hostile company, he began to plunge furiously, and lashed the sand with his long and powerful tail. I was out of reach of the strokes of it, by being near his head. He continued to plunge and strike, and made my seat very uncomfortable. It must have been a fine sight ... it was the first and last time I was on a caiman's back ... Should it be asked how I managed to keep my seat, I would answer [that] I hunted some years with Lord Darlington's fox-hounds.[38]

Doing the Donkey-Work

Apart from wrestling the wildlife, Waterton's main aim in exploring the rainforest was to discover the secret of a fabled substance then known as 'the woorali poison', now better known as curare. Curare is derived from the curare vine, and was used by the Macoushi Indians as a poison for hunting with. Curare-tipped darts, shot from blowpipes into animals, will kill them through paralysing their nervous system, stopping the lungs and causing death by asphyxiation. However, if the animal's lungs can be kept going through a process of artificial respiration, then eventually the effects will wear off and the beast will recover. Because of this unusual property, curare was once used as a form of muscle relaxant and anaesthetic in surgery, although nowadays it has been superseded by other drugs.[39]

However, before it could be put to medical use, curare had to be brought back to Europe; and Waterton was the first man to do so. He was also one of the first to perform experiments with the substance. Most celebrated was the time he injected a female donkey with a dose. Within ten minutes, the donkey was dead – or so it seemed. Then, however, 'An incision was ... made in its windpipe, and through it the lungs were regularly inflated for two hours with a pair of bellows.' Eventually, 'Suspended animation returned. The ass held up her head and looked around.' The poison wore off and the donkey got back up, though she didn't look too well. Feeling pity for the animal, Waterton adopted it, christening it 'Wooralia', and taking it back to Walton Hall to live a stress-free life of luxury. 'Wooralia shall be sheltered from the wintry storm,' promised Waterton, 'and when summer comes, she shall feed in the finest pasture.'[40]

Was this episode cruel, or was it kind? As kind as was possible for an avid naturalist, Waterton would have replied. His opinion was that, just so long as the natural world was not being excessively exploited, then it was still a perfectly valid endeavour to cause an individual animal some harm in the name of science and the greater good. Whether or not an action was sustainable was the key. Mother Nature, he said, will allow thee to slay the fawn, and to cut down the mountain-cabbage for thy support, and to select from every part of her domain whatever may be necessary for the work thou art about; but, having killed a pair of doves in order to enable thee to give mankind a true and proper description of them, thou must not destroy a third through wantonness ... And if, in the cool of the evening, thou art ... deprived of light to write down the information thou hast collected, the firefly ... will be thy candle. Hold it over thy pocket-book, in any position which thou knowest will not hurt it, and it will afford thee ample light. And when thou hast done with it, put it kindly back again on the next branch to thee. It will want no other reward for its services.[41]

He Talks to the Animals

As a boy, you would never have thought that little Charles would grow to be so fond of animals; while studying under Jesuits at Lancashire's famous Stoneyhurst College, he was appointed as the school's official rat-catcher, fox-hunter and rook-killer, the Holy Fathers presenting him with a crossbow to shoot these birds with in their nests.[42] Waterton kept his hatred of rats into adulthood – he accused them of being 'Hanoverians', and devised an unusual method of expelling them using tar[43] – but, while a schoolboy, he seems to have perpetrated acts of extreme violence against a wide variety of God's creatures, whacking his teacher's dog over the head with a brick, for instance, and killing a goose with a sharpened stick. Once he had grown, meanwhile, one of Waterton's pet hates was the act of stealing or breaking birds' eggs; but, as a child, he enjoyed playing a form of 'egg-conkers' with friends during Easter.[44] Clearly, during his earliest days, the infant Charles was not as knowledgeable a naturalist as he would later become. One local animal he dearly wanted to meet in childhood, for instance, was a giant brown ghost rodent called 'The Tudhoe Mouse', which was supposed to haunt the vicinity, scaring the villagers' cats.[45]

During adulthood, however, on such good terms was Squire Waterton with animal-kind that it was not unusual to see him perched halfway up a tree, stroking his favourite birds with the back of his hands in an attempt to show them he cared.[46] Apparently, he even formed the opinion he was able to talk to insects. The Squire could make friends with animals of all kinds; one particularly good pal of his was a Brazilian toad of which he was so fond that, when a visitor jocularly dismissed it as being 'an ugly brute' one day, Waterton got so angry that he simply walked away, later professing himself to be 'grieved to the back-bone' by such a cruel assessment. To Waterton, this toad was genuinely beautiful, and he would spend hours fondling it and gazing into its gorgeous eyes (as well as intermittently burying it underground for experimental purposes). He thought it a genuine wonder of God.[47] Quite typical of this benign if erratic outlook was Waterton's stance upon the sloth, a creature he met in South America, and described thus:

> His looks, his gestures and his cries, all conspire to entreat you to take pity on him. These are the only weapons of defence which nature has given him ... It is said his piteous moans make the tiger relent, and turn out of the way. Do not, then, level your gun at him, or pierce him with a poisoned arrow; he has never hurt one living creature. A few leaves, and those of the commonest and coarsest kind, are all he asks for his support.[48]

So much pity did Waterton feel for sloths that during his travels he went so far as to keep one living in his room with him, allowing it to hang off the back of a chair and wail mournfully to him about the poor hand Mother Nature had dealt it.[49] Regrettably, Waterton's occasional penchant for treating animals as if they were humans did not always turn out so happily; during a trip to Italy, he once managed to collect a large number of owls in cages, intending to bring them back to Walton Hall. Deciding he needed a bath one day, however, Waterton saw no reason not to let his owls join him in the water – with the end result that most of them drowned.[50]

As befits their close position to us on the evolutionary tree, meanwhile, Waterton was particularly adept at forging close friendships with apes. One chimpanzee he came to know, for instance, a poor sick female ailing in captivity, became such a favourite that he took to visiting her daily, kissing her tenderly on the cheek before leaving.[51] The Squire remained forever faithful to the memory of his late wife, Anne Edmonstone, who had died aged eighteen after only a year of marriage in 1830, and it seems likely that this sickly chimp was the only female he ever laid his lips upon following Anne's death.[52] He did, however, once kiss a male orang-utan during a visit to London's Zoological Gardens in 1861. Here, fascinated by the huge orange ape, Waterton implored its dubious keepers to allow him to enter its cage, even though the orangutan was in a 'horrid temper' at the time. What happened next was well-described by Dr Hobson.

The meeting of these two celebrities was clearly a case of love at first sight, as the strangers embraced each other most affectionately; nay, they positively hugged each other, and, in their apparently uncontrollable joy, they kissed one another many times, to the great amusement of the numerous spectators. Mr Waterton, who has written specially on the monkey tribe, had long been anxious to minutely inspect the palm of [one's] hand during life, and was also wishful to examine the teeth of his newly-acquired friend, both of which investigations were graciously conceded to the Squire without a murmur, his fingers being freely admitted within its jaws. These little ceremonies having been accomplished on the part of Mr Waterton, his apeship claimed a similar privilege, which was courteously granted. The ape, true to its natural inclinations, with great familiarity and evident satisfaction, at once set to work in good earnest ... and having most carefully scrutinised every portion of Mr Waterton's face, by pawing as well as by the closest ocular inspection, coolly commenced, to the infinite entertainment of the surrounding spectators, a careful and even critical examination of ... the Squire's head.[53]

The orang-utan didn't find any nits crawling around in Waterton's hair (he actually sported an early crew-cut[54]), but you get the distinct impression that, if he had, the Squire would have experienced not the slightest tinge of embarrassment about the fact.

Flights of Fancy

Maybe the real reason Waterton got on so well with apes was on account of his distinctly monkey-like love of climbing tall trees and other structures. His agility, even in old age, was truly extraordinary. Dr Hobson claimed that, when his friend was seventy-seven years old, he witnessed him scratching the back of his head using his big toe, and said that the Squire, having abnormally long arms, was also able to make his elbows meet behind his back. It was surely because of this 'remarkable suppleness of limb and elasticity of muscle', said Hobson, that Waterton was still able to clamber up the very tallest of trees in search of birds' nests, right into his eighties.[55]

Probably the Squire's most notable climbing expedition occurred during a trip to Rome when, pleased by the sight of St Peter's Dome, he decided to scale it with an old school pal, one Captain Jones. Waterton and Jones made it right to the top, then shinned their way up the Dome's lightning conductor for good measure, leaving behind their gloves as proof of their achievement. Then, Waterton and Jones made their way to Rome's Castello Sant'Angelo, upon whose summit was perched a statue of an angel – which the childhood chums promptly conquered, standing on top of the angel's head and balancing on one foot while gazing out over the Eternal City. Apparently, when he heard, even the Pope was impressed.[56]

Waterton, it appears, simply laughed in the face of danger. Take, for instance, the following account of Dr Hobson:

> I have frequently, in painful suspense and much against my own inclination, seen the Squire, when beyond seventy years of age, hop on one leg along the brink of a rock forming the highest terrace in his [estate's] grotto, while the other leg was dangling over the chasm below; and, while thus hopping at a rapid rate, he would whirl himself entirely round in the air, and dropping on the other foot, would return again by hopping back on the contrary leg. On cautioning him, he would reply [in Latin] 'He falls not from the bridge who walks with prudence!'[57]

Had Waterton really plunged to his doom on the rocks below, then the whole sad business could well have been dismissed as simply the unfortunate yet inevitable result of another of the Squire's bizarre obsessions – namely, the 'crude and ill-digested idea', as Dr Hobson had it, that he was able to fly. Waterton's attempts at flight were similar to those of Colonel Thomas Thorneycroft, examined earlier – with the admirable exception that, instead of getting his butler to jump off a roof in order to test his home-made wings, Waterton at least had the guts to make the leap of faith himself. The specific details of Waterton's human-powered wings are vague – he 'manufactured duplicates of a peculiar character of mechanism as substitutes for natural wings, to be fixed to each arm, and to be united by their surrounding the thoracic and dorsal portion' of his torso, apparently – but, however they worked, Waterton found that there was one thing which prevented him using them properly; namely, his legs. No matter how 'symmetrically formed', said Waterton, a man's legs were 'inconveniently long and heavy' for an 'atmospheric trip' and kept on bringing him back down to ground. He could have chopped them off, but this would probably have proved inconvenient in other ways; another solution would be to float them on some kind of artificial cloud, but he never worked out how to make one.

Regardless of this fact, Waterton did actually manage to test out his wings – though not, thankfully, by jumping onto the breeze from any great height. The Squire's original plan was to leap off a large farm building, trusting that the piles of litter lying below would break any fall, and had actually climbed to the top of this structure intending to do so, when one of his friends appeared on the scene. This man, thankfully, managed to convince the Squire that he should make his first attempt at flight from a lower starting point, just to be on the safe side. Persuaded to err on the side of caution, Waterton jumped off some other platform lower down and spread out his feathered wings – then immediately plummeted to earth like a stone.[58]

Maybe the Squire had simply enjoyed an uncharacteristically heavy meal that day; for, such was his generally abstemious nature, he claimed to be able to 'float' down from heights quite naturally, due to his belly being full of wind and air. For example, when cutting off a rotten tree branch one day, Waterton's ladder slipped, causing him to suffer a twelve-foot drop to the ground. However, in his own words,

> I had just presence of mind, in the act of falling, to forcibly restrain my breath, and from fasting, being meagrely supplied within, when I reached the ground I may say with truth that I literally bounced upon my feet in an instant, and then continued with my occupation. My transit from high to low merely produced a stiffness in my neck and right leg the following day. Had [I] been full of beef at the time, I ... assuredly should have fared worse.[59]

Yet another benefit of going on a diet.

Alternative Medicine

Even Squire Waterton's cures for the occasional minor injury he suffered when performing his acrobatics were somewhat daring in nature. While visiting the United States in 1824, for instance, Waterton sprained his ankle alighting from a carriage. Recalling that, back home in England, doctors had advised him to hold any sprains under a cold-water pump to alleviate the pain, Waterton realised that, given his present location, he had access to the largest source of cold water of all – Niagara Falls! Reasoning that the sheer force of the massive waterfall's cascade could be some kind of hitherto-unrecognised wonder-cure for such injuries,

Waterton held his sore ankle out under the roaring waters; but to little effect. Apparently, 'the magnitude of ... [the water] was too overwhelming, and I was obliged to drop it'.[60]

If sticking your foot under a waterfall didn't work, however, then there was always the option of slitting your afflicted ankle open and letting all the blood spill out. So keen was Waterton on the idea of blood-letting that he even practised it on his horses when they fell ill.[61] It was to this now archaic and discredited medical treatment – combined with his abstemious nature, of course – that Waterton attributed his sprightly good health in old age. Waterton had a real love for what he termed 'a bit of surgery', and solicited donations of sharp medical cutting-implements from Dr Hobson to allow him to pursue his hobby. The Squire first acquired a taste for bloodshed around the year 1800 when, suffering from pulmonary disease, his doctors advised him to give it a go. Finding that the procedure brought him relief, Waterton soon came to relish 'tapping the claret', as he called it, feeling it would come in useful when wandering alone through the South American jungle. Eventually, he became an expert self-practitioner, tying a compress around any given limb then cutting into its veins with a lancet. He always refused any assistance when performing this task, except from one particular servant whom he would allow to hold a bowl into which his ichor spurted – but only, he said, 'as a sort of favour' occasionally, when he wanted to treat the fellow.[62]

Doubtless it was this enthusiasm for blood loss which led to one of Waterton's most notorious experiments, that of offering up his big toe to be sucked by a vampire bat while in South America. Waterton suspected that vampire bats' reputation for feasting on blood was a tad exaggerated – in his view, they probably preferred bananas – but, nonetheless, he wanted to see what it would be like to be bitten by one. Accordingly, Waterton obtained such a creature, installed it in a loft, and deliberately slept in there with his big toe peeping out from his hammock. However, despite sharing sleeping quarters with the bat for several months, it never once took the bait, preferring to drain the blood of the natives instead – either that, or it found some bananas.[63]

Maybe the vampire bat suspected Squire Waterton's blood to be a little thin and tasteless, on account of his notably ascetic lifestyle and diet. The Squire's daily schedule was unforgiving, to say the least; he went to bed at nine and rose at half-past three, getting straight to work on his taxidermy projects. Sleep, said Dr Hobson, 'had no seductive charms for the Squire'; for thirty years,

Waterton refused the vulgar luxury of a bed, preferring to lie on his bare floor-boards with a block of wood for a pillow, his bed sheets being little more than an old and 'much-worn' cloak. Even when travelling overseas, Waterton slept outside on the ship's deck; lacking his handy wooden block, he used the soles of his hobnailed boots as an equally comfortless makeshift pillow.[64]

Partially, this abstemious lifestyle was the result of Charles Waterton's lifelong devotion to God. If luxury was a sin, then Squire Waterton – despite being rich and living in a mansion – wasn't going to be damned to Hell on account of it. Money he failed to spend on comfort for himself could more usefully be used to provide free aid to the poor. He paid for local people's medical treatment, gave them food and shoes, and allowed them access to the pleasant beauties of his estate.[65] It was Waterton's opinion that the greatest imposition upon his private purse was not charity, but Treasury taxation; convinced the old ways were the best, he far preferred to give alms to the poor directly, instead of relying on the State to redistribute his wealth for him. As he liked to point out, there was no need for any poor rates prior to the Reformation, when the Catholic Church had doled out aid to the needy in every parish themselves.[66]

Dedicated Borrower of Fashion

Waterton himself could sometimes have been taken for a charity case, such was his utter disdain for fashion. Like many eccentrics, he wore clothes that were entire decades out of date, donning a faded blue Regency coat with metal buttons well into the reign of Queen Victoria. His shoes, too, were frequently falling apart, but it was his 'shocking bad hat' of which he was most proud; he considered its many holes to be an excellent way of air conditioning his head.[67] It was this very hat, in fact, which nearly led to the Squire falling out with his closest friend, Dr Hobson. While receiving a visit from Waterton one day, Hobson secretly ordered his servant to steal away his friend's hat and clean it. When he found out, Waterton was furious, calling the scrubbed item a 'Miss Nancy-looking concern' which he would be ashamed to wear, and telling his host that, had anyone else ever dared to play such a cruel trick on him, he would never have spoken to that appalling individual ever again.[68]

Because of his dilapidated appearance, Waterton was frequently mistaken for a tramp or tradesman, something which greatly amused him, so much so that people who addressed him as such instantly found him playing the role of one, much to their later embarrassment.[69] The Squire, of course, recognised that these were simply innocent mistakes, but if ever somebody deliberately set out to mock him, his response could be severe. Most notable was a bizarre trick he played on some facetious army officers from a local barracks who, hearing that Waterton was an eccentric, turned up at Walton Hall one day to see the freak, under the excuse of wanting to see his extensive art collection. Waterton was happy to oblige, but it soon transpired that the officers cared little for art, using the visit as an excuse to mock him on the sly. Annoyed, Waterton told them that, if they were unimpressed by his own gallery, perhaps they should go and visit one of his neighbour's houses instead where, he claimed, an even better class of pictures were on display. There was just one problem; they were guarded by an 'odd and eccentric old fellow' whose appearance and manners may well shock them.

Naturally, the officers said they would like to see these interesting sights, so Waterton pointed them on their way, then took a shortcut to his neighbour's house himself, donning a weird disguise which, apparently, he had 'recently prepared for another purpose' – though one wonders quite what this purpose could have been. He wore a red wig, a green eyepatch on one eye and on the other a monocle, long white stockings, and a threadbare old coat which he stuffed with material to give the impression he was a hunchback, then shoved a crutch under his arm. When the officers arrived, the disguised Squire treated them to a deliberately nonsensical lecture on art, while the young men engaged in open ridicule of their recent encounter with the mad old fool up at Walton Hall. When they had finished, the 'hunchback' removed his disguise, bowed down in mock courtesy, then began ranting and raving at them about their lack of respect for so long and so harshly that, in the end, the soldiers were induced to 'hang out the white flag and humbly sue for mercy'.[70]

The Wanderer's End

Waterton's death, when it finally came, was quite ironic, given his propensity for climbing trees and tall buildings without suffering the slightest medical mishap; while crossing a bridge on his estate one May morning in 1865, he got his foot tangled in a bramble and fell onto a log. The fall was a heavy one, and did something terrible to his liver. Less than forty-eight hours later, Charles Waterton was dead.[71] Characteristically, the Squire of Walton Hall bore his fate with acceptance, good humour and a minimum of complaint.

Indeed, throughout three decades of acquaintance, Dr Hobson only ever saw his friend moved to tears the once – and the reason for this abnormal woe was very telling. While walking through his grounds with Hobson one day, Waterton suddenly broke down weeping and gave voice to his fear that, after death, all his labours might be forgotten, his nature reserve, collections, discoveries and ideas being revealed as mere 'moonshine – a flash in the pan – a will-o'the-wisp' rather than anything truly lasting.[72] This would indeed have been a terrible fate; though, in fact, one Waterton need not have feared. He may not exactly be a household name today, but his legacy still endures. Dr Hobson once called him 'a giant in natural history',[73] and so he was. One of the fathers of the conservationist movement, it is to him we owe so many things – each time we visit a nature reserve, buy a nesting box, or are given a muscle relaxant prior to undergoing an operation, we are participating in one of his many gifts to a world which really does owe him a very great debt of gratitude, whether we realise it or not.

Reading over Hobson's biography of Charles Waterton, while it is not hard to spot his various eccentricities, it is also not hard to spot his manifest good nature and borderline saintliness. Perhaps the best tribute to the Immortal Squire's benevolent peculiarity, however, was paid to him not by the Boswell-like Dr Hobson, but by another of his close friends, Father J. Wood, who summed up the worth of his character perfectly

It was perhaps eccentric to have a strong religious faith, and act up to it. It was eccentric ... to dine on a crust, live as cheaply as a hermit, and give his all to the poor. It was eccentric to come into a large estate as a young man, and to have come to extreme old age without having wasted an hour or a shilling. It was eccentric to give bountifully and never allow his name to appear in a subscription-list. It was eccentric to be saturated with the love of nature ... but it was a very agreeable kind of eccentricity. It was eccentric to be child-*like*, but never *childish*. We might multiply instances of his eccentricity to any extent, and we may safely say that the world would be much better than it is if such eccentricity were more common.[74]

I find it hard to disagree.

Conclusion: Britons Ever, Ever, Ever Shall Be Strange

'One of the first signs of a Saint will be that other people do not know what to make of him.'

Thomas Merton[1]

Had you visited the small Leicestershire village of Newton Burgoland, near Ashby-de-la-Zouch, anytime during the 1850s or 1860s, then you may well have encountered a very strange gentleman named William Lole, known locally as 'The Old Hermit', despite the fact that ... well, despite the fact that he wasn't actually a hermit. He drank, he smoked, and he welcomed visitors into his garden – provided they were worthy. In the passageway leading onto his lawn sat a fearsome barrier of Lole's own creation, three benches termed 'The Three Seats of Self-Enquiry'. On each was inscribed a question, which any visitor was required to answer in order to pass. The first asked 'Am I vile?' the second 'Am I a hypocrite?' and the third 'Am I a Christian?' If you answered these queries correctly, then you would be allowed access to the garden, which was remarkable indeed. Descriptions of the place are frustratingly unclear, but it seems to have been designed as one gigantic collection of symbols, a subject with which Lole was seriously obsessed. Apparently, Lole spent so long tending his creations, for whole days and nights at a time, that, had his neighbours not intervened with food, he would actually have forgotten to eat and passed out in his flowerbeds. This was quite ironic, seeing as one of the themed sections of his garden was entitled 'Feast Square', and contained floral displays and arrangements of pebbles designed to resemble things like pasties and pieces of beef. Most other displays, however, had rather more obscure names, like 'Noah's Ark', 'Conjugal Bliss',

'Universal Grave', 'Mount Pisgah', 'Britons Never Shall Be Slaves', 'God Save Our Noble Queen', 'The Christian's Armour' and, of course, 'The Hen-Pecked Husband Put On Water-Gruel'.

Religion and freedom, though, were Lole's main concerns. In the middle of the hermit's garden sat a large tub, with a strange-looking desk before it, to act as a pulpit. Next to it stood a home-made gallows, from which hung a stuffed effigy of the Pope, his pockets filled with Catholic tracts. William Lole viewed the Pope as a tyrant. Whenever he had managed to lure enough visitors into his garden by promising to show them his giant symbolic pasties, he would climb into his tub and begin to deliver what was called by one witness 'a long rambling tirade against Popery', telling his visitors that the Pope was really the Anti-Christ, and expostulating against various forms of religious and political oppression, some of which were real, and others wholly imaginary.

Just as strange as Lole's garden was his appearance. As well as possessing an abnormally long beard, the hermit owned at least twenty special hats and twelve suits, each also of symbolic character, and bearing various mottoes he felt were of the utmost importance to humanity. Again, descriptions are vague, but it appears that these hats were shaped like the objects they were meant to symbolise – so, for example, when wearing a hat entitled 'Bee-Hive of Industry', he presumably walked around with a fake beehive on his head, while his 'Wash-Basin of Reform' no doubt looked like something you could have cleaned your face in. Lole's 'Patent Tea-Pot' hat must have looked the strangest, being, I suppose, short and stout, and coming complete with a handle and a spout. It seems that, when wearing this particular item, Lole wished somehow to pour out the sweet tea of social justice into the world – its motto was 'To draw out the flavour of the tea best – Union and Goodwill'. Lole's weirdest full-length outfit was called, appropriately enough, 'Odd Fellows'. The Victorian writer Robert Chambers described this garb, made from white cotton or linen, thus

It hangs loosely over the body, except being bound round the waist with a white girdle, buckled in the front. Over his left breast is a heart-shaped badge, bearing the words 'Liberty of Conscience', which he calls his 'Order of the Star'.

This particular detail is very telling, particularly when read in conjunction with the motto inscribed upon Lole's militaristic 'Helmet' hat, which read 'Will Fight for the Birthright of Consciences

– Love, Life, Property and National Independence'. Reading between the lines, it appears that Mr Lole believed himself to be some kind of living embodiment – and, perhaps, actual mystical *guarantor* – of the traditional British rights to individual liberty and freedom of thought, speech and action. When interviewed one day and asked why he called himself a hermit despite actively seeking out human company, Lole replied that it was because, in his view, 'True hermits, throughout every age, have been the firm abettors of freedom.' You rather get the impression Lole felt that, if he was ever removed from his Garden of Oddness, or had his Teapot of Justice taken away from him by force, then the Kingdom itself would fall – just like in the old legend about the ravens leaving the Tower of London. Naturally, such bizarre behaviour did not leave Lole with much time left to pursue any kind of career, and he had long-since fallen into poverty through spending all his money on his garden, his Pope-baiting, and the little pamphlets full of invented mottoes which he had printed for callers. Lole's brother did offer to let him come and share his (entirely normal) house with him if he liked, but The Old Hermit of Newton Burgoland refused to do so, wailing that 'My heart is in that garden! I cannot leave it!'[2] If he had ever done so, then the consequences for freedom in these isles may have been truly dire.

The End of Eccentricity?

Lole was clearly a very 'Odd Fellow' indeed, but maybe he was not entirely incorrect in some of his beliefs, at least if examined from a certain angle. Clearly, he did not really possess any mystical powers which guaranteed liberty would prevail within our land; and yet, simply by virtue of existing so strangely, he demonstrated that it in fact does – or did during his own lifetime, at any rate. He was not arrested or institutionalised by the authorities, nor persecuted or assaulted by his neighbours (although some schoolboys did once steal one of his precious hats). Lole was born in Britain, acted like a complete lunatic for around two decades, and yet was left alone to do as he pleased, this being considered his inalienable right, seeing as he wasn't causing anybody any real harm. Could we really say the same thing about our country in this present day and age? Be honest; if your neighbour suddenly started wearing a teapot on his head and inviting crowds into his garden to hear him preach about the Pope, you know full well what would happen to him, whether he bore a badge on his breast reading 'Liberty of Conscience' or not.

We are currently under a kind of assault, from all sides, by the malign twin forces of political correctness and stifling conformity. A person only has to say something even slightly colourful or even vaguely off-message these days and it will be a mere matter of minutes before howling Twitter mobs and the ever-growing ranks of the professionally offended are massing outside your window, demanding a grovelling apology and clamouring for your immediate dismissal/arrest/beheading. Utterly harmless statements, enterprises and pastimes are immediately condemned in overblown terms as being 'inappropriate', 'insensitive', 'tasteless' or even 'evil' by those who simply cannot accept that everybody in this world does not think in exactly the same way as they do.

Take, for instance, the ridiculous recent overreaction to the news that a cafe in London had opened whose owners had dared to stock it entirely with breakfast cereals. The establishment in question, the 'Cereal Killer Cafe', is an eccentric venture stocking around 120 brands of cereal, bowls of which can be bought for £3.20 a pop, playing on customers' nostalgia for the breakfast foods of their 1980s and 1990s childhoods. TVs show old *He-Man* cartoons, radios blare out 80s chart-toppers, and there is even a resident 'mixologist' on-site, who will blend different cereals together for customers desiring to experience unusual tastes. Clearly, the cafe is intended to appeal to trendy-types after a bit of fun novelty – but that was not the way certain people reacted to it. On account of the fact that the cafe is located in a deprived area named Tower Hamlets, Channel Four News, in a pathetic fit of manufactured outrage, sent a reporter out to subject its owners to a series of tedious questions about whether or not it was immoral to charge £3.20 for bowls of cereal in an area where nearly 50 per cent of children lived in poverty. This being the era of social media-inspired idiocy, some people then went online to post their agreement with the reporter's line, kicking up a fuss.[3] If such people can react in this utterly excessive way to some harmless urban hipsters selling people overpriced bowls of Sugar Puffs, then how on earth would they have responded to the outspoken actions and opinions of people like Bill Boaks or Sir Walter Walker?

Suspicious Minds

Eccentricity, I think, is becoming viewed with increasing suspicion and intolerance by a growing number of people. This phenomenon has recently been exacerbated by the disturbing case of Jimmy Savile (1926-2011) who was not only a DJ, TV presenter and child-abuser on an epic scale, but also an eccentric of some note, who dressed and spoke incredibly strangely, never bothered to tie his shoelaces, kept his dead mother's clothes in a wardrobe and still washed them, claimed that having a family would give him 'brain damage', didn't own a cooker and apparently slept in his tracksuit and owned only one pair of underpants. Whenever Jimmy Savile ostentatiously showed off the glass-eyes he had mounted on his gold rings and claimed he'd stolen them from dead people for a laugh, few would ever have considered for a moment he was actually telling the truth, simply 'Jimmy being Jimmy', the eternal joker; but now it turns out he *was* telling the truth about this macabre hobby, after all.[4]

The modern take on his eccentricities, then, is that Savile hid behind them in plain sight somehow, using them as a cover under which to commit his crimes. Maybe so, but most eccentrics are hiding precisely nothing sinister behind their unconventional façades whatsoever. The increasing idea that eccentricity inevitably exists somewhere upon some kind of malign continuum along the path to criminality and outright madness is a demonstrably false one, which can sometimes lead to appalling miscarriages of justice – I'm sure we can all think of certain recent murder investigations in which suspects have been immediately smeared by the gutter-press as being 'weird' and 'obviously guilty' for no reason other than that they were a bit quiet and reclusive, or possessed slightly odd hairstyles and dress sense. The term 'eccentric', I think, is now becoming more and more associated with the words 'suspicious' and 'potentially dangerous', whether this assumption is justified or not. Take, for instance, the case of David Shayler (b.1965), a former MI5 man who has in more recent years remodelled himself as, variously, a conspiracy theorist, a transvestite alter-ego named Delores, and, most radically of all, the Messiah. Shayler's descent into the wilder shores of eccentricity is certainly fascinating, but I do not think it would be right to classify him as being potentially dangerous on account of it – and yet, as we shall see, some people in the media clearly have.

Shayler's story began in 1997, when he went public with sensational revelations about the various alleged misdeeds of Britain's spies, something which led to him being imprisoned under the Official Secrets Act and losing his livelihood. Following his release, Shayler kept monitoring world events for further signs the West was up to no good, hitting the headlines again in 2006 with his peculiar theory that the 'planes' which flew into New York's

Twin Towers on 11 September 2001 were not really planes at all, but missiles the US had sneakily surrounded with holograms to make them *appear* like aircraft. Worse, Shayler then began claiming that America's next plan was to use similar holograms to make it appear that Earth was being invaded by aliens, a wholly fake event which would enable martial law to be declared across the globe, with all our rights then being taken away from us. Better news, however, was soon to follow as, on 5 September 2007, David Shayler sent out an e-mail to his contacts in the media informing them of something wonderful; that, in mankind's 'darkest hour', Jesus was about to return to save humanity. In fact, Jesus had *already* returned to save humanity – indeed, it was Christ who was sending out the e-mail.

Shayler had already outed himself (or Himself, maybe) as the Messiah in August, on both TV and in the pages of the *Daily Mail*, but had found humanity's response underwhelming, so was sending out a press release and attempting something of a Second Coming, PR-wise. Shayler's story went something like this. During a visit to a psychic in June 2007, the spirit of Mary Magdalene had made herself known to Shayler, anointing him as the latest incarnation of Christ. Christ, it seems, was an essentially archetypal being, who had reincarnated Himself in various significant individuals down the ages – Jesus of Nazareth, for instance, Tutankhamen, King Arthur, Mark Antony, Leonardo da Vinci, George Washington and Lawrence of Arabia, all of whom it transpired Shayler had been during previous lives. The fact he had been crucified before, said Shayler, explained why he had 'funny-shaped wrists and ankles', these being a psychic memory of where the Romans had hammered their nails in. Claiming to have found hidden messages saying things like 'David Shayler The Fish' and 'David Shayler, Righteous Chav' in old Hebrew texts, Shayler decided to see if he had the power to work miracles, just like Jesus. It turned out he did. Not only could he control the weather and prevent terrorist outrages using only the power of his mind, he could also influence football results, something he had already discovered when magically powering Middlesbrough FC all the way to the 2006 UEFA Cup Final – where they lost 4-0 to Sevilla. Shayler explained this drubbing by claiming to have been drunk during the game, 'and it turns out it doesn't work if you're drunk.' Also, God got annoyed with him wasting his powers on trying to alter football scores and told him to stop, so he did, Middlesbrough being relegated from the Premier League in 2009.

Predictably, though, almost nobody wanted to hear Shayler's message – other than to laugh at it. Rather more unwarranted, however, was the reaction of one particular media organisation. Only two journalists responded to the Messiah's e-mail and attended his later press conference; the humorous writer Jon Ronson, and a man from Sky News. Apparently, the Sky-man was there to interview Shayler, but his bosses had no intention of broadcasting the footage, just to store it away 'in case something happens in the future'. As Ronson later put it in his own write-up of the event, 'There was no doubting that the "something" he was alluding to would be something truly awful.'[5]

Keeping Us All Sane

Evidently, Sky News were expecting Shayler, at some future point, to harm or even kill himself or others, despite the fact that he has no history of violence whatsoever, having instead repeatedly claimed that his only purpose here on earth is to 'spread the spiritual rules of unconditional love, unconditional sharing, never judging, and having faith in the universe.' Indeed, he claims to have actually *saved* lives not *taken* them, by miraculously ensuring that various bomb plots were foiled. In short, David Shayler was about as likely to go on a murderous rampage as Jesus Christ Himself was – and yet still Sky News thought the worst of him. This is sad. The presence of people like Shayler in our society is, I think, valuable to it in some strange sort of way which is quite difficult to fully define and articulate. Eccentrics – even the most extreme ones – are not mere societal waste products who should be simply cast aside and utterly disregarded. While you can obviously have a damagingly excessive regard for such people, like R. D. Laing did, it would be equally unwise to go too far in the other direction and totally ignore and dismiss them instead.

In his 1991 story *The Quantity Theory of Insanity*, the novelist Will Self memorably proposed that there might be only 'a fixed proportion of sanity available in any given society at any given time', and that any attempt to cure or repress strange or aberrant behaviour in one group of people would just lead to it later popping up again elsewhere in an even worse form.[6] This was just a joke, but like many jokes it may well have contained a grain of truth within it. Perhaps eccentrics fulfil a kind of inoculatory role within any given culture, going a little mad themselves and thus somehow preventing society as a whole from going the same way. The idea of living in a broadly sane society in which the eccentric are at best celebrated, and at worst endured, seems to me infinitely preferable to the idea of living in a wholly insane society in which eccentrics are viewed with outright suspicion and hostility, or even actively persecuted and eliminated. You cannot, I think, be an eccentric in North Korea or Iran. The basic reason for this is obvious. – John Stuart Mill identified it over 150 years ago now. Eccentrics, thinking about things differently, and thus having new ideas, have the potential to act as agents of radical change, and that is the one thing that dictators and totalitarian states fear most of all. Most eccentrics will ultimately achieve little truly world-changing; but, every so often, one truly exceptional member of this peculiar tribe *will* do so. We can never tell for sure, however, who this next exceptional person may be.

When he does come along, though, will we embrace him, or push him away? Current trends suggest the latter. Some of the greatest eccentrics of the past, people like Lord Byron and Geoffrey Pyke, operated upon a much larger stage than their modern contemporaries ever could, living lives which would now be utterly inconceivable in our rule governed, politically correct, increasingly standardised world. A maverick operator like Winston Churchill could never have achieved high office today; Charles Waterton, had he graced our own age, would probably have been damned as an 'imperialist', not celebrated as an adventurer; Colonel Sibthorp would have been charged with perpetrating hate-crimes; Arthur Cravan would have been kept on an even beam with large quantities of prescription drugs. If pride in being British has traditionally meant a corresponding pride in our island race's marked eccentricity, then in a modern, increasingly deracinated and globalised nation in which values such as patriotism are becoming more and more derided and unfashionable, it makes a kind of sense that, nowadays, representative examples of the Great British Eccentric seem to be becoming more marginalised than they ever were. Most are still tolerated by the vast majority – but, increasingly, it seems a rather grudging kind of tolerance. As such, I want to end this book by recounting the life of one final eccentric whose amazing, and now largely forgotten, biography illustrates in the clearest possible way just what it is we are now missing. Examined today, this incredible man's life reads like one long elegy to a sadly vanished world ...

The Last Englishman:
Lieutenant Colonel Alfred
Daniel Wintle, MC (1897–1966)

The one-man army who stole the hearts of an entire nation (and the trousers of a bent solicitor).

We have already examined a few cases of military men who have had a bit of trouble when it came to turning swords into ploughshares. Surely the prime example of an old soldier failing to adapt terribly well to retirement during peace-time, however, was Lieutenant Colonel Alfred Daniel Wintle, MC. Despite dismissing himself as a mere 'donkey-walloper',[1] in the view of many others he was the quintessential old-style Englishman, whose death in 1966 was thought by *The Times* to merit a laudatory editorial entitled 'On Being Oneself', in which he was praised as having been very much his own man.[2] This was certainly true; in Wintle's own words, 'I am never bored when I am present,'[3] and nor was anyone else. The son of a diplomat, Wintle was actually born in Russia, though he did not like to publicise the fact. After all, this was a man so patriotic he claimed to get down on bended knee every night and thank God for making him an Englishman, this being 'the greatest honour He could ever bestow' upon a person. After all, he said, the Good Lord might instead have made him a chimpanzee or a flea – or, even worse, a Frenchman or a German![4]

Wintle's hatred of Germany and its people was truly pathological. As a child, he claimed to have responded to his father's proposal to make him attend a German school during a posting abroad with the words, 'attend a German school, sir? I would rather cut my hands off and blind myself in one eye!'[5] Sadly, the Hun were all too happy to mutilate Wintle in just such a way themselves. Serving during the First World War, Wintle was knocked out when the wheel of a gun-carriage hit an unexploded German shell. Waking up in hospital, in an eerie echo of his childhood words, Wintle found that he was now missing his left eye and most of the fingers from his left hand. His right eye, too, was seriously damaged, obliging him to wear a monocle for life.[6]

Wintle did not despair, though. Refusing to accept his new disabilities meant there was no way back to the Front, he hatched a plan to escape from hospital by disguising himself as a nurse, planning to sneak out and cross the Channel to France without anybody noticing. Sadly, his monocle gave the game away, and he was escorted back to his sickbed. The intervention of his diplomat father allowed Wintle's return to the fight, however, and he was rewarded with the Military Cross for his bravery in personally capturing some thirty-five German soldiers single-handed, an action he later confessed he could not even remember. Life in the trenches suited Wintle; it was where he became a man. On his first night of service, after he had just been introduced to his commanding officer, a shell came whizzing over and killed the man, splattering the new recruit with his entrails. Terrified, the teenage Wintle dealt with this distinctly un-British emotion by standing to attention and saluting his sergeant's shattered corpse. This did the trick. 'Within thirty seconds', he said, he was able to 'become again an Englishman' and carry on with his duties entirely unafraid.[7]

Cursed Are the Peace-Makers

When the war finally ended, Wintle was most disappointed. In June 1919, when the official peace agreements were ratified by all sides following 1918's Armistice, Wintle wrote in his diary 'Great War peace signed at last.' His entry for the next day read, 'I declare private war on Germany!'[8] Convinced this 'peace' was nothing of the kind, and that the Germans were simply 'lying low' waiting for the right moment to attack, he spent so long over the next few years lobbying officials to declare war again immediately that he was eventually posted to Ireland, out of the way. The most notable event of Wintle's inter-war years was his spell in Aldershot Military Hospital after breaking his leg in a fall from a horse. There, he encountered a youthful trumpeter from the Royal Dragoon Guards named Cecil Mays, who was suffering from a deadly combination of mastoiditis and diphtheria. Appalled at this waste of young life, Wintle approached Mays' bedside and issued him with a stern order: 'You will stop dying at once! And, when you get up, get your bloody hair cut!' Mays later claimed to have been so scared of Wintle that, in his own words, he was 'too terrified to die', making a full recovery and living to the ripe old age of ninety-five. This was just as well because, in Wintle's view, a soldier dying away from the battlefield was against army regulations.[9]

This adventure aside, in later life Wintle confessed that he found the years between the two World Wars to be 'intensely boring',[10] and was delighted in September 1939 when Hitler's invasion of Poland signalled a resumption of hostilities. However, there was a problem; now in his forties and half-blind, Wintle was deemed medically unfit to go over to France and fight. Desperate to see action, he at first tried to convince doctors that he didn't have a glass eye at all, and made serious consideration of resigning his commission and forming his own private platoon to take on the Nazis independently.

Instead, he remained in his post on the Home Front but, following news of Britain's disastrous retreat from Dunkirk in May 1940, Wintle became so livid with how the war was going that on 17 June he turned up at the Air Ministry and demanded he be given his own plane. In this, he intended to fly to Bordeaux and command all the French airmen stationed there to fly their planes to Britain and join the RAF that instant, a plan which did not meet with agreement from one Air Commodore A. R. Boyle. Furious at this refusal, Wintle produced a pistol and threatened to shoot Boyle. This was a bluff, however, and Wintle was carted off to the Tower of London to await court martial. The authorities couldn't even do this properly, though, and on his way to the Tower Wintle was disgusted to find that the soldier guarding him had lost his arrest warrant. Considering this kind of thing to be the reason Britain was losing, he marched off to the warrant office himself to get a new one. However, being the only person of sufficient rank there to be allowed to issue such a document, he ended up essentially arresting himself! Once word got out why he had been imprisoned, Wintle was viewed as a hero by his guards, who treated him, said Wintle, 'as if I had been at the Ritz'. Given his own personal servant, he was brought cigars, whisky and ginger ale, and served with various luxuries by his friends, who were allowed to visit whenever they liked. 'I remember one particularly fine duck in aspic,' reminisced Wintle later. 'It gave me indigestion.'[11]

The Trials of War

Once on trial, Wintle refused to back down. Confronted with evidence that he had waved his gun at Air Commodore Boyle and said 'people like you ought to be shot', far from denying the charge, Wintle agreed that this was true and then produced a list of other people he thought should be killed as well, including several high-ranking Cabinet Ministers. It seems that the Government, fearing severe embarrassment should news of this comical escapade get out, soon ordered that all bar one of the charges against Wintle be dropped, issuing him with a 'severe reprimand' in lieu of any meaningful punishment, and sending him off to far-away Syria, to work in intelligence.[12]

Following Allied victory in this arena, in 1941 Wintle was next posted to Occupied France as a spy, where he soon attracted suspicion on account of his bizarre appearance, going around everywhere with gold coins strapped beneath his armpits 'in case of an emergency' and carrying an umbrella, something he considered to be every Englishman's duty to do at all times – although, as he also said, 'No true gentleman would ever *unfurl* one.' Arrested, and guarded over by Vichy French soldiers at a camp in Toulon, Wintle wasted no time informing them that, as an officer in the British Army, it was his solemn duty to try and escape; especially seeing as the people guarding him were such a slovenly lot of what he called 'swivel-eyed sons of syphilitic slime-frogs'.[13]

Disgusted by his guards' shabby dress-sense, he went on a thirteen-day hunger-strike in protest at their appalling lack of standards, dropping down to only seven stone. Constantly berating the guards as cowards and traitors, he said they were not fit to guard an Englishman, as had been proven almost immediately after his initial internment, when he had successfully managed to engineer a temporary escape before being returned into captivity. What kind of way was that to behave, Wintle wanted to know, allowing a prisoner to escape? They should be ashamed of themselves! Seemingly, the guards began to agree. After Wintle had successfully escaped their clutches once more, this time for good, by hiding in a rubbish cart and slipping across the border into Spain, Maurice Molia, the camp commandant, and his men began thinking about the example Wintle had set them. Wasn't he right in what he had said, after all? Feeling guilty about their previous conduct, the entire garrison of 280 men promptly joined the French Resistance![14]

A New Campaign

Following the war, Alfred Wintle refused to settle down to a quiet life, and set his sights upon becoming an MP, standing as the Liberal candidate for Norwood. His purpose in doing so was simple; to destroy the political system itself, which he saw as being corrupt beyond redemption. When asked why he was standing he was quite open about this, answering that 'Guy Fawkes was the last man to enter Parliament with good intentions. You need another man like me to carry on his good work.'[15] The voters of Norwood disagreed, however, and Wintle nearly lost his deposit. Maybe they had heard about a bizarre incident which had occurred to Wintle during the campaign-trail, when he had decided to visit an old friend of his named R. V. Jones, reintroducing himself into Jones' life with a bang by driving his car straight through his living-room window. Speeding, and with poor eyesight in any case, Wintle had taken a corner too sharply, and ended up stepping out of his vehicle amid a mess of shattered glass and bricks to find himself confronted with a shocked Mrs Jones. As always, he took the situation in his stride, greeting her with the words 'My dear lady, I am most frightfully sorry. I must have upset your nerves. What you need most is sherry, which I will now go and get.' He then walked off to the pub to get some, before returning cheerfully as if nothing had happened.[16]

Perhaps Wintle just needed the excitement. Unable to adapt to peace-time conditions, he was involved in a number of bizarre escapades post–1945, including the time when, annoyed by the lack of available first-class carriages on a train, he kicked a ticket collector at Victoria Station and then commandeered the engine-room, refusing to let the driver in until the situation was rectified.[17] His letters to *The Times*, too, were legendary, including the following one, which was sent in 1946 but only printed after his death, as a kind of celebratory illustration of the man's amazing character:

> Sir,
> I have just written you a long letter. On reading it over, I have thrown it into the waste-paper basket. Hoping this will meet with your approval.
> I am, Sir, Your Obedient Servant,
> A. D. Wintle[18]

Goodbye Kitty

Wintle's most famous brush with the headlines, however, was due to a strange legal affair which followed the death of his equally unusual cousin Kitty Wells in 1947. If Wintle was eccentric, then Kitty was outright mad. Of limited mental capacity, Wintle himself called her 'a jelly-fish', and this was not an inaccurate assessment. Living alone in her house at Hove, Kitty's only joy in life was to write herself letters, stuff them into envelopes filled with old bus tickets, then put them in the nearest pillar box in time for the morning post. Then, when these same letters arrived back in the afternoon mail, she would open them in delight, eager to read that morning's latest news *about her own life*. Once read, these letters would be dutifully filed away in her newest handbag. When the handbag was full, it too would dutifully be filed away, beneath her bed. When the space beneath the bed was full, she would remove all of the handbags, and file them away in a cupboard. When the cupboard was full, she would presumably buy another cupboard.

Her own doctor thought Kitty to be so stupid that he refused to allow her to administer her regular insulin doses herself like most adults did, because he considered her incapable of even understanding what a syringe was, let alone how to use it. Kitty never read a newspaper, never talked to anybody else if she could help it, and apparently was entirely unaware that the Second World War had even occurred, despite living in an area of heavy bombing. According to her doctor, she was simply 'inert', had no interests whatsoever, and was just 'content to exist' doing nothing but post letters. Clearly, Kitty could not look after herself, and so Wintle's sister Marjorie heroically stepped into the breach, visiting and caring for her daily for some twenty-five years. After she died, then, it came as some surprise to Marjorie that Kitty had left her only part of her £115,000 estate in her will, with her 'helpful' solicitor, a seventy-one-year-old scoundrel named Frederick Nye, getting the absurd sum of £44,000 for alleged services rendered.

When he heard of this appalling con-trick, Alfred Wintle was outraged, calling Nye 'a cad, a liar, a thief and an embezzler'. The 'jelly-fish' Kitty could not have understood what Nye had tricked her into doing and, naturally, Wintle instituted legal action. However, his main aim in going to court was not necessarily to recover the money from crooked Nye but, rather, to publicly humiliate him. To this end, Wintle hatched a bizarre plan in order to get the case as many column inches as possible in the national newspapers – he would kidnap Nye and then forcibly remove his trousers.[19]

The Wronged Trousers

In 1955, after researching Nye's past, Wintle phoned him up, put on a fake voice, and claimed to be an old business acquaintance named Lord Norbury. Borrowing a flat, Wintle set up a business meeting there with Nye for 6 April, and waited. Opening the door when Nye came to call, Wintle pulled the solicitor inside and jumped on him. Nye, confused, shouted for help, but Wintle produced some rope and said he would tie him up if he didn't shut his mouth. Then, Wintle demanded menacingly (and reputedly at gunpoint) that Nye sign a cheque for £1,000 made out to his sister, as well as a confession, and gave him a big dunce's hat to wear. Then, he commanded that Nye remove his trousers. Having done so, Nye was informed by Wintle that he was now going to take some photographs, including one of 'a particular part of your body' – we can probably guess which one – and send them to the press. These pictures being taken, Wintle locked Nye in a cupboard briefly before kicking him out onto the street, still trouserless, to face public ridicule.

What happened next is disputed, but it seems that Wintle travelled through the local countryside, showing photographs of the debagged Nye and his 'particular part' to everyone he met, before driving to his London club where he had Nye's trousers exhibited in the trophy room. Wintle was arrested that very same night, but there are conflicting accounts of precisely why. In the criminal trial Wintle later faced, our hero claimed that he had originally intended, had he remained at liberty a little longer, to run Nye's trousers up a flagpole 'in triumph', but during a subsequent civil trial Wintle testified that he turned himself in to the police of his own accord, fearing that otherwise Nye might simply be too embarrassed to report the assault, thus rendering it pointless. In July, Wintle faced two criminal charges – assault and fraud, this latter relating to the cheque he had forced Nye to sign. The judge instructed the jury to find Wintle 'Not Guilty' of the second charge, on the grounds that 'if a person honestly believed he was entitled to something he could have no intent to defraud'.[20] Wintle cheerfully admitted to the charge of assault, however, and received six months in Wormwood Scrubs. His words upon hearing this sentence were noble indeed:

> It will be a sad day for this country when an officer and a gentleman is not prepared to go to prison when he thinks he is in the right.[21]

Not only was Wintle prepared to go to prison in order to humiliate Mr Nye, he was also prepared to bankrupt himself. Wintle used his time inside to read up on the law and, following his release, pursued Nye through the courts time and time again, by 1958 eventually reaching the point where he had to dismiss his own lawyers and represent himself in court instead. This suited Wintle down to the ground, as he viewed his crusade against Nye as being essentially war by other means, once telling a courtroom that, when it came to revenge,

> I deal with matters from the military point of view. I regard Mr Nye as an enemy, and I do not disclose my plans [to the enemy] until they are matured. Then I launch my heavy artillery on him and we get busy.[22]

The Last of His Kind
In Wintle's view, he 'had to resort to violence' against Nye 'in order to get the matter into the public eye', and would continue to use any means possible to keep it there and never let his foe forget his vile misdeed – which was why, on the second anniversary of the trouser-stealing incident, Wintle hosted a big party in his home, a celebration to which he actually had the gall to invite his nemesis. Nye didn't turn up, but he and his representatives were nonetheless forced to appear in the courtroom endlessly, seeing as Wintle just wouldn't give up, taking the case to appeal whenever he lost it.

Finally, Wintle took the highly unusual step of taking the case to the House of Lords, where he roped in several of his old army friends (including Cecil Mays, the trumpeter he had previously ordered not to die) to act as his assistants. Remarkably, this time he won! Wintle had made legal history; as far as can be told, this was the first time that a person representing himself had persuaded the Lords to reverse a decision made previously by the Court of Appeal. His triumph had not yet ended, either; in 1960, he again represented himself, this time before the Disciplinary Committee of the Law Society, where he successfully had Nye struck off.[23]

With Wintle's death in 1966 came, it might be said, the end of an era; his was a life which it is simply impossible to imagine being lived by anyone in this country today. When, in 1968, Wintle's biography was published posthumously it was entitled *The Last Englishman*.[24] It could easily be argued that, in the years since, this title has proved itself to have been sadly prophetic. Lieutenant-Colonel Alfred Daniel Wintle would, it is safe to say, have been appalled at the conformist, pygmy nation we have since become. We still have some notable eccentrics here, as I think this book has shown, but never again will they be able to express their cheerful nonconformity across so wide a canvas. We used to have an Empire, you know – an Empire of Eccentricity. That's one Empire, I think, upon which the sun should never have been allowed to set.

Notes and References

Cover Image

The cover image shows another eccentric, Baron Lionel Walter Rothschild (1868-1937), heir to the famous Rothschild banking fortune. Whilst Lionel was expected to enter the family business, he knew from an early age that he would rather do something else with his life. Aged seven, he had informed his parents 'Mama, Papa, I am going to make a museum' – and he was right, he was. By the age of thirteen, Lionel was already corresponding knowledgably with prominent zoological experts, and employing a full-time adult assistant to help catalogue the thousands of insects and other animals he was beginning to amass. Aged twenty-one, he was given some land by his father as a coming-of-age present and promptly built two cottages on it, one to house his books and insects, the other to house a caretaker to look after them. At its largest, Rothschild's collection included some 2,250,000 butterflies, 300,000 birds, 200,000 bird eggs, and thousands upon thousands of assorted mammals, fish, insects and reptiles – the largest private collection ever assembled. Following his death in 1937, it was all donated to what is now the Natural History Museum in London (minus 295,000 birds he had been forced to sell to the American Museum of Natural History in 1937 to pay off a female blackmailer). Undoubtedly, Rothschild made several important contributions towards zoology, but it is not necessarily for his scientific achievements that he is now best remembered. The Baron didn't simply like stuffed animals, but live ones, too, and maintained a large menagerie in the grounds of his Hertfordshire mansion of Tring Park, including a tame wolf, kangaroos, zebras, cassowaries, kiwis and several giant tortoises. His interest in such animals, however, was not always *strictly* academic, as the cover photograph of a top-hatted Lord Rothschild sitting on top of one of his hard-shelled friends, holding out a lettuce leaf in front of its face on a long stick in order to encourage it to bear him ever onwards, clearly shows. Most notoriously, in an attempt to demonstrate to the world that zebras could be tamed, Lionel once hitched up a team to his coach and drove them all the way to Buckingham Palace to visit the Royals. Queen Alexandra was said to have been delighted – the RSPCA doubtless less so.

References

All websites accessed between January 2015 and May 2015.

Introduction

1 Cited at http://www.theguardian.com/stage/2012/may/06/ miranda-raison-ken-campbell-performance

2 *Fortean Times* magazine issue 53, p. 31, citing *The Gentleman's Magazine* for March 1753; Archenholz, 2014, pp. 257, 278; Archenholz claims that Tallis remained so long in bed because he wanted to keep warm, not escape from 'deadly' fresh air, however.

3 Report of 'JD' in *The Gentleman's Magazine* for March 1753; reproduced in an anthology edition, *The Gentleman's Magazine and Historical Chronicle, Vol XXIII*, p. 123, accessed online at https://books.google.co.uk/books?id=8nRIAAAAYAA

4 Greene, 2012, p. 226; Lee, 2009 (no page numbers provided), accessed online at https://books.google.co.uk/books?isbn=0191623016

5 JS Mill, On Liberty, Ch III, paragraph 12

6 JS Mill, On Liberty, Ch III, paragraph 13; Fitzpatrick, 2006, pp. 73–75, also has a good discussion of Mill's ideas relating to eccentricity

7 Diogenes Laërtius, viii., p. 69; Plato *Theaetetus*, section 174a, accessed online at http://www.perseus.tufts.edu/hopper

8 Russell, 2006, p. 15

9 Archenholz, 2014, pp. 256 and 259

10 'England, Your England', in Orwell, 2001, pp. 66–67

11 'England, Your England', in Orwell, 2001, pp. 84

12 Steinmetz, 2008, p. 59, accessed online at https://books.google.co.uk/ books?id=TeT1JJw-yE4C

13 Johnson's Dictionary, p.671 (see johnsonsdictionaryonline.com)

14 Breton, 2009, p. 393

15 Breton, 2009, p. 394

16 Ronson, 2011, pp. 72–73

17 Ronson, 2011, pp. 73–75; http://www.telegraph.co.uk/news/obituaries/1335846/ Mary-Barnes.html

18 Hemming, 2008, Chapter 4 (no page numbers provided), accessed online at https:// books.google.co.uk/books?isbn=1848541546; Interview with Dr David Weeks in *People* magazine, Vol26, No19, 10 Nov 1985; online at http://www.people.com/ people/archive/article/0,,20094970,00.html; average UK IQ-test data taken from http://iq-test.co.uk/stats/

19 Interview with Dr David Weeks in *People* magazine, Vol26, No19, 10 Nov 1985; online at http://www.people.com/people/archive/article/0,,20094970,00.html

20 Adapted from a list cited online at https://classicalbookworm.wordpress. com/2010/10/11/eccentrics-by-dr-david-weeks-and-jamie-james/

21 Interview with Dr David Weeks in *People* magazine, Vol26, No19, 10 Nov 1985; online at http://www.people.com/people/archive/article/0,,20094970,00.html

22 Ronson, 2011, p. 73

23 Archenholz, 2014, p. 257

24 Report of 'JD' in *The Gentleman's Magazine* for March 1753; reproduced in an anthology edition, *The Gentleman's Magazine and Historical Chronicle, Vol XXIII*, p. 123, accessed online at https://books.google.co.uk/books?id=8nRIAAAAYAA

25 These findings have been trotted out repeatedly – see http://www.theguardian.com/ commentisfree/2010/apr/01/eccentricity-einstein-prince-society for a typical example.

26 Michell cited in Clarke & Roberts, 2007, p. 181

Upper-Class Eccentrics

1 Long, 2012, pp. 55–57; http://odnb2.ifactory.com/view/article/38668/38668; http://blog.maryevans.com/2013/04/an-officer-brought-home-to-rest-lieut-norman-de-crespigny.html; *New York Times*, May 19, 1910; Evans, 2004, p. 93

2 Long, 2012, p. 107

3 Shaw, 2009, p. 198

4 Shaw, 2009, p. 216; Grumley-Grennan, 2010, p. 152; Macaulay, 2011, p. 130

5 Eatwell, 2014 (no page numbers provided), accessed online at https://books.google.co.uk/books?isbn=1781856079; Shaw, 2009, pp. 211–213; Long, 2012, pp. 155–156; http://victoriancalendar.blogspot.co.uk/2011/01/january–12–1898-sir-tatton-and-lady.html; http://www.livingnorth.com/yorkshire/people-places/sledmere-house; http://www.spectator.co.uk/books/21022/short-on-names-tall-on-tales/; Shawcross, 2009, p. 120; for Venetia Cavendish-Bentinck, see Long, 2012, pp. 146–147

6 Michell, 1999, pp. 82–83

7 Long, 2012, pp. 116–118; http://www.nottshistory.org.uk/articles/tts/tts1902/spring/spring1902p2.htm

8 Sitwell, 2006, pp.55–65; Michell, 1999, pp. 78–81; Wilson, 1813, pp. 1–17

9 Sitwell, 2006, pp. 124–131; Long, 2012, pp. 130–131; Duducu, 2014, pp. 94–95

10 Cowan, 2007, Chapter 2 (no page numbers provided), accessed online at https://books.google.co.uk/books?isbn=0297865579; Shaw, 2009, pp. 197–198; http://www.meltonmowbraytownestate.co.uk/peace-and-tranquillity/a-walk-in-the-park/swan-porch/painting-the-town-red; http://ahistoryblog.com/2013/01/14/henry-de-la-poer-beresford-third-marquess-of-waterford–1811–1859-beast-and-the-beauty/; http://www.theguardian.com/notesandqueries/query/0,,-5465,00.html

11 Shaw, 2009, p. 205

12 Eatwell, 2014; Archard, 1907, Chapter VII: 'The Eccentric Duke and His Underground Tunnels' accessed online at http://www.nottshistory.org.uk/portland1907/portland7.htm; Obituaries,*The Times*, 8 December 1879; http://www.nottingham.ac.uk/manuscriptsandspecialcollections/collectionsindepth/family/portland/biographies/biographyofwilliamjohncavendish-bentinck-scott,5thdukeofportland(1800–1879).aspx

13 Long, 2012, pp.36–39; http://www.lookandlearn.com/blog/29262/the-brilliant-henry-cavendish-remains-englands-most-eccentric-scientist/; http://www.peakdistrictonline.co.uk/henry-cavendish-famous-derbyshire-people-c2527.html; http://drvitelli.typepad.com/providentia/2010/10/shy-henry.html, Bryson, 2003, pp. 59–62

14 Long, 2012, pp. 148–149; http://www.tettenhall.co.uk/the-fascinating-past-of-tettenhall-towers/; http://www.historywebsite.co.uk/genealogy/Thorneycroft/George.htm

15 Michell, 1999, pp. 107–115; Long, 2012, pp. 81–83; https://www.ucl.ac.uk/news/news-articles/1111/111117-Galton-novel-Kantsaywhere-published-online; http://www.galtoninstitute.org.uk/Newsletters/GINL0209/Sir_Francis_Galton.htm

The Sitwells

1 Greene, 2012, p. 441

2 Evelyn Waugh, 'Urbane Enjoyment Personified: Sir Osbert Sitwell' in the *New York Times Magazine*, 30 November 1952; reprinted in Waugh, 2010, pp. 95–98

3 Sitwell, 2006, pp. 20–21

4 *The Spectator*, 19 May 1933, cited in Greene, 2012, p. 228

5 Sitwell, 2006, p. 20

6   Sitwell, 2006, p. 20

7   Greene, 2012, pp. 412–413

8   Greene, 2012, p. 21–22

9   Greene, 2012, p. 228

10 Greene, 2012, pp. 41–43

11 Greene, 2012, p. 4; Sutton, 1988, p. 76

12 Greene, 2012, pp. 142–243

13 Greene, 2012, pp. 105–106

14 See Sitwell, 1959, pp. 9–10, 113–119 for *The Drum* and a discussion of its craft

15 Greene, 2012, pp. 2-3

16 Greene, 2012, p. 173; Sitwell, 1959, pp. 214–229 has the full tale of the Tedworth Drummer

17 See Sitwell, 1959, pp. 11, 152–153 for the goblin's poem

18 Sitwell, 1959, pp. 65-66

19 Greene, 2012, p. 24

20 Westwood & Simpson, 2005, p. 173

21 Westwood & Simpson, 2005, pp. 172–173; Greene, 2012, p. 24

22 Westwood & Simpson, 2005, p. 173

23 Greene, 2012, p. 24; http://www.dailymail.co.uk/femail/article-459373/Bizarre-exhibition-spiritual-home-British-eccentricity.html

24 Clarke, 2012, pp. 205–206; Greene, 2012, pp. 16–17

25 Cited at http://en.wikiquote.org/wiki/Edith_Sitwell

26 Letter in the *Daily Mail* for 25 June 1928 cited in Greene, 2012, p. 198

27 Cited at http://en.wikiquote.org/wiki/Edith_Sitwell; sometimes she said the pool was actually full of dogfish or goldfish, just for variety's sake.

28 Unreferenced media quote cited in Sitwell, 2006, p. 12

29 Sitwell, 2006, p. 21

30 http://www.independent.co.uk/arts-entertainment/comedy/features/funny-peculiar-the-curious-world-of-vic-reeves-1792545.html

31 Greene, 2012, pp. 12–13

32 Sitwell, 2006, p. 9; Greene, 2012, pp. 8-9

33 Greene, 2012, p. 10

34 Greene, 2012, p. 15; Sitwell, 2006, pp. 9–10

35 Greene, 2012, p. 56; http://www.bbc.co.uk/insideout/yorkslincs/series3/gardening_shotgun_yorkshire_reginald_farrer.shtml

36 Greene, 2012, pp. 25-26

37 All information about Sir George compiled from Greene, 2012, pp. 16–18, 45; Long, 2012, pp. 41-42; Sitwell, 2006, p. 10; Shaw, 2009, pp. 191–194; https://www.nytimes.com/books/first/z/ziegler-sitwell.html; http://www.theage.com.au/articles/2003/01/12/1041990178094.html; http://www.telegraph.co.uk/news/uknews/1530806/Fame-at-last-for-prostitutes-friend-from-the-ladies-loo.html; http://www.dailymail.co.uk/femail/article-459373/Bizarre-exhibition-spiritual-home-British-eccentricity.html

38 https://www.nytimes.com/books/first/z/ziegler-sitwell.html

39 Greene, 2012, p. 29; http://www.telegraph.co.uk/news/uknews/1530806/Fame-at-last-for-prostitutes-friend-from-the-ladies-loo.html

40 Sitwell, 2006, p. 11

41 Long, 2012, p. 42

42 Greene, 2012, pp. 29-30

43 https://www.nytimes.com/books/first/z/ziegler-sitwell.html; Greene, 2012, pp. 17–18

44 Greene, 2012, p. 292

45 Greene, 2012, pp. 35–41

46 Greene, 2012, pp. 9–10, 62, 434

47 Greene, 2012, pp. 11, 284

48 Greene, 2012, pp. 66–67

49 Greene, 2012, p. 156

50 Greene, pp. 152–158, 167–168; Lloyd, 2001, p. 42

51 Leavis, 1932, p. 73

52 Cited in *Who's Who 1961–1970*, 1972, p. 1040

53 Greene, 2012, pp. 168–169

54 Greene, 2012, p. 168; Coward, 2014 (no page numbers provided), accessed online at https://books.google.co.uk/books?isbn=1408177536; some (silent) footage of the Whittlebots at work can be found online at www.youtube.com/watch?v=5rpzleiN2OQ

55 Greene, 2012, pp. 169–70

56 Extract from Coward's diary cited in Greene, 2012, p. 435 57 – Speech cited at http://en.wikiquote.org/wiki/Edith_Sitwell

Political Eccentrics

1 Shaw, 2009, p. 98; Grumley-Grennan, 2010, p. 39; https://www.gov.uk/government/history/past-foreign-secretaries/robert-cecil

2 Shaw, 2009, p. 99; Grumley-Grennan, 2010, p. 40; http://www.leighrayment.com/peers/peersQ.htm

3 http://www.telegraph.co.uk/news/obituaries/politics-obituaries/5496941/Screaming-Lord-Sutch.html; http://www.theguardian.com/news/1999/jun/19/guardianobituaries.nigelfountain; http://news.bbc.co.uk/1/hi/uk/371216.stm; http://www.loonyparty.com/; http://www.independent.co.uk/news/uk/politics/screaming-lord-sutch-the-man-behind-the-monster-6146965.html; http://www.thefreelibrary.com/Lord+Sutch+fought+long+battle+with+depression.-a060467108; http://www.loonyparty.com/about/policy-proposals/; http://usvsth3m.com/post/7-monster-raving-loony-party-policies-which-are-now-part-of-uk-law; Monty Python's 'Election Night Special' is online at http://www.youtube.com/watch?v=31FFTx6AKmU

4 *Fortean Times* magazine issue 170, pp. 44–49; http://news.bbc.co.uk/news/vote2001/hi/english/features/newsid_1370000/1370776.stm; http://www.theguardian.com/uk/2005/aug/15/health.healthandwellbeing; the NLP's 1994 broadcast featuring yogic-flying is online at http://www.youtube.com/watch?v=438UKM1Av1g

5 *The Spectator*, 11 April 2015

6 http://www.theguardian.com/politics/blog/2010/apr/20/seveoaks-mark-ellis-protocols-elders-zion; http://www.courier.co.uk/Independent-Ellis-ducking-issue/story–12011739-detail/story.html; http://www.sevenoakschronicle.co.uk/Eccentric-Sevenoaks-election-candidate-dead-home/story-20675836-detail/story.html

7 Hemming, 2008, Chapter 7 (no page numbers provided), accessed online at https://books.google.co.uk/books?isbn=1848541546; http://www.captainbeany.com/index.html

8 Shaw, 2009, pp. 103–104; http://www.walthamstowmemories.net/pdfs/Bill%20Bayliss%20-%Bill%20Boaks.pdf; http://www.theguardian.com/politics/2015/jan/15/commander-bill-boakes-brightened-electoral-landscape

9 *Fortean Times* magazine issue 288, p. 4, issue 326, p. 6; *Private Eye* magazine issue 1391, p. 18; http://www.dailystar.co.uk/news/latest-news/437064/

simon-parkes-labour-councillor-aliens-abductee-politics-quit-resign-whitby-north-yorks; http://www.theweek.co.uk/people-news/53672/simon-parkes-alien-sex-lovechild; http://www.thescarboroughnews.co.uk/news/local/my-mother-is-a-9ft-green-alien-says-councillor-1-4377481; http://www.dailymail.co.uk/femail/article-2343983/Whitby-Councillor-Simon-Parkes-tells-ITVs-The-Morning-I-lost-virginity-alien-holographic-age-FIVE.html

10 *Fortean Times* magazine issue 250, p. 9

John Conrad Russell

1 'House of Lords Act 1999', accessed at http://www.legislation.gov.uk/ukpga/1999/34/contents

2 Long, 2012, pp. 136–137; http://www.dailymail.co.uk/news/article-1388562/Earl-Onslow-dies-73-The-non-PC-lord-refused-toe-ANY-party-line.html

3 Clarke & Roberts, 2007, pp. 158–159, 167–169; Michell, 1999, pp. 230–231; Clarke, 2011, pp. 96–97

4 Clarke, 2011, pp. 96–101; Michell, 1999, pp. 232–233; Clarke & Roberts, 2007, pp. 205–207; a full transcript of the Lords Debate on UFOs is available online at http://hansard.millbanksystems.com/lords/1979/jan/18/unidentified-flying-objects

5 Robinson & Groves, 2002, pp. 4–6, 13

6 http://www.nndb.com/people/954/000044822/

7 Robinson & Groves, 2002, pp. 96–97

8 Robinson & Groves, 2002, p. 162; http://www.wikipedia.org/wiki/John_Russell_4th_Earl_Russell

9 http://www.wikipedia.org/wiki/John_Russell_4th_Earl_Russell

10 Advert contained in *Fortean Times* magazine issue 29, p.33

11 Advert contained in *Fortean Times* magazine issue 32, p.58

12 Advert contained in *Fortean Times* magazine issue 35, p.58

13 Advert contained in *Fortean Times* magazine, issue 35, p.58

14 Hansard for 18 July 1979, accessed online at http://hansard.millbanksystems.com/lords/1978/jul/18/victims-of-crime-aid-policy

15 http://en.wikipedia.org/wiki/John_Russell_4th_Earl_Russell

16 Russell's speech cited at http://aworldelsewhere-finn.blogspot.co.uk/2010_12_01_archive.html

17 Bertrand Russell, 'A Liberal Decalogue' in *New York Times Magazine* for 16 Dec 1951; accessed online at http://www.notable-quotes.com/r/russell_bertrand_iii.html

18 Robinson & Groves, 2002, p.3

19 Russell, 2009, pp. 1–15

20 Russell, 2009, p. 13

21 Robinson & Groves, 2002, p. 7

22 Robinson & Groves, 2002, pp. 126–127; https://community.tes.co.uk/tom_bennett/b/weblog/archive/2013/07/07/adventures-in-progressive-education-bertrand-and-dora-russell-39-s-beacon-hill-school.aspx

23 Hansard for 7 November 1985, accessed online at http://hansard.millbanksystems.com/lords/1985/nov/07/address-in-reply-to-her-majestys-most#S5LV0468P0_19851107_HOL_94

24 Hansard for 13 June 1986, accessed online at http://hansard.millbanksystems.com/lords/1986/jun/13/public-order-bill#S5LV0476P0_19860613_HOL_130

25 Shaw, 2009, p. 101

Colonel Sibthorp .

1 Wilson, 2003, pp. 39–40
2 Long, 2012, p. 70; Colville, 1971, Chapter 22: 'The Sibthorp Story' accessed online at http://www.brookmans.com/history/colville/chtwentytwo.shtml
3 http://en.wikisource.org/wiki/Sibthorp,_Charles_De_Laet_Waldo_(DNB00)
4 Michell, 1999, p.57; http://brookmans.com/history/house/ch1.shtml
5 http://www.historyofparliamentonline.org/volume/1820–1832/member/waldo-sibthorp-charles–1783–1855; http://www.antiquestradegazette.com/news/2002/apr/03/simmering-sibby/
6 Michell, 1999, p.58; http://www.historyofparliamentonline.org/volume/1820–1832/member/waldo-sibthorp-charles–1783–1855
7 Dickens, 1836, Chapter 18: 'A Parliamentary Sketch' accessed online at http://www.victorianlondon.org/books/boz–118.html
8 Testimony cited at http://www.historyofparliamentonline.org/volume/1820–1832/member/waldo-sibthorp-charles–1783–1855
9 Long, 2012, p. 71; Michell, 1999, p. 60
10 Dickens, 1836, Chapter 18: 'A Parliamentary Sketch' accessed online at http://www.victorianlondon.org/books/boz–118.html
11 Michell, 1999, p. 61
12 Michell, 1999, p. 60
13 Colville, 1971, Chapter 22: 'The Sibthorp Story' accessed online at http://www.brookmans.com/history/colville/chtwentytwo.shtml
14 Michell, 1999, p. 60; Long, 2012, p. 71
15 Evans & Bartholomew, 2009, p. 532;
16 Michell, 1999, p. 61
17 Michell, 1999, p. 61
18 Rev. 8:10–11
19 Dostoyevsky, 2004, p. 443
20 Michell, 1999, pp. 60–61
21 http://www.historyofparliamentonline.org/volume/1820–1832/member/waldo-sibthorp-charles–1783–1855
22 Michell, 1999, p. 59; http://www.lincolnwaites.org.uk/songsibthorp.shtml, citing *Lincolnshire Chronicle* for 29 August 1851
23 http://www.historyofparliamentonline.org/volume/1820–1832/member/waldo-sibthorp-charles–1783–1855
24 Michell, 1999, p. 59
25 http://en.wikipedia.org/wiki/The_Great_Exhibition; Wilson, 2003, pp. 127 and 144
26 Michell, 1999, p. 59; Long, 2012, pp. 71–72
27 *Hansard* for 4 Feb 1851, accessed online at http://hansard.millbanksystems.com/commons/1851/feb/04/address-in-answer-to-the-speech; the Crystal Palace did actually burn down in a fire in 1936, so perhaps these prayers did work after all …
28 Anonymous letter cited in Wilson, 2003, p. 143
29 http://www.historyofparliamentonline.org/volume/1820–1832/member/waldo-sibthorp-charles–1783–1855
30 Colville, 1971, Chapter 22: 'The Sibthorp Story' accessed online at http://www.brookmans.com/history/colville/chtwentytwo.shtml
31 http://www.lincolnwaites.org.uk/songsibthorp.shtml
32 Colville, 1971, Chapter 22: 'The Sibthorp Story' accessed online at http://www.brookmans.com/history/colville/chtwentytwo.shtml

33 http://www.historyofparliamentonline.org/volume/1820–1832/member/waldo-sibthorp-charles–1783–1855; some sources primly prefer 'tavern' for 'bawdy-house'.
34 Long, 2012, p. 72
35 Michell, 1999, p. 60
36 *Hansard* for 1 May 1855, accessed online at http://hansard.millbanksystems.com/commons/1855/may/01/mission-to-vienna#S3V0137P0_18550501_HOC_42

Occult Eccentrics

1 Quentin A. Craufurd, 'Foreword' to Johnson, 2014, pp. 5–7; *Fortean Times* magazine issue 321, pp. 30–32
2 Sleeve-notes to *The Ghost Orchid*, a CD of Cass' recordings released in 1999; http://www.ghostvillage.com/resources/2011/features_06092011.shtml
3 Clarke & Roberts, 2007, pp. 30, 72, 76–77
4 Johnson, 2014, pp. 262–263
5 Clarke & Roberts, 2007, pp. 119–123
6 Michell, pp. 62–74; Long, 2012, pp. 100–102
7 Ronson, 2002, pp. 138–169; McClure, 1996, pp. 111–113; *Sunday Times Magazine*, 16 June 2013, pp. 14–20; *Fortean Times* magazine issue 129, pp. 30–31; http://americanloons.blogspot.co.uk/2015/01/1253-arizona-wilder.html; Icke's *Wogan* interview is online at www.youtube.com/watch?v=Y2MEN4-49dM
8 http://en.wikipedia.org/wiki/L%C3%A8se_majest%C3%A9_in_Thailand

Joe Meek

1 http://en.wikipedia.org/wiki/The_Beatles_in_1966
2 Cited at http://en.wikipedia.org/wiki/Joe_Meek
3 http://www.paranormaldatabase.com/hotspots/brentwood.php
4 'Arena: The Very Strange Story of ... Joe Meek' (first broadcast 8 February 1991, BBC2); this footage is online at www.youtube.com/watch?v=bXtTgKSb4n4
5 Contribution by 'MrRING' made on http://forum.forteantimes.com/index.php?threads/joe-meek-and-the-talking-cat.19759/
6 http://www.nme.com/list/the-50-greatest-producers-ever/262849/article/265277
7 http://www.joemeekpage.info/essay_06_E.htm; http://www.theguardian.com/music/2006/nov/12/popandrock28
8 http://www.joemeekpage.info/essay_01_E.htm; http://www.joemeekpage.info/essay_02_E.htm; http://www.joemeekpage.info/essay_06_E.htm; http://www.islington.gov.uk/publicrecords/library/Leisure-and-culture/Information/Factsheets/2012-2013/(2012-06–15)-Joe-Meek.pdf; *Fortean Times* magazine issue 201, pp.54–55
9 This can be heard online at www.youtube.com/watch?v=pehihWNMgMY
10 http://en.wikipedia.org/wiki/I_Hear_a_New-World; http://www.joemeekpage.info/triumph_3_E.htm
11 http://www.joemeekpage.info/essay_03_E.htm; http://www.joemeekpage.info/essay_05_E.htm; http://en.wikipedia.org/wiki/Joe_Meek; http://www.islington.gov.uk/publicrecords/library/Leisure-and-culture/Information/Factsheets/2012-2013/(2012-06–15)-Joe-Meek.pdf; *Fortean Times* magazine issue 201, pp. 54–55
12 *Fortean Times* magazine issue 201, pp. 54–55
13 http://www.theguardian.com/music/2006/nov/12/popandrock28
14 http://www.walesonline.co.uk/news/wales-news/tom-jones-former-bandmate-recalls-2093911

15 http://www.joemeekpage.info/essay_07_E.htm; http://www.joemeekpage.info/ essay_09_E.htm; http://www.joemeekpage.info/essay_13_E.htm; http://en.wikipedia. org/wiki/Heinz_(singer)

16 http://www.joemeekpage.info/essay_05_E.htm; http://en.wikipedia.org/wiki/ Telstar_(song)

17 All quotes compiled from Meek's sleeve-notes to *I Hear a New World*

18 Lyrics cited at http://www.joemeekpage.info/essay_06_E.htm

19 http://mercurie.blogspot.co.uk/2013/10/teenage-death-songs-someones-going-to.html

20 http:en.wikipedia.org/wiki/Johnny_Remember_Me; http://www.joemeekpage.info/ essay_05_E.htm

21 Psychic *News* for 9 September 1961; http://www.joemeekpage.info/kompositionen_ goddard_E.htm; http://www.joemeekpage.info/essay_05_E.htm; http://en.wikipedia. org/wiki/Geoff_Goddard; http://en.wikipedia.org/wiki/Johnny_Remember_Me; http:// mercurie.blogspot.co.uk/2013/10/teenage-death-songs-someones-going-to.html

22 http://en.wikipedia.org/wiki/Yesterday_(Beatles_song)

23 http://www.theguardian.com/news/2000/may/25/guardianobituaries; http://vaultofevil. proboards.com/thread/932/john-repsch-legendary-joe-meek; *Fortean Times* magazine issue 201, pp. 54–55

24 Patterson, 2004, Chapter 2 (no page numbers provided), accessed online at http:// catdir.loc.gov/catdir/enhancements/fy0641/2004047197-s.html; *Fortean Times* magazine issue 201, pp. 54–55

25 http://forgottenbands.blogspot.co.uk/2009/10/screaming-lord-sutch-savages-in-60s. html; http://en.wikipedia.org/wiki/Screaming_Lord_Sutch_and_the_Savages

26 http://vaultofevil.proboards.com/thread/932/john-repsch-legendary-joe-meek

27 http://www.joemeekpage.info/essay_06_E.htm; http://www.joemeekpage.info/ essay_07_E.htm; http://www.joemeekpage.info/essay_09_E.htm; *Fortean Times* magazine issue 201, pp. 54–55

28 http://www.joemeekpage.info/kompositionen_goddard_E.htm; http://www. theguardian.com/news/2000/may/25/guardianobituaries; http://en.wikipedia.org/wiki/ Geoff_Goddard

29 http://www.joemeekpage.info/essay_09-E.htm

30 http://www.davidfarrant.org/TheHumanTouch/a-life-in-the-death-of-joe-meek/; Farrant, 2014 (no page numbers provided), accessed online at https://books.google. co.uk/books?isbn=075095874X

31 http://www.davidfarrant.org/the-highgate-vampire/; http://en.wikipedia.org/wiki/ Highgate_Vampire

32 http://www.davidfarrant.org/f-a-q/

33 http://en.wikipedia.org/wiki/Joe-Meek

34 Fortean *Times* magazine issue 201, pp. 54–55; http://www.joemeekpage.info/ essay_11_E.htm

Desmond Leslie

1 http://www.turtlebunbury.com/published/published_reviews/pub_rev_leslie.htm; http:// news.bbc.co.uk/1/hi/uk/1518975.stm; Clarke & Roberts, 2007, p.52; some sources say this famous punch happened in 1962, but this does not appear to be correct. Footage of the event can be found at www.youtube.com/watch?v=3EeIRI_oRPY

2 http://www.turtlebunbury.com/published/published_reviews/pub_rev_leslie.htm

3 Clarke & Roberts, 2007, pp. 39–40

4 Price, 1945, pp. 111–113; O'Dell, 2011 (no page numbers provided), accessed online

at https://books.google.co.uk/books?isbn=1445629941; accounts of this event differ wildly, incidentally ...

5　http://www.turtlebunbury.com/published/published_reviews/pub_rev_leslie.htm

6　Clarke & Roberts, 2007, p. 40

7　http://www.turtlebunbury.com/published/published_reviews/pub_rev_leslie.htm

8　Clarke & Roberts, 2007, p.40; http://en.wikipedia.org/wiki/Desmond_Leslie; some sound-footage of Leslie's album 'Music of the Future' can be found at www.youtube.com/watch?v=4I2bmxXVtYw

9　http://www.turtlebunbury.com/published/published_reviews/pub_rev_leslie.htm

10　Redfern, 2010, pp. 25–31; Clarke & Roberts, 2007, pp. 42–43

11　Clarke & Roberts, 2007, pp. 38, 43

12　Clarke & Roberts, 2007, pp. 4–5

13　*Sunday Dispatch*, 11 June 1954; Clarke & Roberts, 2007, pp. 58-62

14　Redfern, 2010, pp. 86–87; Clarke & Roberts, 2007, pp. 72–75, 79–81, 85–89

15　Tucker, 2013, pp. 187–194

16　Clarke & Roberts, 2007, pp. 95–103

17　Clarke & Roberts, 2007, pp. 48–49, 68-69, 91–93

18　http://www.bbc.co.uk/news/uk-northern-ireland–10985156

19　Clarke & Roberts, 2007, pp. 49–50

20　Clarke & Roberts, 2007, pp. 40–42, 51

21　Clarke & Roberts, pp. 57–58

22　Redfern, 2010, p. 89

23　Michell, 1999, p. 227; Clarke & Roberts, 2007, pp. 58–60

24　Clarke & Roberts, 2007, pp. 56-57

25　Redfern, 2010, p. 88; Clarke & Roberts, 2007, pp. 58–60

26　Clarke & Roberts, 2007, p. 51; http://www.turtlebunbury.com/published/published_reviews/pub_rev_leslie.htm

27　http://www.turtlebunbury.com/published/published_reviews/pub_rev_leslie.htm;

28　http://en.wikipedia.org/wiki/Castle_Leslie

Literary and Artistic Eccentrics

1　Lachman, 2003, pp. 55–61

2　Blake, 2006, p. vii

3　Wilson, 2006, pp. 73–74, 78, 83, 113, 123–124, 131, 138

4　Sandbrook, 2006, pp. 164–171

5　*Fortean Times* magazine issue 188, pp. 40–43

6　All material and quotes taken from McDiarmaid, 1936, pp. 57–75; http://en.wikipedia.org/wiki/William_McGonagall

7　*The Sunday Times 'Culture'* magazine, 1 February 2015, pp. 24–25; http://www.theguardian.com/culture/2001/nov/21/artsfeatures1; http://www.theguardian.com/society/2009/apr/09/kim-noble-will-die-mental-health; http://www.independent.co.uk/arts-entertainment/comedy/reviews/kim-noble-youre-not-alone-soho-theatre-review-a-show-that-runs-on-surprise-and-shock–10036119.html; http://www.theartsdesk.com/comedy/kim-noble-soho-theatre-0; http://www.independent.co.uk/arts-entertainment/comedy/features/has-comedian-kim-noble-exploited-his-mental-illness-to-create-one-of-the-most-shocking-standup-shows-ever–1832815.html

8　http://www.theguardian.com/artanddesign/2015/jan/28/Leonora-carrington-wild-at-heart

9　Hopkins, 2004, p. 127

10 Downes, 1997, particularly pp. 10, 19–21, 31–33; http://en.wikipedia.org/wiki/
    Tony_Doc_Shiels

11 http://listverse.com/2014/06/16/10-truly-bizarre-facts-about-
    englands-most-insane-prisoner/; http://www.thefreelibrary.com/
    Cockroaches+are+my+best+friends...+I+get+spiders+to+do+tricks+by...-a060300192;
    http://en.wikipedia.org/wiki/Charles_Salvador; http://www.telegraph.co.uk/lifestyle/
    wellbeing/diet/4712171/Are-you-fit-and-mad-enough-to-flatten-a-cow.html; http://
    www.independent.co.uk/news/people/charles-bronson-changes-name-to-charles-
    salvador-the-old-me-dried-up-9645908.html; http://www.dailymail.co.uk/news/
    article-2785326/Artwork-notorious-prisoner-Charles-Bronson-set-sell-thousands-
    auction-Salvador-changed-tribute-favourite-artist-Dali.html

Arthur Cravan

NOTE: *Various English translations of Cravan's texts are available, from a number of sources (he wrote only in French), and they do vary quite a bit. Thus, as far as was possible, I chose to quote from the ones I personally found to be the most comic.*

 1 *Maintenant* issue 3; accessed online at http://www.academia.edu/3751101/
    English_Translation_of_Maintenant_3_by_Arthur_Cravan

 2 Breton, 2009, p. 303; *Flux* magazine issue 70, pp. 54–57, accessed online at http://
    andrewgallix.com/tag/marie-laurencin/

 3 Nicholl, 2011, Chapter 20 (no page numbers provided), accessed online at https://
    books.google.co.uk/books?isbn=0713994940

 4 Cited at http://www.brooklynrail.org/2004/06/books/
    the-provocations-of-arthur-cravan

 5 http://www .mr-oscar-wilde.de/about/g/gide.htm

 6 Raby, 1988, p. 7

 7 Friedman, David, *Wilde in America: Oscar Wilde and the Invention of Modern
    Celebrity* (London: WW Norton & Co, 2014)

 8 Well, when he *allegedly* said this, in any case; see http://www.oscarwildeinamerica.
    org/quotations/nothing-to-declare.html

 9 See, for example, Evelyn Waugh, 'Let Us Return to the Nineties – BUT NOT TO
    OSCAR WILDE' in *Harper's Bazaar*, November 1930; reprinted in Waugh, 2010, pp.
    19–22

10 http://www .mr-oscar-wilde.de/about/g/gide.htm

11 All quotes taken from *Maintenant* issue 2; reproduced in Breton, 2009, pp. 306–310.
    A curious point about this meeting, incidentally, is that Gide knew of Cravan and
    his reputation beforehand, having based a character from his 1914 novel *Les Caves
    du Vatican* – the murderous anarchist conman Lafcadio – upon him. Surely, then, he
    must have known the kind of revenge-treatment he would be letting himself in for by
    agreeing to the interview? See Various, 2005, p. 20

12 Polizzotti, 2009, p. 32

13 All quotes taken from *Maintenant* issue 4; accessed online at http://www.academia.
    edu/4291483/English_Translation_of_Maintenant_4_by_Arthur_Cravan

14 Cited in Nicholl, 2011, Chapter 20 (no page numbers provided), accessed online at
    https://books.google.co.uk/books?isbn=0713994940

15 Maintenant issue 4; accessed online at http://www.academia.edu/4291483/
    English_Translation_of_Maintenant_4_by_Arthur_Cravan

16 Frieze magazine issue 61, accessed online at http://www.frieze.com/issue/article/
    the_lyrical_heavyweight/

17   Flux magazine issue 70, pp. 54–57, accessed online at http://andrewgallix.com/tag/
     marie-laurencin/

18   http://en.wikipedia.org/wiki/Arthur_Cravan

19   Nicholl, 2011, Chapter 20 (no page numbers provided), accessed online at https://
     books.google.co.uk/books?isbn=0713994940

20   Nicholl, 2011, Chapter 20 (no page numbers provided), accessed online at https://
     books.google.co.uk/books?isbn=0713994940

21   http://www.booktryst.com/2011/09/day-boxings-jack-johnson-put-dada.html; Various,
     2005, p.21

22   Flux magazine issue 70, pp. 54–57, accessed online at http://andrewgallix.com/tag/
     marie-laurencin/

23   Trotsky cited in Nicholl, 2011, Chapter 20 (no page numbers provided), accessed
     online at https://books.google.co.uk/books?isbn=0713994940

24   Maintenant issue 4; accessed online at http://www.academia.edu/4291483/
     English_Translation_of_Maintenant_4_by_Arthur_Cravan

25   http://boxrec.com/list_bouts.php?human_id=58873&cat=boxer

26   Nicholl, 2011, Chapter 20 (no page numbers provided), accessed online at https://
     books.google.co.uk/books?isbn=0713994940

27   See www.youtube.com/watch?v=CCktHSUAFM for the footage in question

28   Nicholl, 2011, Chapter 20 (no page numbers provided), accessed online at https://
     books.google.co.uk/books?isbn=0713994940; *Frieze* magazine issue 61, accessed
     online at http://www.frieze.com/issue/article/the_lyrical_heavyweight/

29   'Hie!' originally appeared in issue two of *Maintenant*; translation cited in *Jacket*
     magazine issue 24, accessed online at http://jacketmagazine.com/34/parmar-loy.shtml

30   Cited at http://www.brooklynrail.org/2004/06/books/
     the-provocations-of-arthur-cravan

31   Hopkins, 2004, p. 56

32   Hopkins, 2004, pp. 41–42

33   Nicholl, 2011, Chapter 20 (no page numbers provided), accessed online at https://
     books.google.co.uk/books?isbn=0713994940

34   http://www.brooklynrail.org/2004/06/books/the-provocations-of-arthur-cravan

35   Flux magazine issue 70, pp. 54–57, accessed online at http://andrewgallix.com/tag/
     marie-laurencin/; Nicholl, 2011, Chapter 20 (no page numbers provided), accessed
     online at https://books.google.co.uk/books?isbn=0713994940; Various, 2005, p. 24

36   Schenkar, 2001 (no page numbers provided), accessed online at https://books.google.
     co.uk/books?isbn=0786752629; *Flux* magazine issue 70, pp. 54–57, accessed online
     at http://andrewgallix.com/tag/marie-laurencin/; Various, 2005, p. 76

37   Nicholl, 2011, Chapter 20 (no page numbers provided), accessed online at https://
     books.google.co.uk/books?isbn=0713994940

38   Jacket magazine issue 24, accessed online at http://jacketmagazine.com/34/parmar-loy.
     shtml

39   Flux magazine issue 70, pp. 54–57, accessed online at http://andrewgallix.com/tag/
     marie-laurencin/

40   Frieze magazine issue 61, accessed online at http://www.frieze.com/issue/article/the_
     lyrical_heavyweight/; Various, 2005, p. 20

41   Nicholl, 2011, Chapter 20 (no page numbers provided), accessed online at https://
     books.google.co.uk/books?isbn=0713994940

42   http://en.wikipedia.org/wiki/B_Traven

43   http://www.anthonygardner.co.uk/features/oscar_wilde.html; Vyvyan Holland quoted

in Nicholl, 2011, Chapter 20 (no page numbers provided), accessed online at https://books.google.co.uk/books?isbn=0713994940

44 New *York Times*, 9 November 1913

45 New *York Times*, 9 November 1913

46 *Maintenant* issue 3; accessed online at http://www.academia.edu/3751101/English_Translation_of_Maintenant_3_by_Arthur_Cravan

47 All quotes taken from *Maintenant* issue 3; accessed online at http://www.academia.edu/3751101/English_Translation_of_Maintenant_3_by_Arthur_Cravan

48 Maintenant issue 3; accessed online at http://www.academia.edu/3751101/English_Translation_of_Maintenant_3_by_Arthur_Cravan

49 Wilde, 2003, p.3

Evelyn Waugh

1 Waugh, 1983, p. 173

2 http://en.wikipedia.org/wiki/C._R._M._F._Cruttwell

3 'Fathers and Sons: The Waughs', TV documentary broadcast on BBC Four, 21 June 2010

4 Evelyn Waugh, 'People Who Want to Sue Me' in the *Daily Mail*, 31 May 1930; reprinted in Waugh, 2010, pp. 13–15

5 Waugh, 2000, p. 94

6 http://en.wikipedia.org/wiki/Evelyn_Waugh

7 http://www.telegraph.co.uk/culture/books/bookreviews/6023040/Evelyn-Waughs-mad-world.html

8 Long, 2012, pp. 122–123; Shaw, 2009, pp. 204–205; http://en.wikipedia.org/wiki/Lord_Berners

9 http://www.literaryreview.co.uk/Waugh_10_14.php

10 Evelyn Waugh, 'I See Nothing But Boredom ... Everywhere' in the *Daily Mail*, 28 December 1959; reprinted in Waugh, 2010, pp. 45–48

11 http://en.wikiquote.org/wiki/Evelyn_Waugh

12 Auberon Waugh, 'Death in the Family' in *The Spectator*, 6 May 1966; reprinted in Cook, 2010, pp. 65–70; the actual quote is on p. 68

13 Relevant transcripts from these interviews are included as an Appendix to Waugh, 2006, pp. 135–143; the actual quotes are on pp. 141–143

14 Letter cited in Waugh, 2006, p. xxii

15 http://en.wikipedia.org/wiki/Evelyn_Waugh

16 Auberon Waugh, 'Rejoice in the Plague of Literary Biographies' in *The Oldie*, May 1996; reprinted in Cook, 2010, pp. 301–302

17 http://www.goodreads.com/author/quotes/65325.Auberon_Waugh

18 Cited in Cook, 2010, pp. 2–3; http://www.telegraph.co.uk/news/obituaries/1318325/Auberon-Waugh.html

19 Sandbrook, 2013, pp. 455–456

20 Auberon Waugh, 'The Joys of Being Burgled' in *The Spectator*, 29 August 1987; reprinted in Cook, 2010, pp. 147–148

21 'Fathers and Sons: The Waughs', TV documentary broadcast on BBC Four, 21 June 2010

Military Eccentrics

1 Shaw, 2009, p. 228

2 Shaw, 2009, pp. 234–235; http://www.theguardian.com/books/2005/dec/10/featuresreviews.guardianreview2

3 *Daily Mail*, 16 Jan 2015, p. 64

4 Sebag-Montefiore, 2006, pp. 424–425; http://ww2talk.com/forums/topic/4629-eccentricity/

5 Shaw, 2009, p. 229; http://spotlights.fold3.com/2012/03/23/orde-wingate/; http://en.wikipedia.org/wiki/Orde_Wingate

6 http://warfarehistorynetwork.com/daily/wwii/mad-jack-churchill-a-rare-breed-of-warrior/; http://www.telegraph.co.uk/news/obituaries/7733516/Lieutenant-Colonel-Jack-Churchill.html; http://www.dailymail.co.uk/news/article-2255533/The-amazing-story-Mad-Jack-hero-took-Nazis-bow-arrow-later-professional-bagpipe-player.html;

7 Sitwell, 2006, pp. 120–124; http://en.wikisource.org/wiki/Thornton,_Thomas_(1757–1823)_(DNB00); http://www.britishmuseum.org/research/collection_online/collection_object_details.aspx?objectId=1596913&partId=1

8 Westwood & Simpson, 2005, pp. 711–712; http://www.surreymirror.co.uk/Eccentric-major-predicted-death/story-19567828-detail/story.html

9 For the full story of Spicer-Simson, see Foden, 2005; useful summaries of his life also appear in Shaw, 2009, pp. 235–237 and online at http://en.wikipedia.org/wiki/Geoffrey_Spicer-Simson; http://www.spiegel.de/international/world/a-century-in-service-kaiser-s-african-gunship-enjoys-new-lease-on-life-a-690396-3.html; http://www.spiegel.de/international/world/a-century-in-service-kaiser-s-african-gunship-enjoys-new-lease-on-life-a-690396-4.html; http://www.nytimes.com/2005/04/10/books/review/10MACIN.html?pagewanted=print&position=

General Sir Walter Walker

1 Walker, 1997, cited online at http://www.telegraph.co.uk/news/obituaries/military-obituaries/gurkha-obituaries/1337219/General-Sir-Walter-walker.html

2 Walker's letter cited in Sandbrook, 2013, p. 137

3 Interview cited in Sandbrook, 2013, p. 138

4 Leigh, 1988, p. 221; Walker was not to the only one to hold this theory at the time, but that is another story altogether …

5 Sandbrook, 2013, p. 136

6 Sandbrook, 2013, pp. 136–137

7 For a discussion about whether or not Unison and Civil Assistance were actually the same thing, see *Lobster* magazine #11; (online at http://www.8bitmode.com/rogerdog/lobster/lobster11.pdf)

8 Garnett, 2008, p. 75

9 http://www.telegraph.co.uk/news/obituaries/military-obituaries/gurkha-obituaries/1337219/General-Sir-Walter-walker.html

10 http://en.wikipedia/.org/wiki/Civil_Assistance

11 http://archive.spectator.co.uk/article/5th-october–1974/15/general-sir-walter-walker

12 Sandbrook, 2013, pp. 138–139

13 Beckett, 2003, p. 198

14 http://www.wsws.org/en/articles/2006/04/wil2-a20.html

15 Lobster #11

16 Sandbrook, 2013, pp. 139–140; *Lobster* #11

17 Wheen, 2010, pp. 252 and 255; *Lobster* #11

18 Playboy magazine, Sept 1976; cited in Sandbrook, 2013, p. 343 (Bowie's comments have since been reclaimed as 'ironic')
19 Sandbrook, 2013, p. 138
20 Sandbrook, 2013, p. 364
21 Fortean *Times* magazine issue 171, p. 35
22 Sandbrook, 2013, p. 365
23 Sandbrook, 2013, pp. 382–384
24 Sandbrook, 2013, p. 138
25 http://www.independent.co.uk/news/bentine-brains-behind-sas–1082289.html; http://news.bbc.co.uk/1/hi/in_depth/uk/2000/iranian_embassy_siege/717047.stm; although, in truth, the formation of the SAS' counter-terrorist wing probably had more to do with the 1972 hostage crisis at the Munich Olympics than the intervention of one of The Goons ...
26 Series 2, Episode 3 (1977); script cited in Sandbrook, 2013, pp. 140–141 & Wheen, 2010, pp. 253–254
27 http://en.wikipedia.org/wiki/Fairly_Secret_Army
28 Wheen, 2010, p. 257
29 Lobster #11
30 Inman, 2007, p. 43

Geoffrey Pyke

1 *Fortean Times* magazine issue 197, p. 49
2 *Daily Mail*, 29 Jan 2015, p. 62; *The Times* 'T2' supplement, 23 Jan 2015, pp. 4–5; http://www.bbc.co.uk/news/science-environment-30915445
3 *Daily Mail*, 29 Jan 2015, p. 62; http://en.wikipedia.org/wiki/Landships_Committee; http://en.wikipedia.org/wiki/History_of_the_tank; see Wells, 1998, p.611 for the author's quite inaccurate version of how these 'landships' would actually move ...
4 *Fortean Times* magazine issue 149, p. 22 and issue 131, p. 10; http://en.wikipedia.org/wiki/Explosive_rat; no 'rat-bombs' ever actually exploded, but the Nazis, having discovered the plan, wasted much time and effort looking for such devices.
5 Felton, 2007, pp. 40–41; http://www.telegraph.co.uk/history/world-war-two/8701034/Revealed-sex-hormone-plan-to-feminise-Hitler.html; http://en.wikipedia.org/wiki/Sticky_bomb
6 *The Times* 'T2' supplement, 23 Jan 2015, pp. 4–5; http://en.wikipedia.org/wiki/Solly_Zuckermann,_Baron_Zuckermann; http://en.wikipedia.org/wiki/Frederick_Lindemann,_1st_Viscount_Cherwell
7 *The Spectator* for 30 Oct 1959, p. 30; online at http://archive.spectator.co.uk/article/30th-october–1959/30/patents-and-precedents
8 *The Spectator* for 30 Oct 1959, p. 30; online at http://archive.spectator.co.uk/article/30th-october–1959/30/patents-and-precedents
9 *Fortean Times* magazine issue 197, p. 47
10 *Fortean Times* magazine issue 197, p. 47
11 Michell, 1999, p. 122; http://en.wikipedia.org/wiki/Geoffrey_Pyke
12 *Manchester Guardian*, 20, 21, 24 August 1945; this newspaper was actually the forerunner of today's *Guardian*.
13 Michell, 1999, p. 121; *Fortean Times* magazine issue 197, p. 51; *The Economist*, 11 Aug 1945
14 Michell, 1999, p. 118
15 Fortean *Times* magazine issue 197, p. 51; http://en.wikipedia.org/wiki/Geoffrey_Pyke

16 Manchester *Guardian*, 7 March 1951

17 Lampe, 1959, pp. 164–168; http://en.wikipedia.org/wiki/Geoffrey_Pyke

18 Michell, 1999, p. 119; *Fortean Times* magazine issue 197, p. 48; letter in *New Scientist* magazine for 20 August 1981, p. 490

19 Michell, 1999, pp. 121–122; *The Times*, 26 February 1948; *Fortean Times* magazine issue 197, p. 51; http://en.wikipedia.org/wiki/Geoffrey_Pyke

20 A facsimile of *To Ruhleben and Back* is available online at https://archive.org/details/toruhlebenandbac00pykeiala; additional information gleaned from Michell, 1999, pp. 116–117; http://en.wikipedia.org/wiki/Geoffrey_Pyke

21 Michell, 1999, p. 117

22 Michell, 1999, pp. 117–118; Shaw, 2009, p. 241; *Fortean Times* magazine issue 197, p. 46, http://en.wikipedia.org/wiki/Geoffrey_Pyke

23 Adverts in *New Statesman* and *Nature* for 22 March 1924

24 The *Times*, 26 April 1927

25 http://www.thearchitectureofearlychildhood.com/2012/07/susan-isaacs-malting-house-child.html

26 Advert in *The Times* 7 July 1927

27 For Health and Safety Executive-baiting photographs of small children using such devices, see http://www.thearchitectureofearlychildhood.com/2012/07/susan-isaacs-malting-house-child.html; the ages of pupils admitted to Malting House seems to have kept on changing from advert to advert – my phrase 'three to ten' represents the most extreme boundaries.

28 Fortean *Times* magazine issue 197, p. 44

29 Advert in *The Times* 7 July 1927

30 Fortean *Times* magazine issue 197, p. 46

31 General information about Malting House compiled from http://en.wikipedia.org/wiki/Malting_House_School; http://www.thearchitectureofearlychildhood.com/2012/07/susan-isaacs-malting-house-child.html

32 http://en.wikipedia.org/wiki/Geoffrey_Pyke; *Fortean Times* magazine issue 197, pp. 46–47

33 Michell, 1999, pp. 119–120; *Fortean Times* magazine issue 197, pp. 47–48

34 Michell, 1999, pp. 120–121

35 Fortean *Times* magazine issue 197, p. 48; http://en.wikipedia.org/wiki/Geoffrey_Pyke

36 http://en.wikipedia.org/wiki/Project_Habakkuk provides the original sources for these two alleged incidents

37 A mis-spelling of 'Habakkuk', a book in the Bible which features an appropriate quote: 'I will work a work in your days which ye will not believe, though it be told to you.' Hab1:5

38 All information about ice-ships compiled from Michell, 1999, pp. 120–121; *Fortean Times* magazine issue197, pp. 48–51; http://en.wikipedia.org/wiki/Geoffrey_Pyke; http://en.wikipedia.org/wiki/Project_Habakkuk; http://en.wikipedia.org/wiki/Pykrete; http://www.royalnavalmuseum.org/info_sheets_habbakkuk.htm

Zoological Eccentrics

1 *Fortean Times* magazine issue 284, pp. 76–77

2 Sitwell, 2006, pp. 65–66; Kirby, 1820, pp.49-50

3 http://www.praxxis.co.uk/credebyron/menagerie.htm

4 Long, 2012, pp. 54–55; http://www.thurrock-history.org/fatherh.htm

5 http://www.dailymail.co.uk/news/article-2530436/Shameless-Asda-Nazi-dresses-dog-Swastika-covered-sheepskin-jacket.html

6 Long, 2012, pp. 63–64; http://ahistoryblog.com/2012/10/11/francis-henry-egerton-8th-earl-of-bridgewater–1756–1829-privilege-done-right/; http://en.wikisource.org/wiki/Egerton,_Francis_Henry_(DNB00); http://en.wikipedia.org/wiki/Francis_Egerton,_8th_Earl_of_Bridgewater

7 Long, 2012, pp. 84–86; http://www.telegraph.co.uk/news/obituaries/1345656/John-Aspinall.html; http://en.wikipedia.org/wiki/John_Aspinall_(zoo_owner)

8 http://www.praxxis.co.uk/credebyron/menagerie.htm

9 Long, 2012, pp. 11–12; https://henrypoole.com/hall_of_fame/12th-duke-of-bedford/; http://www.theguardian.com/uk/2002/may/09/humanities.research; http://en.wikipedia.org/wiki/Hastings_Russell,_12th_Duke_of_Bedford

10 https://victoriannaturalist.wordpress.com/tag/frank-buckland/; http://www.improbable.com/airchives/paperair/volume6/v6i6/buckland-6-6.htm; http://www.theguardian.com/lifeandstyle/wordofmouth/2008/feb/25/foodherowilliambuckland; http://www.mhs.ox.ac.uk/eccentric-eating; http://en.wikipedia.org/wiki/William_Buckland; http://en.wikipedia.org/wiki/Francis_Trevelyan_Buckland

11 Grumley-Grennan, 2010, p. 158; Sitwell, 2006, pp. 118–120; http://en.wikipedia.org/wiki/Jemmy_Hirst

12 All material about Hawker taken from Brendon, 2002, particularly pp. 61, 101, 142–144 for the animal-related details, pp. 139–40 for his clothes and pp. 41–42 for his practical jokes. Other material taken from pp. 23–24, 56, 62, 77, 96, 152, 154, 174, 218

13 For these stories, see *Illustrated Police News*, 7 August 1880, cited in Clay, 2013, pp. 27–28 and *Royal Cornwall Gazette*, 20 March 1890, cited in Clay, 2013, pp. 31–32

14 All information and quotes relating to Lindsay taken from Richard Barnett & Michael Neve, 'Dr Lauder Lindsay's Lemmings' in Pilkington, 2011, pp. 140–163

15 Michell, 1999, pp. 97–106; http://en.wikipedia.org/wiki/James_Burnett,_Lord_Monboddo; http://en.wikipedia.org/wiki/Monboddo_House

Charles Waterton

1 The enlarged edition I consulted was published in 1867, at any rate; there was an earlier one.

2 Sitwell, 2006, pp. 274–275

3 Hobson, 1867, Contents Pages; the full text is online at https://archive.org/stream/charleswaterton02hobsgoog/charleswaterton02hobsgoog_djvu.txt

4 Sitwell, 2006, p. 281

5 Hobson, 1867, pp.5–6, 78–79

6 Hobson, 1867, pp.33–34

7 http://en.wikipedia.org/wiki/Charles_Waterton

8 Hobson, 1867, pp. 41–42, 78–79, 317, 307

9 Hobson, 1867, p. 284

10 Hobson, 1867, pp. 53–54

11 Edgington, 1996, p. 96; http://en.wikipedia.org/wiki/Waterton_Lakes_National_Park

12 http://en.wikipedia.org/wiki/Charles_Waterton

13 Hobson, 1867, p. 40

14 Hobson, 1867, p. 251

15 Hobson, 1867, pp. 248–252

16 Hobson, 1867, pp. 30–32

17 Hobson, 1867, pp. 26, 95
18 Hobson, 1867, p. 253
19 Norman Moore, 'Introduction', in Waterton, 1891, p. 31
20 Cited in Sitwell, 2006, p. 263
21 Hobson, 1867, pp. 213, 246
22 Hobson, 1867, pp. 19–20
23 Hobson, 1867, pp. 123–124
24 Hobson, 1867, pp. 212, 305–306
25 Hobson, 1867, p. 212
26 http://wakefieldmuseumsandlibraries.blogspot.co.uk/2014/03/charles-watertons-creations-museumweek_25.html
27 Hobson, 1867, pp. 192–193; http://wakefieldmuseumsandlibraries.blogspot.co.uk/2014/03/charles-watertons-creations-museumweek_25.html
28 Hobson, 1867, p. 300
29 Hobson, 1867, pp. 292–297
30 Hobson, 1867, pp. 261–262, 265–267, 341–342; http://www.improbable.com/airchives/paperair/volume6/v6i6/waterton-6-6.html
31 Hobson, 1867, pp.209-210; http://www.wakefield.gov.uk/Documents/culture-museums/charles-watertons-creations.pdf
32 Hobson, 1867, pp. 189–90, 342–343
33 Waterton, 1891, pp. 19–22
34 Waterton, 1891, pp. 151–152
35 Waterton, 1891, p. 188
36 Waterton, 1891, pp. 79-80, 117–118, 139–140
37 Sitwell, 2006, pp. 276-277
38 Waterton, 1891, pp. 24-28
39 http://en.wikipedia.org/wiki/Curare
40 Waterton, 1891, pp. 118–119
41 Waterton, 1891, pp. 50-51
42 http://en.wikipedia.org/wiki/Charles-Waterton
43 Hobson, 1867, pp. 6, 125–126
44 Moore in Waterton, 1891, pp. 12–14
45 Moore in Waterton, 1891, pp. 14–15
46 Hobson, 1867, p. 41
47 Hobson, 1867, p. 322–324
48 Waterton, 1891, p. 43
49 Sitwell, 2006, p. 271
50 Sitwell, 2006, p. 268
51 Sitwell, 2006, p. 268
52 Sitwell, 2006, p. 281-282; http://en.wikipedia.org/wiki/Charles_Waterton
53 Hobson, 1867, pp. 74–75
54 Hobson, 1867, p. 213
55 Hobson, 1867, pp. 66, 218, 220
56 Hobson, 1867, p. 305; Sitwell, 2006, p. 266
57 Hobson, 1867, pp. 142–143
58 Hobson, 1867, pp. 193–196
59 Hobson, 1867, pp. 218-219
60 Cited in Sitwell, 2006, p. 267
61 Hobson, 1867, p. 230
62 Hobson, 1867, pp. 146–152

63 Sitwell, 2006, p. 272
64 Hobson, 1867, pp. 154–155, 241
65 Hobson, 1867, pp. 204–207
66 Hobson, 1867, pp. 156–157
67 Hobson, 1867, pp. 245–246
68 Hobson, 1867, pp. 252–253
69 Hobson, 1867, p. 163
70 Hobson, 1867, pp. 133–135
71 Moore in Waterton, 1891, pp. 32–34
72 Hobson, 1867, pp. 255–257
73 Hobson, 1867, p. 101
74 Father J Wood cited in Sitwell, 2006, p. 285

CONCLUSION

1 Cited in Feuerstein, 2006, p. ix
2 Chambers, 1864, p. 27 Entry for 6 July accessed online at https://books.google.co.uk/books?id=K0UJAAAAIAAJ ; Sitwell, 2006, pp. 51–55
3 http://www.dailymail.co.uk/news/article-2869969/Excruciating-encounter-hipster-twin-Cereal-Killer-cafe-challenged-selling-bowl-cornflakes-3-20-one-London-s-poorest-areas.html
4 http://www.telegraph.co.uk/culture/4730532/Its-every-one-else-whos-odd.html; http://www.imdb.com/title/tt0304938/quotes; http://www.dailymail.co.uk/news/article-2672395/Glass-eye-stolen-corpse-Savile-necklace-sold-charity-auction-75-wore-final-Top-Pops-groped-child.html
5 Ronson, 2011, pp. 189–222; http://www.dailymail.co.uk/news/article-475616/The-M15-Messiah-Why-David-Shayler-believes-hes-son-God.html; http://www.dailymail.co.uk/news/article-474364/Im-God-says-renegade-spy-David-Shayler.html; http://en.wikipedia.org/wiki/David-Shayler
6 Self, 1994, pp.126–127

Alfred Daniel Wintle

1 Park, Malcolm, 'A Layman's Triumph' in *Victorian Bar News* magazine for Spring 1989, p. 1; page numbers cited are for the version of this article available online
2 *The Times*, 13 May 1966
3 Cited at http://en.wikipedia.org/wiki/Alfred_Wintle
4 Cited at http://en.wikipedia.org/wiki/Alfred_Wintle; Quinn & Leaver, 2008, p. 31
5 Cited at http://en.wikipedia.org/wiki/Alfred_Wintle
6 Quinn & Leaver, 2008, p. 31
7 Quinn & Leaver, 2008, p. 31; http://en.wikipedia.org/wiki/Alfred_Wintle
8 Cited at http://en.wikipedia.org/wiki/Alfred_Wintle
9 Long, 2012, pp. 78–81; Shaw, 2009, pp. 222–228; Quinn & Leaver, 2008, p. 31
10 Cited at http://en.wikipedia.org/wiki/Alfred_Wintle
11 Park, 1989, p. 3; http://en.wikipedia.org/wiki/Alfred_Wintle
12 Park, 1989, p. 3; http://en.wikipedia.org/wiki/Alfred_Wintle
13 Shaw, 2009, pp. 222–228; http://en.wikipedia.org/wiki/Alfred_Wintle
14 Shaw, 2009, pp. 222–228; http://en.wikipedia.org/wiki/Alfred_Wintle
15 Cited at http://en.wikipedia.org/wiki/Alfred_Wintle
16 Park, 1989, p. 4

17 Shaw, 2009, pp. 222–228
18 *The Times*, 15 May 1966
19 Park, 1989, pp.4-5; Shaw, 2009, pp. 222–228
20 Park, 1989, pp.5-7; Shaw, 2009, pp. 222–228
21 Cited in Shaw, 2009, p. 227
22 Cited in Park, 1989, p. 7
23 Park, 1989, pp. 8–12
24 http://en.wikipedia.org/wiki/Alfred_Wintle

Bibliography

Archard, Charles J., *The Portland Peerage Romance* (London: Greening & Co, 1907)

Archenholz, Johann Wilhelm von, *England* (Maryland: University Press of America, 2014)

Beckett, Andy, *Pinochet in Piccadilly: Britain and Chile's Hidden History* (London: Faber & Faber, 2003)

Blake, William, *Songs of Innocence and of Experience* (London: Tate Books, 2006)

Brendon, Piers, *Hawker of Morwenstow: Portrait of a Victorian Eccentric* (London: Pimlico, 2002)

Breton, André, *Anthology of Black Humour* (London: Telegram Books, 2009)

Chambers, Robert, *The Book of Days: A Miscellany of Popular Antiquaries* (London & Edinburgh: W&R Chambers, 1864)

Bryson, Bill, *A Short History of Nearly Everything* (London, Black Swan, 2003)

Clarke, David, *The UFO Files: The Inside Story of Real-Life Sightings* (London: Bloomsbury, 2011)

Clarke, David & Roberts, Andy, *Flying Saucerers: A Social History of UFOlogy* (Loughborough: Heart of Albion Press, 2007)

Clarke, Roger, *A Natural History of Ghosts: 500 Years of Hunting for Proof* (London: Particular Books, 2012)

Clay, Jeremy, *The Burglar Caught by a Skeleton – and Other Singular Tales from the Victorian Press* (London: Icon Books, 2013)

Colville, Dorothy, *North Mymms, Parish and People* (Hertfordshire: Letchworth Printers, 1972)

Cook, William (Ed.) *Kiss Me, Chudleigh: The World According to Auberon Waugh* (London: Coronet, 2010)

Cowan, Ruth, *Relish: The Extraordinary Life of Alexis Soyer, Victorian Celebrity Chef* (London: Phoenix, 2007)

Coward, Noël, *Collected Revue Sketches and Parodies* (London: Bloomsbury/Methuen, 2014)

Dickens, Charles, *Sketches by Boz* (London: John Macrone, 1836)

Dostoyevsky, Fyodor, *The Idiot* (London: Penguin Classics, 2004)

Downes, Jonathan, *The Owlman and Others* (Exeter: CFZ Press, 1996)

Duducu, Jem, *The British Empire in 100 Facts* (Stroud, Amberley, 2014)

Eatwell, Piu Marie, *The Dead Duke, His Secret Wife and the Missing Corpse* (London: Head of Zeus, 2014)

Edgington, Brian W., *Charles Waterton: A Biography* (Cambridge: Lutterworth Press, 1996)

Evans, Stewart P., *Executioner: The Chronicles of James Berry, Victorian Hangman* (Stroud, Sutton Publishing, 2004)

Evans, Hilary & Bartholomew, Robert E., *Outbreak! The Encyclopedia of Extraordinary Social Behaviour* (San Antonio: Anomalist Books, 2009)

Farrant, Della, *Haunted Highgate* (Stroud: The History Press, 2014)

Felton, Bruce, *What Were They Thinking? Really Bad Ideas Throughout History* (Connecticut: The Lyons Press, 2007)

Feurstein, Georg, *Holy Madness* (Arizona: Hohm Press, 2006)

Fitzpatrick, John R., *John Stuart Mill's Political Philosophy* (London: Continuum, 2006)

Foden, Giles, *Mimi and Toutou Go Forth: The Bizarre Battle of Lake Tanganyika* (London: Penguin, 2005)

Garnett, Mark, *From Anger to Apathy: The Story of Politics, Society and Popular Culture in Britain Since 1975* (London: Vintage, 2008)

Greene, Richard, *Edith Sitwell: Avant-Garde Poet, English Genius* (London: Virago, 2012)

Grumley-Grennan, Tony, *Tales of English Eccentrics* (North Carolina: Lulu, 2010)

Hemming, Henry, *In Search of the English Eccentric* (London: John Murray, 2008)

Hobson, Dr Richard, *Charles Waterton: His Home, Habits and Handiwork, Second Edition* (London: Whittaker & Co, 1867)

Hopkins, David, *Dada and Surrealism: A Very Short Introduction* (Oxford: Oxford University Press, 2004)

Inman, Nick, *Politipedia: A Compendium of Useful and Curious Facts about British Politics* (Hampshire: Harriman House, 2007)

Johnson, Marjorie T., *Seeing Fairies* (San Antonio: Anomalist Press, 2014)

Kirby, R. S., *Kirby's Wonderful and Eccentric Museum: Or, Magazine of Remarkable Characters, Vol.2* (London: RS Kirby, 1820)

Lachman, Gary, *The Dedalus Book of the Occult: A Dark Muse* (Cambridge: Dedalus, 2003)

Lampe, David, *Pyke, the Unknown Genius* (London: Evans Brothers, 1959)

Leavis, F. R., *New Bearings in English Poetry* (London: Chatto & Windus, 1932)

Lee, Hermione, *Biography: A Very Short Introduction* (Oxford: Oxford University Press, 2009)

Leigh, David, *The Wilson Plot: The Intelligence Services and the Discrediting of a Prime Minister* (London: Heinemann, 1988)

Lloyd, Stephen, *William Walton: Muse of Fire* (Suffolk, Boydell Press, 2001)

Long, David, *English Country House Eccentrics* (Stroud: The History Press, 2012)

MacDiarmid, Hugh, *Scottish Eccentrics* (London: Routledge, 1936)

McClure, Kevin, *The Fortean Times Book of the Millennium* (London: John Brown, 1996)

Macaulay, Thomas Babington, *The History of England: Vol II* (New York, Digireads, 2011)

Michell, John, *Eccentric Lives and Peculiar Notions* (Illinois: Adventures Unlimited, 1999)

Nicholl, Charles, *Traces Remain: Essays and Explorations* (London: Penguin, 2011)

O'Dell, Damien, *Paranormal Cambridgeshire* (Stroud: Amberley, 2011)

Orwell, George, *Inside the Whale and Other Essays* (London: Penguin, 2001)

Patterson, R. Gary, *Take a Walk on the Dark Side: Rock and Roll Myths, Legends and Curses* (New York: Fireside/Simon & Schuster, 2004)

Pilkington, Mark (Ed.) *Strange Attractor Journal Four* (London: Strange Attractor Press, 2011)

Polizzotti, Mark, *Revolution of the Mind: The Life of André Breton* (Massachusetts: Black Widow Press, 2009)

Price, Harry, *Poltergeist Over England* (London: Country Life, 1945)

Quinn, Tom & Leaver, Ricky, *Eccentric London* (London: New Holland Publishers, 2008)

Raby, Peter, *Oscar Wilde* (Cambridge: Cambridge University Press, 1988)

Redfern, Nick, *Contactees: A History of Alien-Human Interaction* (New Jersey: New Page Books, 2010)

Robinson, Dave & Groves, Judy, *Introducing Bertrand Russell* (Cambridge: Icon Books, 2002)

Ronson, Jon, *Them! Adventures with Extremists* (London: Picador, 2002)

Ronson, Jon, *The Psychopath Test* (London: Picador, 2011)

Russell, Bertrand, *History of Western Philosophy* (Abingdon: Routledge, 2006)

Russell, Bertrand, *In Praise of Idleness and Other Essays* (Abingdon: Routledge, 2009)

Sandbrook, Dominic, *Never Had It So Good: A History of Britain from Suez to The Beatles* (London: Abacus, 2006)

Sandbrook, Dominic, *Seasons in the Sun: The Battle for Britain, 1974–1979* (London: Penguin, 2013)

Schenkar, Joan, *Truly Wilde: The Unsettling Story of Dolly Wilde, Oscar Wilde's Niece* (Massachusetts: Da Capo Press, 2001)

Sebag-Montefiore, Hugh, *Dunkirk: Fight to the Last Man* (London: Viking, 2006)

Self, Will, *The Quantity Theory of Insanity* (London: Penguin, 1994)

Shaw, Karl, *Curing Hiccups with Small Fires: A Delightful Miscellany of Great British Eccentrics* (London: Boxtree, 2009)

Shawcross, William, *Queen Elizabeth: The Queen Mother: The Official Biography* (London, Pan Macmillan, 2009)

Sitwell, Edith, *The English Eccentrics* (London: Pallas Athene, 2006)

Sitwell, Sacheverell, *Poltergeists: An Introduction and Examination Followed by Chosen Instances* (New York: University Books, 1959)

Steinmetz, Sol, *Semantic Antics* (New York, Random House, 2005)

Sutton, Jonathan, *The Religious Philosophy of Vladimir Solovyov* (London, Palgrave Macmillan, 1988)

Tucker, S. D., *Paranormal Merseyside* (Stroud: Amberley, 2013)

Various, *4 Dada Suicides* (London: Atlas Press, 2005)

Various, *Who's Who 19611970* (London, A & C Black, 1972)

Walker, General Sir Walter, *Fighting On* (London: New Millennium, 1997)

Waterton, Charles, *Wanderings in South America* (London: Cassell, 1891)

Waugh, Evelyn, *A Little Learning* (London: Penguin Modern Classics, 1983)

Waugh, Evelyn, *Vile Bodies* (London: Penguin Modern Classics, 2000)

Waugh, Evelyn, *The Ordeal of Gilbert Pinfold* (London: Penguin Modern Classics, 2006)

Waugh, Evelyn, *A Little Order: Selected Journalism* (London: Penguin Modern Classics, 2010)

Wells, H. G., *The Complete Short Stories* (London: JM Dent/Weidenfeld & Nicolson, 1998)

Westwood, Jennifer & Simpson, Jacqueline, *The Lore of the Land: A Guide to England's Legends, from Spring-Heeled Jack to the Witches of Warboys* (London: Penguin, 2005)

Wheen, Francis, *Strange Days Indeed: The Golden Age of Paranoia* (London: Fourth Estate, 2010)

Wilde, Oscar, *The Picture of Dorian Gray* (London: Penguin Classics, 2003)

Wilson, A. N., *The Victorians* (London: Arrow, 2003)

Wilson, Colin, *The Occult* (London: Watkins, 2006)

Wilson, G. H., *The Eccentric Mirror (Volume I)* (London, J. and J. Cundee, 1813)

Index